UNDERSTANDING

PROGRAMMING

LANGUAGES

Thi   or be

2

UNDERSTANDING

PROGRAMMING

LANGUAGES

M. BEN-ARI

JOHN WILEY & SONS
Chichester · New York · Brisbane · Toronto · Singapore

Copyright © 1996 by John Wiley & Sons Ltd,
Baffins Lane, Chichester,
West Sussex PO19 1UD, England

National   01243 779777
International (+44) 1243 779777

Other Wiley Editorial Offices

John Wiley & Sons, Inc., 605 Third Avenue,
New York, NY 10158-0012, USA

Jacaranda Wiley Ltd, 33 Park Road, Milton,
Queensland 4064, Australia

John Wiley & Sons (Canada) Ltd, 22 Worcester Road,
Rexdale, Ontario M9W 1L1, Canada

John Wiley & Sons (SEA) Pte Ltd, 37 Jalan Pemimpin #05-04,
Block B, Union Industrial Building, Singapore 2057

British Library Cataloguing in Publication Data

A catalogue record for this book is available from the British Library

ISBN 0 471 95846 8

Produced from camera-ready copy supplied by the authors using LaTeX
Printed and bound in Great Britain by Redwood Books, Trowbridge, Wilts
This book is printed on acid-free paper responsibly manufactured from
sustainable forestation for which at least two trees are planted for each one
used for paper production.

Contents

Preface

The importance of programming languages

To say that a good programmer can write good software in any language is like saying that a good pilot can fly any aircraft: true, but irrelevant. A passenger aircraft is designed for safety, comfort and economic viability; a military aircraft is designed for performance and mission capability; an ultralite aircraft is designed for low cost and operational simplicity.

The role of language in programming has been downgraded in favor of software methodology and tools; not just downgraded, but totally repudiated when it is claimed that a well-designed system can be implemented equally well in any language. But programming languages are not just a tool; they furnish the raw material of software, the thing we look at on our screens most of the day. I believe that the programming language is one of the *most* important, not one of the *least* important, factors that influence the ultimate quality of a software system. Unfortunately, too many programmers have poor linguistic skills. He/she is passionately in love with his/her "native" programming language, but is not able to analyze and compare language constructs, nor to understand the advantages and disadvantages of modern languages and language concepts. Too often, one hears statements that demonstrate conceptual confusion: "Language L1 is more powerful (or more efficient) than language L2".

This lack of knowledge is a contributing factor to two serious problems in software. The first is the ultra-conservatism that exists in the choice of programming languages. Despite the explosive advances in computer hardware and the sophistication of modern software systems, most programming is still done in languages that were developed about 1970, if not earlier. Extensive research in programming languages is never tested in practice, and software developers are forced to use tools and methodologies to compensate for obsolete language technology. It is as if airlines would refuse to try jet aircraft on the grounds that an old-fashioned propeller aircraft is perfectly capable of getting you from here to there.

The second problem is that language constructs are used indiscriminately, with little or no regard for safety or efficiency. This leads to unreliable software that cannot be maintained, as well as to inefficiencies that are solved by assembly language coding, rather than by refinement of the algorithms and the programming paradigms.

Programming languages exist *only* for the purpose of bridging the gap in the level of abstraction between the hardware and the real world. There is an inevitable tension between higher levels of abstraction that are easier to understand and safer to use, and lower levels of abstraction that are more flexible and can often be implemented more efficiently. To design or choose a programming language is to select an appropriate level of abstraction, and it is not surprising that different programmers prefer different levels, or that one language may be appropriate for one project and not for another. Within a specific language, a programmer should understand in depth the safety and efficiency implications of each construct in the language.

The aim of the book

The aim of this book is to help the student understand programming languages by analyzing and contrasting language constructs:

- What alternatives are available to the language designer?

- How are language constructs implemented?

- How should they be used?

We have not hesitated to be prescriptive: to claim that accumulated experience shows that certain constructs are to be preferred, and others to be avoided or at least used with caution.

Of course, any book on programming languages should not be taken as a reference manual for any particular language. The goal is to learn to analyze languages and not to study the peculiarities of any language in depth. Nor is the book a guide to the choice of a language for any particular project. The goal is to supply the student with the conceptual tools needed to make such a decision.

Selection of the material

The author of a text on programming languages must necessarily offend at least 3975 of the 4000 or so inventors of programming languages! I made the conscious decision to focus on a *very* small number of languages (even if it means offending 3994 people), because I believe that I can explain most language concepts using these languages. Other languages are mentioned or surveyed only if they demonstrate some concept that is not found in the languages chosen for the mainstream of the presentation.

Much of the book is concerned with "ordinary" imperative languages and two languages have been chosen from this class. Representing languages with a low level of abstraction is C, which has overtaken Fortran as the dominant language in this category. To represent a higher level of abstraction we have chosen Ada which offers a much cleaner definition than the more widely known Pascal.

An additional justification for these choices is that both languages have extensions (C++ and Ada 95) that we can use to study language support for object-oriented programming, currently the dominant programming method.

Unfortunately (I believe) most programming today is still done in imperative languages, but in recent years the quality of implementations for non-imperative languages has improved so that they can be used to develop "real" software. The final chapters introduce functional (ML) and logic programming (Prolog) languages in the hope of convincing the student that imperative languages are not conceptual necessities for programming.

The theory of programming language syntax and semantics is beyond the scope of this text. These important subjects are best left to more advanced courses.

To prevent confusion when comparing examples from different languages, an indication like C++ is attached to each example. In a section that discusses constructs in a specific language, no indication will be given.

Overview of the material

Part I is descriptive, defining and surveying programming languages and environments. Part II explains in great detail the basic constructs of programming languages: types, statements and subprograms. Part III continues the discussion of more advanced programming constructs such as: real numbers, static polymorphism, error handling and concurrency. Part IV is devoted to programming large systems with emphasis on language support for object-oriented programming. Finally, Part V surveys the basic concepts of functional and logic programming.

Teaching recommendations

The prerequisite for this book is at least one year of programming in some language such as Pascal or C. In any case, the student should have a basic reading knowledge of C. A familiarity with the structure and machine code of some computer will also be helpful.

There is too much material for a single course. Parts I and II together with portions of Part IV on modules and object-oriented programming can form the basis of a one-semester course for second-year undergraduates. For advanced undergraduates, the first half can be quickly reviewed in order to concentrate on the more difficult material in Parts III and IV. An advanced course should certainly include Part V supplemented by more material on some non-imperative language chosen by the instructor. Starred sections are more appropriate for advanced students.

It is possible to obtain free compilers for most languages as discussed in Appendix A. Students should also be taught how to examine the assembly language instructions that are emitted by the compilers that they use.

Exercises: since this is a book on programming languages and not on programming, the emphasis in the exercises is not on programming projects. Instead, we ask the students to dig into language descriptions, compare languages and verify compiler implementations of language constructs. The instructor is encouraged to tailor the exercises and append others, according to personal taste and the availability of tools.

The book will also be useful to programmers who wish to deepen their knowledge of the tools they use daily: programming languages.

A personal note

I admit that I prefer higher to lower levels of abstraction. This is not a prejudice, but a "post-judice". We software engineers have an exceedingly dismal record when it comes to producing reliable software systems, and I believe that *part* of the solution lies in higher levels of abstraction in programming languages. To expand on Dijkstra's saying: if you have a 100,000-line program that you can't understand, you should rewrite it as a 10,000-line program in a higher-level programming language.

My formative experience was in the early 1970's as a member of a large team of programmers working on a financial transaction system. We actually installed a new on-line system, even though we knew the system had a bug that we could not locate. Several weeks later the bug was finally trapped: it turned out that poor design of the programming language being used had turned a trivial typographical mistake into a type mismatch. A couple of years later when I first saw Pascal, I was hooked. The addiction deepened each time I helped a scientist who had wasted weeks of his/her life searching for a bug that would not have *compiled* successfully in Pascal. While type mismatch is certainly not the only source of programming error, it is so common and so dangerous, yet so simple to catch, that I would no more abandon strong type checking than I would drive without a seat-belt: it may be uncomfortable but even the best drivers can be involved in an accident and the discomfort is trivial relative to the potential damage.

I do not wish to get involved in language "wars" claiming that one language is better than another *for any specific* machine or application. I have attempted to analyze language constructs as objectively as I can in the hope that this will contribute to making discussions about language more scientific.

Acknowledgements

I would like to thank Kevlin A.P. Henney and David W. Barron for comprehensive reviews of the manuscript, as well as Harry Mairson, Tamar Benaya and Bruria Haberman who read portions of the manuscript. I am indebted to Amiram Yehudai for serving as my object-oriented guru: guiding me during numerous discussions and carefully checking the relevant chapters. Edmond Schonberg, Robert Dewar and their team at NYU quickly responded to my questions on GNAT, making it possible for me to learn and to write about Ada 95 even before a full compiler was available. Ian Joyner kindly provided his unpublished analysis of C++ which was most helpful. Like my previous books, this book would probably not have been written without Leslie Lamport's LaTeX!

It has been my privilege to work with a very professional and efficient publishing team at John Wiley, and I would like to thank them, especially my editor Gaynor Redvers-Mutton, for this opportunity.

M. Ben-Ari

Rehovot, Israel
October 1995

PART I

Introduction to Programming Languages

1   What Are Programming Languages?

1.1 The wrong question

When one first encounters a new programming language, the first question is usually:

> What can this language "do"?

Implicitly we are comparing the new language with other languages. The answer is very simple: all languages can "do" exactly the same computations! Section 1.8 outlines the justification for this answer. If they can all do the same computations, surely there must be other reasons for the existence of hundreds of programming languages.

Let us start with some definitions:

> A *program* is a sequence of symbols that specifies a computation.
> A *programming language* is a set of rules that specify which sequences of symbols constitute a program, and what computation the program describes.

You may find it interesting that the definition does not mention the word computer! Programs and languages can be defined as purely formal mathematical objects. However, more people are interested in programs than in other mathematical objects such as groups, precisely because it is possible to use the program—the sequence of symbols—to control the execution of a computer. While we highly recommend the study of the theory of programming, this text will generally limit itself to the study of programs *as they are executed* on a computer.

These definitions are very general and should be interpreted as generally as possible. For example, sophisticated word processors usually have a facility that enables you to "capture" a sequence of key-presses and store

3

them as a *macro* so that you can execute the entire sequence by pressing a single key. This is certainly a program because the sequence of key-presses specifies a computation and the software manual will clearly specify the macro language: how to initiate, terminate and name a macro definition.

To answer the question in the title of the chapter, we first go back to early digital computers, which were very much like the simple calculators used today by your grocer in that the computation that such computers perform is "wired-in" and cannot be changed.

The most significant early advance in computers was the realization (attributed to John von Neumann) that the specification of the computation, the program, can be *stored* in the computer just as easily as the data used in the computation. The *stored-program computer* thus becomes a general-purpose calculating machine and we can change the program just by changing a plugboard of wires, feeding a punched card, inserting a diskette, or connecting to a telephone line.

Since computers are binary machines that recognize only zeros and ones, storing programs in a computer is technically easy but practically inconvenient, since each instruction has to be written as binary digits (*bits*) that can be represented mechanically or electronically. One of the first software tools was the *symbolic assembler*. An assembler takes a program written in *assembly language*, which represents each instruction as a symbol, and translates the symbols into a binary representation suitable for execution on the computer. For example, the instruction:

```
load        R3,54
```

meaning "load register 3 with the data in memory location 54", is much more readable than the equivalent string of bits. Believe it or not, the term *automatic programming* originally referred to assemblers since they automatically selected the right bit sequence for each symbol. Familiar programming languages like C and Pascal are more sophisticated than assemblers because they "automatically" choose addresses and registers, and even "automatically" choose instruction sequences to specify loops and arithmetical expressions.

We are now ready to answer the question in the title of this chapter:

> A programming language is an abstraction mechanism. It enables a programmer to specify a computation abstractly, and to let a program (usually called an assembler, compiler or interpreter) implement the specification in the detailed form needed for execution on a computer.

We can also understand why there are hundreds of programming languages: two different classes of problems may demand different levels of abstraction, and different programmers have different ideas on how abstraction should be done. A C programmer is perfectly content to work at a level of abstraction that requires specification of computations using arrays and indices, while an author of a report prefers to "program" using a language consisting of the functions of a word-processor.

Levels of abstraction can be clearly seen in computer hardware. Originally, discrete components like transistors and resistors were wired directly to one another. Then standard plug-in modules were used, followed by small-scale integrated circuits. Today, entire computers can be constructed from a handful of chips each containing hundreds of thousands of components. No computer engineer would dare to design an "optimal" circuit from individual components if there exists a set of chips that can be adapted do to the same function.

There is a general truth that arises from the concept of abstraction:

The higher the abstraction, the more detail is lost.

If you write a program in C, you lose the ability you had in assembly language to specify register allocation; if you write in Prolog, you lose the ability you had in C to specify arbitrary linked structures using pointers. There is a natural tension between striving for the concise, clear and reliable expression of a computation in a high-level abstraction, and wanting the flexibility of specifying the computation in detail. An abstraction can never be as exact or optimal as a low-level specification.

In this textbook you will study languages at three levels of abstraction: skipping assembly language, we start with "ordinary" programming languages like Fortran, C, Pascal and the Pascal-like constructs of Ada. Then in Part IV, we discuss languages like Ada and C++ that enable the programmer to construct higher-level abstractions from statements in ordinary languages. Finally, we will describe functional and logic programming languages that work at even higher levels of abstractions.

1.2 Imperative languages

Fortran

Fortran was the first programming language that significantly rose above the level of assembly language. It was developed in the 1950's by an IBM team led by John Backus, and was intended to provide an abstract way of specifying scientific computations. The opposition to Fortran was strong for reasons similar to those advanced against all subsequent proposals for higher-level abstractions, namely, most programmers believed that a compiler could not produce optimal code relative to hand-coded assembly language.

Like most first efforts in programming languages, Fortran was seriously flawed, both in details of the language design and more importantly in the lack of support for modern concepts of data and module structuring. As Backus himself said in retrospect:

> As far as we were aware, we simply made up the language as we went along. We did not regard language design as a difficult problem, merely a simple prelude to the real problem: designing a compiler which could produce efficient programs.[1]

Nevertheless, the advantages of the abstraction quickly won over most programmers: quicker and more reliable development, and less machine dependence since register and machine instructions are abstracted away. Because most early computing was on scientific problems, Fortran became the standard language in science and engineering, and is only now being replaced by other languages. Fortran has undergone extensive modernization (1966, 1977, 1990) to adapt it to the requirements of modern software development.

Cobol and PL/I

The Cobol language was developed in the 1950's for business data processing. The language was designed by a committee consisting of representatives of the US Department of Defense, computer manufacturers and commercial organizations such as insurance companies. Cobol was intended to be only a short-range solution until a better design could be created; instead, the language as defined quickly became the most widespread language in its field (as Fortran has in science), and for a similar reason: the language provides a natural means of expressing computations that are typical in its field. Business data processing is characterized by the need to do relatively simple calculations on vast numbers of complex data records, and Cobol's data structuring capabilities far surpass those of algorithmic languages like Fortran or C.

IBM later created the language PL/I as a universal language having all the features of Fortran, Cobol and Algol. PL/I has replaced Fortran and Cobol on many IBM computers, but this very large language was never widely supported outside of IBM, especially on the mini- and micro-computers that are increasingly used in data processing organizations.

---

[1]R.L. Wexelblat, *History of Programming Languages*, Academic Press, 1981, page 30. Copyright by the ACM, Inc., reprinted by permission.

Algol and its descendants

Of the early programming languages, Algol has influenced language design more than any other. Originally designed by an international team for general and scientific applications, it never achieved widespread popularity compared to Fortran because of the support that Fortran received from most computer manufacturers. The first version of Algol was published in 1958; the revised version Algol 60 was extensively used in computer science research and implemented on many computers, especially in Europe. A third version of the language, Algol 68, has been influential among language theorists, though it was never widely implemented.

Two important languages that were derived from Algol are Jovial, used by the US Air Force for real-time systems, and Simula, one of the first simulation languages. But perhaps the most famous descendent of Algol is Pascal, developed in the late 1960's by Niklaus Wirth. The motivation for Pascal was to create a language that could be used to demonstrate ideas about type declarations and type checking. In later chapters, we will argue that these ideas are among the most significant concepts ever proposed in language design.

As a practical language, Pascal has one big advantage and one big disadvantage. The original Pascal compiler was itself written in Pascal,[2] and thus could easily be ported to any computer. The language spread quickly, especially to the mini- and micro-computers that were then being constructed. Unfortunately, the Pascal language is too small. The standard language has no facilities whatsoever for dividing a program into modules on separate files, and thus cannot be used for programs larger than several thousand lines. Practical compilers for Pascal support decomposition into modules, but there is no standard method so large programs are not portable.

Wirth immediately recognized that modules were an essential part of any practical language and developed the Modula language. Modula (now in version 3 which supports object-oriented programming) is a popular alternative to non-standard Pascal dialects.

C

C was developed by Dennis Ritchie of Bell Laboratories in the early 1970's as an implementation language for the UNIX operating system. Operating systems were traditionally written in assembly language because high-level languages were considered inefficient. C abstracts away the details of assembly language programming by offering structured control statements and

---

[2]We won't discuss here how this can be done!

data structures (arrays and records), while at the same time it retains all the flexibility of low-level programming in assembly language (pointers and bit-level operations).

Since UNIX was readily available to universities, and since it is written in a portable language rather than in raw assembly language, it quickly became the system of choice in academic and research institutions. When new computers and applications moved from these institutions to the commercial marketplace, they took UNIX and C with them.

C is designed to be close to assembly language so it is extremely flexible; the problem is that this flexibility makes it extremely easy to write programs with obscure bugs because unsafe constructs are not checked by the compiler as they would be in Pascal. C is a sharp tool when used expertly on small programs, but can cause serious trouble when used on large software systems developed by teams of varying ability. We will point out many of the dangers of constructs in C and show how to avoid major pitfalls.

The C language was standardized in 1989 by the American National Standards Institute (ANSI); essentially the same standard was adopted by the International Standards Organization (ISO) a year later. References to C in this book are to ANSI C[3] and not to earlier versions of the language.

C++

In the 1980's Bjarne Stroustrup, also from Bell Laboratories, used C as the basis of the C++ language, extending C to include support for object-oriented programming similar to that provided by the Simula language. In addition, C++ fixes many mistakes in C and should be used in preference to C, even on small programs where the object-oriented features may not be needed. C++ is the natural language to use when upgrading a system written in C.

Note that C++ is an evolving language and your reference manual or compiler may not be fully up-to-date. The discussion in this book follows *The Annotated C++ Reference Manual* by Ellis and Stroustrup (as reprinted in 1994) which is the basis for the standard now being considered.

Ada

In 1977 the United States Department of Defense decided to standardize on one programming language, mainly to save on training and on the cost of maintaining program development environments for each military system. After evaluating existing languages, they chose to ask for the development

---

[3]Technically, the ANSI standard was withdrawn with the appearance of the ISO standard, but colloquially the language is still known as ANSI C.

of a new language to be based on a good existing language such as Pascal. Eventually one proposal was chosen for a language which was named Ada, and a standard was adopted in 1983. Ada is unique in several aspects:

- Most languages (Fortran, C, Pascal) were proposed and developed by a single team, and only standardized after they were in widespread use. For compatibility, all the unintentional mistakes of the original teams were included in the standard. Ada was subjected to intense review and criticism before standardization.

- Most languages were initially implemented on a single computer and were heavily influenced by the quirks of that computer. Ada was designed to support writing portable programs.

- Ada extends the scope of programming languages by supporting error handling and concurrent programming which are traditionally left to (non-standard) operating system functions.

Despite technical excellence and advantages of early standardization, Ada has not achieved widespread popularity outside of military and other large-scale projects (such as commercial aviation and rail transportation). Ada has received a reputation as a difficult language. This is because the language supports many aspects of programming (concurrency, exception handling, portable numerics) that other languages (like C and Pascal) leave to the operating system, so there is simply more to learn. Also, good and inexpensive development environments for education were not initially available. Now with free compilers (see Appendix A) and good introductory textbooks available, Ada is increasingly used in the academic curriculum, even as a "first" language.

Ada 95

Exactly twelve years after the finalization of the first standard for the Ada language in 1983, a new standard for the Ada language has been published. The new version, called Ada 95, corrects some mistakes in the original version. But the main extension is support for true object-oriented programming including inheritance which was left out of Ada 83 because it was thought to be inefficient. In addition, the Ada 95 standard contains annexes that describe standard (but optional) extensions for real-time systems, distributed systems, information systems, numerics and secure systems.

In this text, the name "Ada" will be used unless the discussion is specific to one version: "Ada 83" or "Ada 95". Note that in the literature, Ada 95 was referred to as Ada 9X since the exact date of standardization was not known during the development.

1.3   Data-oriented languages

In the early days of programming several very influential languages were designed and implemented that had one characteristic in common: the languages each had a preferred data structure and an extensive set of operations for the preferred structure. These languages made it possible to create sophisticated programs that were otherwise difficult to write in languages such as Fortran that simply manipulated computer words. In the following subsections we will survey some of these languages.[4]

Lisp

Lisp's basic data structure is the linked list. Originally designed for research in the theory of computation, much work on artificial intelligence was carried out in Lisp. The language was so important that computers were designed and built to be optimized for the execution of Lisp programs. One problem with the language was the proliferation of different dialects as the language was implemented on different machines. The Common Lisp language was later developed to enable programs to be ported from one computer to another. Currently, a popular dialect of Lisp is CLOS which supports object-oriented programming.

The three elementary operations of Lisp are: car(L) and cdr(L)[5] which extract the head and tail of a list L, respectively, and cons(E, L) which creates a new list from an element E and an existing list L. Using these operations, functions can be defined to process lists containing non-numeric data; such functions would be extremely difficult to program in Fortran.

We will not discuss Lisp further because many of its basic ideas have been carried over in modern functional programming languages such as ML which we will discuss in Chapter 16.

APL

The APL language evolved from a mathematical formalism used to describe calculations. The basic data structures are vectors and matrices, and oper-

---

[4]You may wish to defer reading this section and return to it after studying Parts I and II.

[5]The strange notation is a historical artifact of the first computer on which Lisp was implemented.

ations work directly on such structures without loops. Thus programs are very concise compared with similar programs in ordinary languages. A difficulty with APL is that the language carried over a large set of mathematical symbols from the original formalism. This requires a special terminal and makes it difficult to experiment with APL without investing in costly hardware; modern graphical user interfaces which use software fonts have solved this problem that slowed acceptance of APL.

Given a vector:

V = 1 5 10 15 20 25

APL operators can work directly on V without writing loops on the vector indices:

+/V	= 76	Reduction of addition (add elements)
ϕ V	= 25 20 15 10 5 1	Reverse the vector

$$2\ 3\rho\ V\ =\ \begin{matrix} 1 & 5 & 10 \\ 15 & 20 & 25 \end{matrix}$$ Redimension V as 2×3 matrix

In addition, vector and matrix addition and multiplication can be done directly on such values.

Snobol, Icon

Early languages dealt almost exclusively with numbers. For work in fields such as natural language processing, Snobol (and its successor Icon) are ideally suited because their basic data structure is the string. The basic operation in Snobol is matching a pattern to a string, and as a side-effect of the match, the string can be decomposed into substrings. In Icon, the basic operation is expression evaluation, where expressions include complex string operations.

An important predefined function in Icon is find(s1, s2) which searches for occurrences of the string s1 in the string s2. Unlike similar functions in C, find *generates* a list of all positions in s2 in which s1 occurs:

```
line := 0                      # Initialize line counter
while s := read() {            # Read until end of file
    every col := find("the", s) do
                               # Generate column positions
        write(line, " ", col)  # Write (line,col) of "the"
    line := line + 1
}
```

This program will write the line and column numbers of all occurrences of the string "the" in a file. If find does not find an occurrence, it will fail and the evaluation of the expression is terminated. The keyword every forces the repeated evaluation of the function as long as it is successful.

Icon expressions are not limited to strings which are sequences of characters; they are also defined on *csets*, which are sets of characters. Thus:

```
vowels := 'aeiou'
```

gives the variable vowel a value that is the set of characters shown. This can be used in functions like upto(vowels,s) which generates the sequence of locations of vowels in s, and many(vowels,s) which returns the longest initial sequence of vowels in s.

A more complex function is bal which is like upto except that it generates sequences of locations which are balanced with respect to bracketing characters:

```
bal('+-*/', '([', ')]', s)
```

This expression could be used in a compiler to generate balanced arithmetic sub-strings. Given the string "x+(y[u/v]-1)*z", the above expression will generate the indices corresponding to the sub-strings:

```
x
x + (y[u/v] - 1)
```

The first sub-string is balanced because it is terminated by "+" and there are no bracketing characters; the second is balanced because it is terminated by "*" and has square brackets correctly nested within parentheses.

Since an expression can fail, *backtracking* can be used to continue the search from earlier generators. The following program prints the occurrences of vowels except those that begin in column 1:

```
line := 0                      # Initialize line counter
while s := read() {            # Read until end of file
    every col := (upto(vowels, line) > 1) do
                               # Generate column positions
        write(line, " ", col)  # Write (line,col) of vowel
    line := line + 1
}
```

The function find will generate an index which will then be tested by ">". If the test fails (don't say: "if the result is false"), the program returns to the generator function upto to ask for a new index.

Icon is a practical language for programs that require complex string manipulation. Most of the explicit computation with indices is abstracted away, producing programs that are extremely concise relative to ordinary languages that were designed for numeric or systems programming. In addition, Icon is very interesting because of the built-in mechanism for generation and backtracking which offers a further level of control abstraction.

SETL

SETL's basic data structure is the set. Since sets are the most general mathematical structure from which all other mathematical structures are defined, SETL can be used to create generalized programs that are very abstract and thus very concise. The programs resemble logic programs (Chapter 17) in that mathematical descriptions can be directly executed. The notation used is that of set theory: $\{x \mid p(x)\}$ meaning the set of all x such that the logical formula $p(x)$ is true. For example, a mathematical specification of the set of prime numbers can be written:

$$\{n \mid \neg \exists m[(2 \le m \le n - 1) \wedge (n \bmod m = 0)]\}$$

This formula is read: the set of numbers such that there does not exist a number m between 2 and $n - 1$ that divides n without a remainder.

To print all primes in the range 2 to 100, we just translate the definition into a one-line SETL program:

```
print({n in {2..100} | not exists m in {2..n-1} | (n mod m) = 0});
```

What all these languages have in common is that they approach language design from a mathematical viewpoint—how can a well-understood theory be implemented, rather than from an engineering viewpoint—how can instructions be issued to the CPU and memory. In practice, these advanced languages are very useful for difficult programming tasks where it is important to concentrate on the problem and not on low-level details.

Data-oriented languages are somewhat less popular than they once were, partly because by using object-oriented techniques it is possible to embed such data-oriented operations into ordinary languages like C++ and Ada, but also because of competition from newer language concepts like functional and logic programming. Nevertheless, the languages are technically interesting and quite practical for the programming tasks for which they were designed. Students should make an effort to learn one or more of these languages, because they broaden one's vision of how a programming language can be structured.

1.4 Object-oriented languages

Object-oriented programming (OOP) is a method of structuring programs by identifying real-world or other objects, and then writing modules each of which contains all the data and executable statements needed to represent one *class* of objects. Within such a module, there is a clear distinction between the abstract properties of the class which are exported for use by other objects, and the implementation which is hidden so that it can be modified without affecting the rest of the system.

The first object-oriented programming language, Simula, was created in the 1960's by K. Nygaard and O.-J. Dahl for system simulation: each subsystem taking part in the simulation was programmed as an object. Since there can be more than one instance of each subsystem, a class can be written to describe each subsystem and objects of this class can then be allocated.

The Xerox Palo Alto Research Center popularized OOP with the Smalltalk[6] language. The same research also led to the windowing systems so popular today, and in fact, an important advantage of Smalltalk is that it is not just a language, but a complete programming environment. The technical achievement of Smalltalk was to show that a language can be defined in which classes and objects are the *only* structuring constructs, so there is no need to introduce these concepts into an "ordinary" language.

There is a technical aspect of these pioneering object-oriented languages that prevented wider acceptance of OOP: allocation, operation dispatching and type checking are dynamic (run-time) as opposed to static (compile-time). Without going into detail here (see the appropriate material in Chapters 8 and 14), the result is that there is a time and memory overhead to programs in these languages which can be prohibitive in many types of systems. In addition, static type checking (see Chapter 4) is now considered essential for developing reliable software. For these reasons, Ada 83 only implemented a subset of the language support required for OOP.

C++ showed that it was possible to implement the entire machinery of OOP in a manner that is consistent with *static* allocation and type-checking, and with fixed overhead for dispatching; the dynamic requirements of OOP are used only as needed. Ada 95 based its support for OOP on ideas similar to those found in C++.

However, it is not necessary to graft support for OOP onto existing languages to obtain these advantages. The Eiffel language is similar to Smalltalk in that the only structuring method is that of classes and objects, and it is similar to C++ and Ada 95 in that it is statically type-checked and the imple-

---

[6]Smalltalk is a trademark of Xerox Corporation.

mentation of objects can be static or dynamic as needed. The simplicity of
the language relative to the "hybrids", combined with full support for OOP,
make Eiffel an excellent choice for a first programming language.

We will discuss language support for OOP in great detail, first using C++
and then Ada 95. In addition, a short description of Eiffel will show what a
"pure" OOP language is like.

1.5 Non-imperative languages

All the languages we have discussed have one trait in common: the basic
statement is the assignment statement which commands the computer to
move data from one place to another. This is actually a relatively low level
of abstraction compared to the level of the problems we want to solve with
computers. Newer languages prefer to describe a problem and let the computer figure out how to solve it, rather than specifying in great detail how to
move data around.

Modern software packages are really highly abstract programming languages. An application generator lets you *describe* a series of screen and
database structures, and then automatically creates the low-level commands
needed to implement the program. Similarly, spreadsheets, desktop publishing software, simulation packages and so on have extensive facilities for
abstract programming. The disadvantage of this type of software is that they
are usually limited in the type of application that can be easily programmed.
It seems appropriate to called them *parameterized programs*, in the sense
that by supplying descriptions as parameters, the package will configure
itself to execute the program you need.

Another approach to abstract programming is to describe a computation
using equations, functions, logical implications, or some similar formalism.
Since mathematical formalisms are used, languages defined this way are true
general-purpose programming languages, not limited to any particular application domain. The compiler does not really translate the program into
machine code; rather it attempts to solve the mathematical problem, whose
solution is considered to be the output of the program. Since indices, pointers, loops, etc. are abstracted away, these programs can be an order of
magnitude shorter than ordinary programs. The main problem with descriptive programming is that computational tasks like I/O to a screen or disk do
not fit in well with the concept, and the languages must be extended with
ordinary programming constructs for these purposes.

We will discuss two non-imperative language formalisms: (1) functional
programming (Chapter 16), which is based on the mathematical concept of

pure functions, like sin and log that do not modify their environments, unlike so-called functions in an ordinary language like C which can have side-effects; (2) logic programming (Chapter 17), in which programs are expressed as formulas in mathematical logic, and the "compiler" attempts to infer logical consequences of these formulas in order to solve problems.

It should be obvious that programs in an abstract, non-imperative language cannot hope to be as efficient as hand-coded C programs. Non-imperative languages are to be preferred whenever a software system must search through large amounts of data, or solve problems whose solution cannot be precisely described. Examples are: language processing (translation, style checking), pattern matching (vision, genetics) and process optimization (scheduling). As implementation techniques improve and as it becomes ever more difficult to develop reliable software systems in ordinary languages, these languages will become more widespread.

Functional and logic programming languages are highly recommended as first programming languages, so that students learn from the start to work at higher levels of abstraction than they would if they were introduced to programming via Pascal or C.

1.6 Standardization

The importance of standardization must be emphasized. *If* a standard exists for a language and *if* compilers adhere to the standard, programs can be ported from one computer to another. If you are writing a software package that is to run on a wide range of computers, you should strictly adhere to a standard. Otherwise your maintenance task will be extremely complicated because you must keep track of dozens or hundreds of machine-specific items.

Standards exist (or are in preparation) for most languages discussed here. Unfortunately, the standards were proposed years after the languages became popular and must preserve machine-specific quirks of early implementations. The Ada language is an exception in that the standards (1983 and 1995) were created and evaluated at the same time as the language design and initial implementation. Furthermore, the standard is enforced so that compilers can be compared based on performance and cost, rather than on adherence to the standard. Compilers for other languages may have a mode that will warn you if you are using a non-standard construct. If such constructs must be used, they should be concentrated in a few well-documented modules.

1.7 Computer architecture

Since we are dealing with programming languages as they are used in practice, we include a short section on computer architecture so that a minimal set of terms can be agreed upon. A computer is composed of a *central processing unit* (CPU) and *memory* (Figure 1.1). Input/output devices can be considered

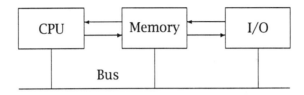

Figure 1.1 Computer architecture

to be a special case of memory. All components of a computer are normally connect together on a *bus*. Physically a bus is a set of connectors wired in parallel; logically a bus is a definition of the signals that enable the components to exchange data. As shown in the figure, modern computers may have more direct connections between the components to improve performance (by specializing the interface and by avoiding bottlenecks). From the point of view of the software, the only difference that need be considered is the rate at which data can be transferred between components.

The CPU contains a set of *registers* which are special memory locations in which computation is be done. The CPU can execute any one of a set of *instructions* which are stored in memory; the CPU maintains an *instruction pointer* which points to the location of the next instruction to be executed. Instructions are divided into the following classes:

- Memory access: Load the contents of a memory word into a register, and Store the contents of a register into a memory word.

- Arithmetic instructions such as add and subtract. These operations are performed on the contents of two registers (or sometimes between the content of a register and the content of a memory word). The result is left in a register. For example:

      add   R1,N

  adds the contents of the memory word N to the contents of the register R1 and leaves the result in the register.

• Compare and jump. The CPU can compare two values such as the contents of two registers; depending on the result (equal, greater than, etc.), the instruction pointer is changed to point to another instruction. For example:

```
        jump_eq    R1,L1
           ...
    L1:    ...
```

causes the computation to continue with the instruction labeled L1 if the contents of R1 are zero; otherwise, the computation continues with the next instruction.

Many computers, called *Reduced Instruction Set Computers* (RISC), limit themselves to these elementary instructions; the rationale is that a CPU that only needs to execute a few simple instructions can be very fast. Other computers define more Complex Instructions (CISC) to simplify both assembly language programming and compiler construction. The debate between these two approaches is beyond the scope of this book; they have enough in common that the choice does not materially affect our discussion.

Memory is a set of locations that can be used to store data. Each memory location, called a memory *word*, has an *address*, and each word consists of a fixed number of bits, typically 16, 32, or 64 bits. The computer may be able to load and store 8 bit *bytes*, or double words of 64 bits.

It is important to know what kind of addressing modes can be used in an instruction. The simplest mode is immediate addressing which means that the operand is part of the instruction. The value of the operand may be the address of a variable and we will use the C notation in this case:

```
        load       R3,#54          Load value 54 into R3
        load       R2,&N           Load address of N into R2
```

Next we have the absolute addressing mode, which is usually used with the symbolic address of a variable:

```
        load       R3,54           Load contents of address 54
        load       R4,N            Load contents of variable N
```

Modern computers make extensive use of *index registers*. Index registers are not necessarily separate from registers used for computation; what is important is that the register has the property that the address of an operand of an instruction can be obtained from the content of the register. For example:

```
load        R3,54(R2)          Load contents of addr(R2)+54
load        R4,(R1)            Load contents of addr(R1)+0
```

where the first instruction means "load into register R3 the contents of the memory word whose address is obtained by adding 54 to the contents of the (index) register R2"; the second instruction is a special case which just uses the contents of register R1 as the address of a memory word whose contents are loaded into R4. Index registers are essential to efficient implementation of loops and arrays.

Cache and virtual memory

One of the hardest problems confronting computer architects is matching the performance of the CPU to the performance of the memory. CPU processing speeds are so fast compared with memory access times, that the memory cannot supply data fast enough for the CPU to be kept continuously working. There are two reasons for this: (1) there are only a few CPU's (usually one) in a computer, and the fastest, most expensive technology can be used, but memory is installed in ever increasing amounts and must use less-expensive technology; (2) the speeds are so fast that a limiting factor is the speed at which electricity flows in the wires between the CPU and the memory.

The solution is to use a hierarchy of memories as shown in Figure 1.2. The idea is to store unlimited amounts of program instructions and data in

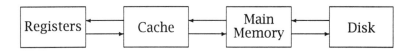

Figure 1.2 Cache and virtual memory

relatively slow (and inexpensive) memory, and to load relevant portions of the instructions and data into smaller amounts of fast (and expensive) memory. When the slow memory is disk and the fast memory is ordinary RAM (Random Access Memory), the concept is called *virtual memory* or *paged memory*. When the slow memory is RAM and the fast memory is RAM implemented in a faster technology, the concept is called *cache memory*.

A discussion of these concepts is beyond the scope of this book, but the programmer must be aware of the potential effect of cache or virtual memory on a program, even though the maintenance of these memories is done by the computer hardware or operating system software, and is totally transparent to the programmer. Instructions and data are moved between slower and faster memory in blocks, not in single words. This means that a sequence of instructions without jumps, and a sequence of consecutive data accesses (such as indexing through an array) are likely to be much more efficient than jumps and random accesses, which require the computer to move different blocks between levels of the memory hierarchy. If you are attempting to improve the efficiency of a program, you should resist the temptation to write portions in lower-level languages or assembly language; instead, attempt to rearrange the computation taking into consideration the influence of the cache and virtual memory. The rearrangement of statements in a high-level language does not affect the portability of the program, though of course the efficiency improvement may not carry over to another computer with a different architecture.

1.8 * Computability

In the 1930's, even before digital computers were invented, logicians studied abstract concepts of computation. Alan Turing and Alonzo Church each proposed extremely simple models of computation (called *Turing machines* and *Lambda calculus*, respectively) and then advanced the following claim (known as the *Church-Turing Thesis*):

> Any effective computation can be done in one of these models.

Turing machines are extremely simple; expressed in the syntax of C, there are two data declarations:

```
char tape[...];
int current = 0;
```

where the tape is potentially infinite.[7] A program consists of any number of statements of the form:

```
L17:   if (tape[current] == 'g') {
            tape[current++] = 'j';
            goto L43;
        }
```

Executing a statement of a Turing machine is done in four stages:

- Read and examine the current character[8] on the current cell of the tape.

---

[7]This does not mean that an infinite number of memory words need be allocated, only that we can always plug in more memory if needed.

[8]In fact, it is sufficient to use just two characters, blank and non-blank.

- Replace the character with another character (optional).

- Increment or decrement the pointer to the current cell.

- Jump to any other statement.

According to the Church-Turing Thesis, any computation that you can effectively describe can be programmed on this primitive machine. The evidence for the Thesis rests on two foundations:

- Researchers have proposed dozens of models of computation and all of them have been proven to be equivalent to Turing machines.

- No one has ever described a computation that cannot be computed by a Turing machine.

Since a Turing machine can easily be simulated in any programming language, all programming languages "do" the same thing.

1.9 Exercises

1. Describe how to implement a compiler for a language in the same language ("bootstrapping").

2. Invent a syntax for an APL-like matrix-based language that uses ordinary characters.

3. Write a list of interesting operations on strings and compare your list with the predefined operations of Snobol and Icon.

4. Write a list of interesting operations on sets and compare your list with the predefined operations of SETL.

5. Simulate a (universal) Turing machine in several programming languages.

2   Elements of Programming Languages

2.1 Syntax

Like ordinary languages, programming languages have syntax:

> The *syntax* of a (programming) language is a set of rules that define what sequences of symbols are considered to be valid expressions (programs) in the language.

The syntax (set of rules) is expressed using a formal notation.

The most widespread formal notation for syntax is *Extended Backus-Naur Form* (*EBNF*) In EBNF, we start with a highest level entity *program* and use rules to decompose entities until single characters are reached. For example, in C the syntax of an if-statement is given by the rule:

> *if-statement* ::= **if** (*expression*) *statement* [**else** *statement*]

Names in italic represent syntactic categories, while names and symbols in boldface represent actual characters that must appear in the program. Each rule contains the symbol "::=" which means "is composed of". Various other symbols are used to make the rules more concise:

> [ ]   Optional   { }   Zero or more repetitions | Or

Thus the else-clause of an if-statement is optional. The use of braces is demonstrated by the (simplified) rule for the declaration of a list of variables:

> *variable-declaration* ::= *type-specifier identifier* {**,** *identifier*}**;**

This is read: a variable declaration *is composed of* a type specifier followed by an identifier (the variable name), optionally followed by a sequence of identifiers preceded by commas, and terminated by a semicolon.

Syntax rules are easier to learn if they are given as syntax diagrams (Figure 2.1). Circles or ovals denote actual characters, while rectangles denote

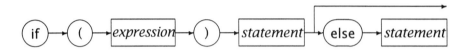

Figure 2.1 Syntax diagram

syntactic categories which have their own diagram. A sequence of symbols constructed by tracing a path in the diagrams is a (syntactically) valid program.

While many programmers have a passionate attachment to the syntax of a specific language, this aspect of a language is perhaps the least important. It is easy to learn and to develop familiarity with any reasonable syntax; furthermore, bugs with syntax are caught by the compiler and rarely cause problems with a working program. We will restrict ourselves to noting several possible pitfalls with syntax that can cause run-time bugs:

- Be careful with limitations on the significance of the length of identifiers. If only the first 10 characters are significant, current_winner and current_width will represent the same identifier.

- Many languages are case-insensitive, that is, COUNT and count represent the same name. C is case-sensitive, so that the strings represent two distinct identifiers. In case-sensitive languages, a project should establish clear conventions on the use of case so that accidental typing mistakes do not cause errors. For example, one convention in C requires that everything be in lower-case, except defined constant names which are all in upper-case.

- There are two forms of comments: Fortran, Ada and C++ comments begin with a symbol (C, --, and //, respectively) and extend to the end of a line, while C[1] and Pascal comments have both begin- and end-symbols: /*...*/ in C, and (*...*) or {...} in Pascal. The second form is convenient for "commenting-out" unused code that may have been inserted for testing, but it is possible to omit an end-symbol causing a sequence of statements to be ignored:

```
/*                        Comment should end here     [C]
a = b+c;                  Statement will be ignored
/* ... */                 Comment ends here
```

---

[1]C++ also allows the use of C-style comments.

- Beware of similar but distinct symbols. If you have ever studied mathematics, you should be surprised that the familiar symbol "=" is used for the assignment operator in C and Fortran, while new symbols "==" in C and ".eq." in Fortran are used for the familiar equality operator. The tendency to write:

> if (a = b) ...   `C`

is so common that many compilers will issue a warning even though the statement has a valid meaning.

- For its historical interest, we mention a notorious problem with the syntax of Fortran. Most languages require that words in a program be separated by one or more spaces (or other *whitespace* characters such as tabs), while in Fortran whitespace is ignored. Consider then the following statement, which specifies "loop until label 10 as the index i counts from 1 to 100":

> do 10 i = 1, 100   `Fortran`

If the comma is accidentally replaced by a period, the statement becomes a valid assignment statement, assigning 1.100 to the variable whose name is obtained by concatenating all characters before the "=":

> do10i = 1.100   `Fortran`

This bug is reported to have caused a rocket to explode upon launch into space!

2.2 * Semantics

Semantics is the meaning of an expression (program) in a (programming) language.

While the syntax of languages is very well understood, semantics is much more difficult. To give an example from English, consider the sentences:

> The pig is in the pen.
> The ink is in the pen.

It requires quite a lot of general knowledge that has nothing to do with the English language to know that "pen" does not have the same meaning in the two sentences.

Formal notations for programming language semantics are beyond the scope of this book. We will restrict ourselves to a few sentences that give the basic idea. At any point in its execution, we can describe the *state* of a program which is composed of: (1) a pointer to the next instruction to be executed, and (2) the contents of the program's memory.[2] The semantics of a statement is given by specifying the change in state caused by the execution of the statement. For example, executing:

   a := 25

will change the state s to a new state s' that is exactly like s except that the memory location assigned to a contains 25.

For control statements, mathematical logic is used to describe the computation. Assume that we already know the meaning of two statements S1 and S2 in an arbitrary state s. This is denoted by the formulas $p(S1, s)$ and $p(S2, s)$, respectively. Then the meaning of the if-statement:

   if C then S1 else S2

is given by the formula:

$$(C(s) \Rightarrow p(S1, s)) \& (\neg C(s) \Rightarrow p(S2, s))$$

If C evaluates to *true* in state s then the meaning of the if-statement is the same as the meaning of S1; otherwise, C evaluates to *not true* and the meaning is the same as that of S2.

As you can imagine, specifying the semantics of loop statements and procedure calls with parameters can be very difficult. In this book, we will content ourselves with the informal explanations of the semantics of language constructs as commonly written in reference manuals:

> The condition following if is evaluated; if the result is True, the statement following then is executed, otherwise the statement following else is executed.

An additional advantage to a formalization of the semantics of programming languages is that it becomes possible to *prove* the correctness of a program. The effect of an execution of the program can be formalized by axioms that describe how the statement transforms a state that satisfies an input *assertion* (logical formula) to a state that satisfies an output assertion. The meaning of a program is obtained by building input and output assertions for the whole program based on the individual statements. The result

---

[2]More exactly a mapping from every variable to its value.

is a proof that *if* the input data satisfies the input assertion, *then* the output data satisfies the output assertion.

Of course, the proof of correctness is only relative to the input and output assertions: it does you no good to prove that a program computes a square root if you need a program to compute a cube root! Nevertheless, program verification is a powerful method that has been used in systems that must be highly reliable. More importantly, studying verification will improve your ability to write correct programs, because you will learn to think in terms of the requirements for correctness. We also recommend studying and using the Eiffel programming language which includes support for assertions within the language (Section 11.5).

2.3 Data

When first learning a programming language there is a tendency to concentrate on actions: statements or commands. Only when the statements of the language have been studied and exercised, do we turn to study the support that the language provides for structuring data. In modern views of programming such as object-oriented programming, statements are seen as manipulating the data used to represent some object. Thus you should study the data structuring aspects of a language before the statements.

Assembly language programs can be seen as specifications of actions to be performed on *physical* entities such as registers and memory cells. Early programming languages continued this tradition of identifying language entities like *variables* with memory words, even though mathematical names like *integer* were attributed to these variables. In Chapters 4 and 9 we will explain why int and float are not mathematical, but rather physical representations of memory.

We now define the central concept of programming:

> A *type* is a set of *values* and a set of *operations* on those values.

The correct meaning of int in C is: int is a type consisting of a finite set of values (about 65,000 or 4 billion, depending on the computer), and a set of operations (denoted by +, <=, etc.) on these values. Modern programming languages like Ada and C++ are characterized by their ability to create new types. Thus, we are no longer restricted to the handful of types predefined by the inventor of the language; instead, we can create our own types that correspond more exactly to the problem that we are trying to solve.

The discussion of data types in this book will follow this approach, namely, define a set of values and the operations on these values. Only later will we discuss how such a type can be implemented on a computer. For example, an array is an indexed collection of elements with operations such as indexing. Note that the definition of a type varies with the language: assignment is an operation defined on arrays in Ada but not in C. Following the definition of an array type, the implementation of arrays as sequences of memory cells can be studied.

To conclude this section, we define the following terms that will be used when discussing data:

Value A value is an undefined primitive concept.

Literal A specific value is denoted in a program by a literal, which is a sequence of symbols, for example: 154, 45.6, FALSE, 'x', "Hello world".

Representation A value is represented within a computer by a specific string of bits. For example, the character value denoted by 'x' may be represented by the string of eight bits 0111 1000.

Variable A variable is a name given to the memory cell or cells that can hold the representation of a value of a specific type. The value may be changed during the execution of the program.

Constant A constant is a name given to the memory cell or cells that can hold the representation of a value of a specific type. The value may *not* be changed during the execution of the program.

Object An object is a variable or a constant.

Note that a variable must be defined to be of a specific type for the simple reason that the compiler must know how much memory to allocate! A constant is simply a variable that can not be modified. Until we discuss object-oriented programming, we will generally use the familiar term variable, rather than the precise term object to denote either a constant or a variable.

2.4 The assignment statement

Surprisingly, ordinary programming languages have only one statement that actually does anything: the assignment statement. All other statements such as if-statements and procedure calls exist only to control the sequence of execution of the assignment statements. Unfortunately, it is difficult to give a formal meaning to the assignment statement (as opposed to describing what it does when executed); in fact, you never encountered anything similar when you studied mathematics in high school and college. What you studied was *equations*:

$$ax^2 + bx + c = 0 \qquad \int \sin x \, dx = -\cos x$$

You transformed equations, you solved them and you evaluated them. Never did you modify them: if x represented a number in one part of the equation, it represented the same number in the rest of the equation.

The lowly assignment statement is actually quite complex, executing three separate tasks:

1. Compute the value of the expression on the right-hand side of the statement.

2. Compute the expression on the left-hand side of the statement; the expression must evaluate to the address of a memory cell.

3. Copy the value obtained in step (1) to memory cells starting with the address obtained in step (2).

Thus the assignment statement:

```
a(i+1) = b + c;
```

despite its superficial resemblance to an equation specifies a complex computation.

2.5 Type checking

In the three-step description of assignment, the evaluation of the expression produces a value of a specific type, while the computation of the left-hand-side produces only the starting address of a block of memory. There is no guarantee that the address is associated with a variable of the same type as that of the expression; in fact there is not even a guarantee that the *size* of the value to be copied is the same as the size of the receiving variable.

> *Type checking* is a check that the type of the expression is compatible with the type of the target variable during assignment. This includes the assignment of an actual parameter to a formal parameter when a procedure is called.

Possible approaches to type checking are:

- Do nothing; it is the programmer's responsibility to ensure that the assignment is meaningful.

- Implicitly convert the value of the expression to the type required by the left-hand side.

- *Strong* type checking: refuse to execute the assignment if the types are not the same.

There is a clear trade-off between flexibility and reliability: the more type checking that is done the more reliable a program will be, but it will require more programming effort to define an appropriate set of types. In addition, provision must be made to bypass type checking if needed. Conversely, if little type checking is done it is easy to write a program, but it then becomes difficult to find bugs and to ensure the reliability of the program. A further disadvantage to type checking is that it may require run-time overhead to implement. Implicit type conversion can be as bad as, if not worse than, doing nothing because it gives a false sense of security that all is well.

Strong type checking can eliminate obscure bugs which are usually caused by such errors or misunderstandings. It is especially important in large software projects which are developed by teams of programmers; breakdowns in communications, personnel turnovers, etc. make it difficult to integrate such software without the constant checking done by strong type checking. In effect, strong type checking attempts to transform run-time errors into compile-time errors. Run-time errors can be extremely difficult to find, dangerous to the users of the software and expensive for the developer of the software in terms of delayed delivery and damaged reputation. The cost of a compile-time error is trivial; in fact, you probably don't even have to tell your boss that you made a compile-time error.

2.6 Control statements

Assignment statements are normally executed in the sequence in which they are written. Control statements are used to modify the order of execution. Assembly language programs use arbitrary jumps from one instruction address to another. By analogy, a programming language can include a goto-statement which jumps to a label on an arbitrary statement. Programs using arbitrary jumps are difficult to read, and hence to modify and maintain.

Structured programming is the name given to the programming style which restricts the use of control statements to those which yield well-structured programs that are easy to read and understand. There are two classes of well-structured control statements:

- Choice statements that select one alternative from two or more possible execution sequences: if-statements and case- or switch-statements.

- Loop statements that repeatedly execute a sequence of statements: for-statements and while-statements.

A good understanding of loop statements is particularly important for two reasons: (1) most of the execution time will (obviously) be spent within loop statements, and (2) many bugs are caused by incorrect coding at the beginning or end of a loop.

2.7 Subprograms

A *subprogram* is a unit consisting of data declarations and executable statements that can be invoked (*called*) repeatedly from different parts of a program. Subprograms (called *procedures, functions, subroutines* or *methods*) were originally used just to enable such reuse of a program segment. The more modern view is that subprograms are an essential element of program structure, and that every program segment that does some identifiable task should be placed in a separate subprogram.

When a subprogram is called, it is passed a sequence of values called *parameters*. Parameters are used to modify each execution of the subprogram, to send data to the subprogram, and to receive the results of a computation. Parameter passing mechanisms differ widely from one language to another, and programmers must fully understand their effect on the reliability and efficiency of a program.

2.8 Modules

The elements of the language discussed thus far are sufficient for writing *programs*; they are not sufficient for writing a *software system*: a very large program or set of programs developed by teams of programmers. Students often extrapolate from their talent at writing (small) programs, and conclude that writing a software system is no different, but bitter experience has shown that writing a large system requires additional methods and tools beyond mere programming. The term *software engineering* is used to denote the methods and tools for designing, managing and constructing software systems. In this text we limit ourselves to discussing support for large systems that can be given by programming languages.

You may have been told that a single subprogram should be limited to 40 or 50 lines, because a programmer cannot easily read and comprehend larger segments of code. By the same measure, it should be easy to understand the interactions of 40 or 50 subprograms. The obvious conclusion is that any program larger than 1600-2500 lines is hard to understand! Since useful programs can have tens of thousands of lines, and systems of hundreds of thousands of lines are not uncommon, it is clear that additional structures are needed to construct large systems.

If older programming languages are used, the only recourse is to "bureaucracy": sets of rules and conventions that prescribe to the team members how programs are to be written. Modern programming languages contain an additional structuring method for *encapsulating*[3] data and subprograms within larger entities called *modules*. The advantage of modules over bureaucracy is that the interfaces between modules can be checked during compilation to prevent errors and misunderstandings. Furthermore, the actual executable statements, and most (or all) of the data of a module, can be hidden so that they cannot be modified or used except as specified by the interface.

The are two potential difficulties with the practical use of modules:

- A powerful program development environment is needed to keep track of the modules and to check the interfaces.

- Modularization encourages the use of many small subprograms with the corresponding run-time overhead of the subprogram call.

Neither of these is now a problem: the average personal computer is more than adequate to run an environment for C++ or Ada, and modern computer architectures and compilation techniques minimize the overhead of calls.

The fact that a language has support for modules does not help us to decide what to put in a module. In other words, how do we decompose a software system into modules? Since the quality of the system is directly dependent on the quality of the decomposition, the competence of a software engineer should be judged on his/her ability to analyze a project's requirements and to create the best software structure to implement the project. It requires much experience to develop this ability; perhaps the best way is to study existing software systems.

Despite the fact that sound engineering judgement cannot be taught, there are certain principles that can be studied. One of the leading methods for guiding program decomposition is *object-oriented programming* (OOP) which builds on the concept of type discussed above. According to OOP, a module should be constructed for any real-world or abstract "object" that can be represented by a set of data and operations on that data. Chapters 14 and 15 contain a detailed discussion of language support for OOP.

---

[3]From the word "capsule", container.

2.9 Exercises

1. Translate (part of) the BNF syntax of C or Ada into syntax diagrams.

2. Write a program in Pascal or C that compiles and executes, but computes the wrong answer because of a comment that was not closed.

3. Even if Ada used the style of comments used in C and Pascal, bugs caused by not closing comments would be less frequent. Why?

4. In most languages, keywords like begin and while are reserved and may not be used as identifiers. Other languages like Fortran and PL/I do not have reserved keywords. What are the advantages and disadvantages of reserved words?

3 Programming Environments

A language is a set of rules for writing programs which are no more than sequences of symbols. This chapter will review the components of a *programming environment*—the set of tools used to transform symbols into executable computations:

Editor An editor is a tool used to create and modify *source* files, which are files of characters that comprise a program in a language.

Compiler A compiler translates the symbols in a source file into an *object module*, which contains machine code instructions for a specific computer.

Librarian A librarian maintains collections of object files called libraries.

Linker A linker collects the object files of the components of the program and *resolves* external references from one component to another in order to form an *executable* file.

Loader A loader copies the executable file from the disk into memory, and initializes the computer before executing the program.

Debugger A debugger is a tool that enables the programmer to control the execution of a program at the level of individual statements, so that bugs can be diagnosed.

Profiler A profiler measures the relative amount of time spent in each component of a program. The programmer can then concentrate on improving the efficiency of *bottlenecks*: components responsible for most of the execution time.

Testing tools Testing tools automate aspects of the software testing process by creating and running tests, and analyzing the test results.

35

Configuration tools Configuration tools automate the creation of programs and track modifications to source files.

Interpreter An interpreter directly executes the source code of a program, rather than translating the source into an object file.

A programming environment can be constructed from separate tools; alternatively, many vendors sell *integrated* programming environments, which are systems containing most or all of these tools. The advantage of an integrated environment is that the user interface is extremely simple: each tool is initiated using a single key or menu selection, rather than typing file names and parameters.

3.1 Editor

Every programmer has his/her favorite general-purpose editor. Even so, you may wish to consider using a *language-sensitive* editor, which is an editor that can create an entire language construct such as an if-statement with one key-press. The advantage of a language-sensitive editor is that syntax errors are prevented. However, touch-typists may find that it is easier to type language constructs rather than to search for the menu selection.

The reference manual for a language may specify a recommended layout for the source code: indentation, line breaks, upper/lower case. These rules do not affect the correctness of the program, but for the benefit of future generations that will read your program, such conventions should be respected. If you have failed to follow the conventions while writing the program, you can use a tool called a *pretty-printer* which rewrites the source code in the recommended format. Since a pretty-printer can inadvertently introduce mistakes, it is preferable to respect conventions from the beginning.

3.2 Compiler

A programming language without a compiler (or interpreter) may be of great theoretical interest, but you cannot execute a program in the language on a computer. The relationship between languages and compilers is so close that the distinction can become blurred, and one often hears such nonsense as:

Language L1 is more efficient than language L2.

What *is* true is that compiler C1 may emit more efficient code than compiler C2, or that a construct of L1 may be easier to compile efficiently than a corresponding construct of L2. One of the aims of this text is to show the relation between language constructs and resulting machine code after compilation.

The structure of a compiler is shown in Figure 3.1. The *front-end* of a

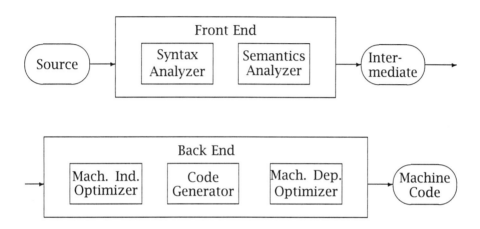

Figure 3.1 The structure of a compiler

compiler "understands" the program by analyzing its syntax and semantics according to the rules of the language. The syntax analyzer is responsible for transforming sequences of characters into abstract syntactical entities called *tokens*. For example, the character "=" in C is transformed into the assignment operator, unless it is followed by another "="; in that case the two characters together "==" are transformed into the equality operator. The semantics analyzer is responsible for assigning a meaning to these abstract entities. For example, in the following program the semantic analyzer assigns a global address to the first i, and a parameter offset to the second i:

```
static int i;                                    C
void proc(int i) { ... }
```

The output of the front-end of the compiler is an abstract representation of the program called the *intermediate representation*. From it you could reconstruct the source program except for the names of the identifiers and the physical format of lines, spaces, comments, etc.

Research into compilers has advanced to the point where a front-end can be automatically generated from a *grammar* (a formal description) of the language. Readers who are interested in designing a programming language are strongly advised to study compilation in depth, so that the language can be easy to compile using automated techniques.

The *back-end* of a compiler takes the intermediate representation and emits *machine code* for a specific computer. Thus the front-end is *language-dependent* while the back-end is *computer-dependent*. A compiler vendor can produce a family of compilers from some language L to a set of widely differing computers C1, C2, ..., by writing a set of back-ends which use the intermediate representation of a common front-end. Similarly, a computer vendor can create a high-quality back-end for a computer C, and then support a large number of languages L1, L2, ..., by writing front-ends that translate the source of each language to the common intermediate code. In this case, it truly makes no sense to ask which language is most efficient on the computer.

Associated with the code generator is the *optimizer* which attempts to improve the code to make it more efficient. Several classes of optimization are possible:

- Optimization on the intermediate representation, for example, common subexpression extraction:

    a = f1(x+y) + f2(x+y);

  Rather than compute the expression x+y twice, it can be computed once and stored in a temporary variable or register. Optimizations such as this do not depend on a specific target computer and can be done before code generation. This means that even part of the back-end can be shared by compilers for different computers.

- Computer-specific optimization. Optimizations such as storing intermediate results in registers rather than in memory must clearly be done during code generation, because the number and type of registers differ from one computer to another.

- *Peephole optimization* is usually done on the generated instructions, though sometimes it can be done on the intermediate representation. This optimization technique attempts to replace short sequences of instructions with a single, more efficient instruction. For example, the C expression n++ might be compiled into:

```
load      R1,n
add       R1,#1
store     R1,n
```

but a peephole optimizer for a specific computer might be able to replace
the three instructions with one that directly increments a memory word:[1]

```
incr        n
```

Optimizers must be used with care. Since by definition an optimizer
modifies a program, it may be difficult to debug using a source debugger,
because the order of the statements as executed may be different from the
order in the source code. It is usually necessary to turn off the optimizer
when debugging. Furthermore, the complexity of an optimizer means that
it is more likely to contain bugs than any other component of the compiler.
An optimizer bug is difficult to diagnose because the debugger is designed
to work on source code, not on optimized (that is, modified) object code. In
no circumstances should a program be tested without using the optimizer
and then distributed after optimization. Finally, the optimizer may make
assumptions that are incorrect in any given situation. For example, when
using memory-mapped I/O devices, a variable may have a value assigned to
it twice without an intervening read:

```
transmit_register = 0x70;                        C
/* Wait 1 second */
transmit_register = 0x70;
```

The optimizer will assume that the second assignment is redundant and will
remove it from the generated object code.

3.3 Librarian

Object modules can be stored as individual files, or a set of modules can
be stored in a single file called a library. Libraries can be provided with the
compiler, purchased separately or created by the programmer.

Many of the constructs in a programming language are not implemented
by compiled code within the program, but by calls to procedures that are
stored in a library provided by the compiler vendor. As languages grow
larger, there is a trend towards placing more functionality into "standard"
libraries that are an indivisible part of the language. Since the library is just
a structured collection of types and subprograms and does not contain new

---

[1]In fact C was first implemented on the DEC PDP-11 computer which has increment memory
and decrement memory instructions. These instructions were the motivation for the corresponding operators in C.

language constructs, it simplifies the tasks of both the student who must learn the language and the implementor of a compiler.

The essential set of procedures needed for initialization, memory management, expression evaluation, etc., is called the *run-time system*. It is essential that a programmer be familiar with the run-time system of the compiler being used: innocent-looking language constructs may in fact invoke time-consuming procedures in the run-time system. For example, if high-precision arithmetic is implemented by library procedures, then changing all integers to long integers will significantly increase execution time.

3.4 Linker

It is perfectly possible to write a program that is several thousand lines long in a single file or module. However, large software systems, especially those that are developed by teams, require that the software be decomposed into modules (Chapter 13). If a call is made to a procedure not in the current module, the compiler has no way of knowing the address of the procedure. Instead a note of the *external reference* is made in the object module. If a language allows access to global variables from several modules, external references must be created for each such access. When all modules have been compiled, the linker resolves these references by searching for definitions of procedures and variables that have been *exported* from a module for non-local use.

Modern programming practice calls for extensive use of modules to decompose a program. A side-effect of this practice is that compilations are usually short and fast, while the linker is called upon to link hundreds of modules with thousands of external references. The efficiency of the linker can be critical to a software team's performance in the final stages of a project: even a small change to one source module will require a time-consuming link.

One solution to this problem is to link subsystems together and only then resolve the links between the subsystems. Another solution is to use *dynamic linking* if available on the system. In dynamic linking, external references are not resolved; instead the first call to a procedure is trapped by the operating system and resolved. Dynamic linking may be combined with *dynamic loading*: not only are the references unresolved, but a module is not even loaded until one of its exported procedures is needed. Of course dynamic linking or loading entails additional overhead at run-time, but it is a powerful method of adapting systems to changing requirements without relinking.

3.5 Loader

As its name implies, the loader loads a program into memory and initializes it for execution. On older computers, the loader was non-trivial because it had to *relocate* programs. An instruction such as load 140 referred to an absolute memory address and had to be fixed according to the actual address where the program was loaded. Modern computers address code and data relative to registers. A register will be allocated to point to each code and data area, so all the loader has to do is to copy the executable program into memory and initialize a set of registers. The instruction load 140 now means "load the value located in the address obtained by adding 140 to the contents of the register that points to the data area".

3.6 Debugger

Debuggers support three functions:

Tracing The execution of a program step-by-step so that the programmer can precisely follow the order in which statements are executed.

Breakpoints A means to specify that a program will run until a specific line in the program has been reached. A special form of a breakpoint is a *watchpoint*, which causes the program to run until a specific memory location is accessed.

Examine/modify data The ability to examine and modify the value of any variable at any point in the computation.

Symbolic debuggers work in terms of symbols of the source code (variable and procedure names) rather than in terms of absolute machine addresses. A symbolic debugger requires the cooperation of the compiler and linker to create tables relating symbols and their addresses.

Modern debuggers are extremely powerful and flexible, to the point where they can be abused as a substitute for thinking. Often, just trying to explain a procedure to another programmer can locate a bug faster than days of tracing.

Some problems are not easily solved even using a debugger. For example, dynamic data structures such as lists and trees cannot be examined as a whole; instead you must manually traverse each link. More serious are problems like smearing memory (see Section 5.3), which are caused by bugs that are far removed from the area where the symptoms appear. Debuggers are used for investigating symptoms such as "zero-divide in procedure p1", and are of limited use in solving such bugs.

Finally, some systems cannot be "debugged" as such: you cannot create a medical emergency at will just to debug the software for a heart monitor; you cannot send a team of programmers along on a spaceflight to debug the flight control program. Such systems must be tested using special hardware and software to simulate the program inputs and outputs; the software is thus never tested and debugged in actual use! Critical software systems motivate research into language constructs improving program reliability and formal methods of program verification.

3.7 Profiler

It is often said that more bugs are caused by attempts at efficiency than by all other causes. What makes this saying so tragic is that most attempts at improving efficiency achieve nothing, or at most, improvements that are not commensurate with the effort invested. Throughout this book we will discuss the relative efficiency of various program constructs, but this information should be used only if three conditions are met:

- The current performance of the program is unacceptable.

- There is no better way to improve efficiency. In general, choosing a more efficient algorithm will give better results than improving the programming of an existing one (see Section 6.5 for an example).

- The cause of the inefficiency can be identified.

Identifying inefficiencies is extremely difficult without the aid of a measuring tool. The reason is that there are so many orders of magnitude between time intervals that we instinctively understand (seconds), and the time intervals in which computers work (micro- or nano-seconds). A function which seems difficult to us may have little effect on the overall execution time of a program.

A profiler samples the instruction pointer of the computer at regular intervals and then builds a histogram displaying the percentage of execution time that can be attributed to each procedure or statement. Very often the result will surprise the programmer by identifying bottlenecks that are not at all evident. Investing effort in optimizing a program without the use of a profiler is totally unprofessional.

Even with a profiler, improving the efficiency of a program can be difficult. One reason is that much of the execution time is being spent in externally provided components such as database or windowing subsystems, which are often designed more for flexibility than for performance.

3.8 Testing tools

Testing a large system can take as much time as the initial programming and debugging. Software tools have been developed to automate several aspects of testing. One tool is a *coverage analyzer* which keeps track of which statements have been tested. However, such a tool does nothing to help create and execute the tests.

More sophisticated tools execute predefined tests and then compare the output to a specification. Tests may also be generated automatically by *capturing* input from an external source such as a user pressing keys on a keyboard. The captured input sequence can then be run repeatedly. Whenever a new version of a software system is to be released, previous tests should be rerun. Such *regression testing* is essential because the assumptions underlying a program are so interconnected, that any modification may cause bugs even in modules where "nothing has changed".

3.9 Configuration tools

Configuration tools are used to automate bureaucratic tasks associated with software. A *make* tool creates an executable file from source code by invoking the compiler, linker, etc. In a large project, it can be difficult to keep track of exactly which files need to be recompiled, in which order, and with which parameters, and it is very easy to fix a bug and then cause another one by using an outdated object module. A make tool automatically ensures that a new module is correctly created with a minimum amount of recompilation.

A *source control* or *revision control* tool is used to maintain a record of all changes to the source code modules. This is important because in a large project it is often necessary to "back off" a modification that causes unforeseen problems, or to be able to trace a modification to a specific version or programmer. In addition, a program may be delivered in different versions to different customers; without a software tool, we would have to fix a common bug in all the versions. A source control tool simplifies these tasks because it only maintains changes (called *deltas*) from the original version, and can easily reconstruct any previous version from the changes.

3.10 Interpreters

An *interpreter* is a program that directly executes the source code of a program. The advantage of an interpreter over a compiler is that it can be extremely convenient to use, because it does not require that a sequence of tools be invoked: compiler, linker, loader, etc. Interpreters are also easy to write because they need not be computer-specific; since they directly execute the program they have no machine code output. Thus an interpreter written in a standardized language is portable. An additional simplification comes from the fact that traditionally interpreters do not attempt any optimization.

In fact, it can be very difficult to distinguish an interpreter from a compiler. Very few interpreters actually execute the source code of a program; instead they translate (that is, compile) the source into the machine code of an imaginary machine, and then execute the abstract machine code (Figure 3.2).

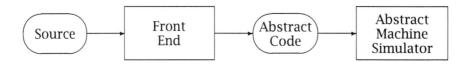

Figure 3.2 The structure of an interpreter

Suppose now that someone invents a computer whose machine code is exactly this abstract code; alternatively, suppose that someone writes a set of macros that replace the abstract machine code by the actual machine code of an existing computer. In either case, the so-called interpreter has become a compiler without changing a single line of the program.

The original Pascal compiler was written to produce machine code for a specific machine (CDC 6400). Soon afterwards, Niklaus Wirth created a compiler that produced code, called *P-Code*, for an abstract stack-based machine. By writing an interpreter for P-Code, or by compiling the P-Code into machine code for a specific machine, it is possible to create a Pascal interpreter or compiler with relatively little effort. The compiler for P-Code was a decisive factor in making Pascal the widespread language that it is today.

The logic programming language Prolog (see Chapter 17) was considered at first to be a language that was only suitable for interpretation. David Warren produced the first true compiler for Prolog by defining an abstract machine (the *Warren Abstract Machine*, or *WAM*) that manipulated the basic data structures required to execute programs in the language. Both compiling

Prolog to WAM programs and compiling WAM programs into machine code are not too difficult; Warren's achievement was to define the WAM at the right intermediate level between the two. Much research on compilation of logic programming languages has been based on the WAM.

There does not seem to be much practical value in arguing about the difference between a compiler and interpreter. When comparing programming environments, the emphasis should be on reliability, correct translation, high performance, efficient code generation, good debugging facilities and so on, and not on the implementation techniques used to create the environment.

3.11 Exercises

1. Study your compiler's documentation and list the optimizations that it performs. Write programs and check the resulting object code for the optimizations.

2. What information does the debugger need from the compiler and linker?

3. Run a profiler and study how it works.

4. How can you write your own simple testing tool? What influence does automated testing have on program design?

5. AdaS is an interpreter for a subset of Ada written in Pascal. It works by compiling the source into P-Code and then executing the P-Code. Study the AdaS program (see Appendix A) and write a description of the P-Code machine.

PART II

Essential Concepts

4   Elementary Data Types

4.1 Integer types

The word *integer* is familiar from mathematics where it denotes the unbounded, ordered sequence of numbers:

$$\ldots, -3, -2, -1, 0, 1, 2, 3, \ldots$$

The term is used in programming to denote something quite different: a
specific data type. Recall that a data type is a set of values and a set of
operations on those values. Let us begin by defining the set of values of the
Integer data type.

Given a word of memory, we can simply define a set of values by the
usual interpretation of the bits of the word as a binary value. For example,
if a word with 8 bits contains the sequence 1010 0011, it is interpreted as:

$$(1 \times 2^7) + (1 \times 2^5) + (1 \times 2^1) + (1 \times 2^0) = 128 + 32 + 2 + 1 = 163$$

The range of possible values is 0..255, or in general $0..2^B - 1$ for a word of
B bits. A data type with this set of values is called an *unsigned integer* and
a variable of this type can be declared in C as:

> unsigned int v;   <kbd>C</kbd>

Note that the number of bits in a value of this type varies from one computer
to another.[1] Today the most common word size is 32 bits and an (unsigned)
integer value is in the range $0..2^{32} - 1 \approx 4 \times 10^9$. Thus, the set of mathematical
integers is unbounded while integer types are limited to a finite range of
values.

Since they cannot represent negative numbers, unsigned integers are
mostly useful as representations of values read from external equipment.

---

[1] In fact, unsigned int need not be the same size as a word of memory.

For example, a temperature probe may return 10 bits of information; the unsigned value in the range 0..1023 must then be translated into ordinary (positive and negative) numbers. Unsigned integers are also used to represent characters (see below). Unsigned integers should not be used for ordinary computation, because most computer instructions work on signed integers and a compiler may emit extra instructions for unsigned values.

The range of values that a variable can have may not fit into a single word, or it may fit into a partial word. Length specifiers can be added to indicate different integer types:

```
unsigned int v1;
unsigned short int v2;
unsigned long int v3;
```
C

In Ada, additional types such as Long_Integer are predefined along with ordinary Integer. The actual interpretation of length specifiers like long and short varies from one compiler to another; some compilers may even give the same interpretation to two or more specifiers.

The representation of signed numbers in mathematics uses a special character "−" followed by the usual representation of the absolute value of the number. This representation is not convenient for computer instructions to work with. Instead most computers represent signed integers in a notation called *two's complement*. A positive number is represented by a leading zero bit followed by the usual binary representation of the value. It follows that the largest positive integer that can be represented in a word with w bits is only $2^{w-1} - 1$.

To obtain the representation of $-n$ from the binary representation $B = b_1 b_2 \ldots b_w$ of n:

- Take the logical *complement* of B, that is, change each b_i from zero to one or from one to zero.

- Add one.

For example, the representations of -1, -2 and -127 as 8-bit words are:

$$
\begin{array}{rclclclcr}
1 & = & 0000\,0001 & \rightarrow & 1111\,1110 & \rightarrow & 1111\,1111 & = & -1 \\
2 & = & 0000\,0010 & \rightarrow & 1111\,1101 & \rightarrow & 1111\,1110 & = & -2 \\
127 & = & 0111\,1111 & \rightarrow & 1000\,0000 & \rightarrow & 1000\,0001 & = & -127
\end{array}
$$

A negative value will always have a one in the high-order bit.

Two's complement is convenient because if you do ordinary binary arithmetic on values, the result is correct:

$$
\begin{array}{rcl}
(-1) - 1 & = & -2 \\
1111\,1111 - 0000\,0001 & = & 1111\,1110
\end{array}
$$

Note that the bit string 1000 0000 cannot be obtained from any positive value. It represents −128, even though its positive counterpart 128 cannot be represented as an 8-bit two's complement number. This asymmetry in the range of integer types must be kept in mind, especially when dealing with short types.

An alternative representation of signed numbers is *one's complement*, in which the representation of −*n* is just the complement of *n*. The set of values is then symmetric, but there are two representations of zero: 0000 0000 called positive zero, and 1111 1111 called negative zero.

If you do not use a special syntax like unsigned in a declaration, the default is to use signed integers:

```
int i;              /* Signed integer in C */
I: Integer;         -- Signed integer in Ada
```

Integer operations

Integer operations include the four basic operations: addition, subtraction, multiplication and division. They can be used to form *expressions*:

```
a + b / c - 25 * (d - e)
```

Normal mathematical rules of precedence apply to integer operations; parentheses can be used to change the order of computation.

The result of an operation on a signed integer must not be outside the range of values; otherwise, overflow will occur as discussed below. For unsigned integers, arithmetic is cyclic. If short int is stored in one 16-bit word, then:

```
unsigned short int i;    /* Range of i = 0..65535 */        C
i = 65535;               /* Largest possible value */
i = i + 1;               /* Cyclic arithmetic, i = 0 */
```

The designers of Ada 83 made the mistake of not including unsigned integers. Ada 95 generalizes the concept of unsigned integers to *modular types*, which are integer types with cyclic arithmetic on an arbitrary modulus. A standard unsigned byte can be declared:

```
type Unsigned_Byte is mod 256;                              Ada
```

while a modulus that is not a power of two can be used for hash tables or random numbers:

type Random_Integer is mod 41;

Ada

Note that modular types in Ada are portable since only the cyclic range is part of the definition, not the *size* of the representation as in C.

Division

In mathematics, division of two integers a/b produces two values, a *quotient* q and a *remainder r* such that:

$$a = q * b + r$$

Since arithmetical expressions in programs return a single value, the "/" operator is used to return the quotient, and a distinct operator (called "%" in C and rem in Ada) returns the remainder. The expression 54/10 yields the value 5, and we say that the result of the operation has been *truncated*. Pascal uses a separate operator div for integer division.

The definition of integer division is not trivial when we consider negative numbers. Is the expression – 54/10 equal to −5 or −6? In other words, is truncation done to smaller (more negative) values or to values closer to zero? One choice is to truncate towards zero, since the equation for integer division can be maintained just by changing the sign of the remainder:

$$-54 = -5 * 10 + (-4)$$

There is another mathematical operation called *modulo* which corresponds to truncation of negative numbers to smaller (more negative) values:

$$-54 = -6 * 10 + 6$$
$$-54 \bmod 10 = 6$$

Modulo arithmetic has applications whenever arithmetic is done on finite ranges, such as error-correcting codes used in communications systems.

The meaning of "/" and "%" in C is implementation dependent, so programs using these integer operators may not be portable. In Ada, "/" always truncates towards zero. The operator rem returns the remainder corresponding to truncation towards zero, while the operator mod returns the remainder corresponding to truncation towards minus infinity.

Overflow

An operation is said to *overflow* if it produces a result that is not within the range of defined values. The following discussion is given in terms of 8-bit integers for clarity.

Suppose that the signed integer variable i has the value 127 and that we increment i. The computer will simply add one to the integer representation of 127:

$$0111\ 1111 + 0000\ 0001 = 1000\ 0000$$

to obtain −128. This is not the correct result and the error is called overflow.

Overflow may cause strange bugs:

```
for (i = 0; i < j*k; i++) ...
```

C

If the expression j*k overflows, the upper bound may be negative and the loop will not be executed.

Suppose now that the variables a, b and c have the values 90, 60 and 80, respectively. The expression (a−b+c) evaluates to 110, because (a−b) evaluates to 30, and then the addition gives 110. However, the optimizer may choose to evaluate the expression in a different order, (a+c−b), giving an incorrect answer because the addition (a+c) gives the value 170 which overflows. If your high-school teacher told you that addition is commutative and associative, he/she was talking about mathematics and not about programming!

Some compilers have the option of checking every integer operation for overflow, but this may be prohibitive in terms of run-time overhead unless the detection of overflow is done by hardware. Now that most computers use 32-bit memory words, integer overflow is rarely a problem, but you must be aware of it and take care not to fall into the traps demonstrated above.

Implementation

Integer values are stored directly in memory words. Some computers have instructions to compute with partial words or even individual bytes. Compilers for these computers will usually map short int into partial words, while compilers for computers that recognize only full words will implement all integer types identically. long int will be mapped into two words to achieve a larger range of values.

Addition and subtraction are compiled directly into the corresponding instructions. Multiplication is also implemented as a single instruction but requires significantly more processing time than addition and subtraction. Multiplication of two words stored in registers R1 and R2 produces a result that is two words long and will require two registers to store. If the register containing the high-order value is not zero, the result has overflowed.

Division requires the computer to perform an iterative algorithm similar to "long division" done by hand. This is done in hardware and you need not concern yourself with the details, but if efficiency is important it is best to avoid division.

Arithmetic on long int takes more than twice the amount of time as it does on int. The reason is that an instruction must be used to transfer a possible "carry" from the low-order words to the high-order words.

4.2 Enumeration types

Programming languages such as Fortran and C define data in terms of the underlying computer. Real-world data must be explicitly mapped onto data types that exist on the computer, in most cases one of the integer types. For example, if you are writing a program to control a heater you might have a variable dial that stores the current position of the dial. Suppose that the real-world dial has four positions: *off, low, medium, high*. How would you declare the variable and denote the positions? Since the computer does not have instructions that work on four-valued memory words, you will choose to declare the variable as an integer, and you will choose four specific integers (say 1, 2, 3, 4) to denote the positions:

```
int dial;                /* Current position of dial */        C
if (dial < 4) dial++;    /* Increment heater level*/
```

The obvious problem with using integers is that the program becomes hard to read and maintain. You must write extensive documentation and continually refer to it in order to understand the code. The first improvement that can be made is to document the intended values internally:

```
#define    Off        1                                        C
#define    Low        2
#define    Medium     3
#define    High       4

int dial;
if (dial < High) dial++;
```

Improving the documentation, however, does nothing to prevent the following problems:

```
dial = -1;          /* No such value */                        C
dial = High + 1;    /* Undetected overflow */
dial = dial * 3;    /* Meaningless operation */
```

To be precise, representing the four-position dial as an integer allows the programmer to assign values that are not within the intended range, and to execute operations that are meaningless for the real-world object. Even if the programmer does not intentionally create any of these problems, experience has shown that they frequently arise from misunderstandings among software team members, typographical errors and other mistakes typical in the development of complex systems.

The solution is to allow the program designer to create *new* types that correspond exactly to the real-world objects being modeled. The requirement discussed here—a short ordered sequence of values—is so common that modern programming languages support creation of types called *enumeration types*. In Ada, the above example would be:

```
type Heat is (Off, Low, Medium, High);                    Ada
Dial: Heat;

Dial := Low;
if Dial < High then Dial := Heat'Succ(Dial);

Dial := -1;                          -- Error
Dial := Heat'Succ(High);             -- Error
Dial := Dial * 3;                    -- Error
```

Before explaining the example in detail, note that C has a construct that is superficially the same:

```
typedef enum {Off, Low, Medium, High} Heat;              C
```

However, variables declared to be of type Heat are still *integers* and none of the above statements are considered to be errors (though a compiler may issue a warning):

```
Heat dial;                                               C

dial = -1;              /* Not an error! */
dial = High + 1;        /* Not an error! */
dial = dial * 3;        /* Not an error! */
```

In other words, the enum construct is just a means of documentation that is more convenient than a long series of define's, but it does not create a new type.

Fortunately, C++ takes a stricter interpretation of enumeration types and does not allow assignment of an integer value to a variable of an enumeration type; the above three statements are in error. However, values of enumeration types can be implicitly converted to integers so the type checking is not complete. Unfortunately, C++ provides no operations on enumeration types so there is no predefined way to increment a variable of enumeration type. You can write your own function that takes the result of an integer expression and then explicitly converts it back to the enumeration type:

dial = (Heat) (dial + 1);   `C++`

Note the implicit conversion of dial to integer, followed by the explicit conversion of the result back to Heat. The "++" and "--" operators can be overloaded in C++ (Section 10.2), so they can be used for defining operations on enumeration types that are syntactically the same as those of integer types.

In Ada, the type definition creates a new type Heat. The values of this type are *not* integers. Any attempt to exceed the range or to use integer operations will be detected as an error. If your finger slips and you enter Higj instead of High, an error will be detected, because the type contains exactly the four values that were declared; if you had used integers, 5 would be as valid an integer as 4.

Enumeration types are types just like integers: you can declare variables and parameters to be of these types. However, they are restricted in the set of operations that can be performed on values of the type. These include assignment (:=), equality (=) and inequality (/=). Since the set of values in the declaration is interpreted as an ordered sequence, the relational operators (<,>,>=,<=) are defined.

Given an enumeration type T and a value V of type T, the following functions called *attributes* are defined in Ada:

- T'First returns the first value of T.

- T'Last returns the last value of T.

- T'Succ(V) returns the successor of V.

- T'Pred(V) returns the predecessor of V.

- T'Pos(V) returns the position[2] of V within the list of values of T.

- T'Val(I) returns the value at the I'th position in T.

Attributes make the program robust to modifications: if values are added to an enumeration type, or if the values are rearranged, loops and indices remain unaltered:

---

[2]The position of a value is defined by its position (starting from zero) in the declaration of the type.

```ada
for I in Heat'First .. Heat'Last – 1 loop
    A(I) := A(Heat'Succ(I));
end loop;
```

Not every language designer believes in enumeration types. Eiffel does not contain enumeration types for the following reasons:

- A desire to keep the language as small as possible.

- The same level of safety can be obtained using assertions (Section 11.5).

- Enumeration types are often used with variant records (Section 10.4); when inheritance (Section 14.3) is used correctly there is less need for enumeration types.

Enumeration types should be used whenever possible in preference to ordinary integers with lists of defined constants; their contribution to the reliability of a program cannot be overestimated. C programmers do not have the benefit of type-checking as in Ada and C++, but they should still use enum for its significant contribution to readability.

Implementation

I will let you in on a secret and tell you that the values of an enumeration type are represented in the computer as consecutive integers starting from zero. The Ada type checking is purely compile-time, and operations such as "<" are ordinary integer operations.

It is possible to request the compiler to use a non-standard representation of enumeration types. In C this is specified directly in the type definition:

```c
typedef enum {Off=1, Low=2, Medium=4, High=8} Heat;
```

while in Ada a representation specification is used:

```ada
type Heat is (Off, Low, Medium, High);
for Heat use (Off=>1, Low=>2, Medium=>4, High=>8);
```

4.3 Character type

Though computers were originally invented in order to do numerical calculations, it quickly became apparent that non-numerical applications are just as important. Today non-numerical applications, such as word-processors, educational programs and databases, probably outnumber mathematical applications. Even mathematical applications such as financial software need text for input and output.

From the point of view of a software developer, text processing is extremely complicated because of the variety of natural languages and writing systems. From the point of view of programming languages text processing is relatively simple, because the language assumes that the set of characters forms a short, ordered sequence of values, that is, characters can be defined as an enumeration type. In fact, except for languages like Chinese and Japanese that use thousands of symbols, the 128 or 256 possible values of a signed or unsigned 8-bit integer suffice.

The difference in the way that Ada and C define characters is similar to the difference in the way that they define enumeration types. In Ada, there is a predefined enumeration type:

Ada

```
type Character is (..., 'A', 'B', ...);
```

and all the usual operations on enumeration types (assignment, relations, successor, predecessor, etc.) apply to characters. In Ada 83, Character is limited to the 128 values of the American standard ASCII, while in Ada 95, the type is assumed to be represented in an unsigned byte, so the 256 values required by international standards are available.

In C, char is just a very small integer type and all the following statements are accepted since char and int are essentially the same:

C

```
char c;
int i;
c = 'A' + 10;          /* Convert char to int and back */
i = 'A';               /* Convert char to int */
c = i;                 /* Convert int to char */
```

char is a distinct type in C++, but is convertible to and from integers so the above statements remain valid.

For non-alphabetic languages, 16-bit characters can be defined. These are called wchar_t in C and C++, and Wide_Character in Ada 95.

The only thing that distinguishes characters from ordinary enumeration or integer types is the special syntax ('A') for the set of values, and more importantly the special syntax that exists for arrays of characters called *strings* (Section 5.5).

4.4 Boolean type

Boolean is a predefined enumeration type in Ada:

type Boolean is (False, True); | Ada |

The Boolean type is extremely important because:

- Relational operators (=, >, etc.) are functions which return a value of Boolean type.

- The if-statement takes an expression of Boolean type.

- Operators for Boolean algebra (and, or, not, xor) are defined on the Boolean type.

C does not define a separate type; instead integers are used with the following interpretation:

- Relational operators return 1 if successful and 0 if not.

- The if-statement takes the false branch if the integer expression evaluates to zero, and the true branch otherwise.

There are several methods for introducing Boolean types into C. One possibility is to define a type which will allow declaration of functions with Boolean result:

typedef enum {false, true} bool; | C |

bool data_valid(int a, float b);

if (data_valid(x, y)) ...

but of course this is purely for documentation and readability, because a statement like:

bool b; | C |
b = i + 56;   /* Add 56 to "true" ?? */

is still accepted and can cause obscure bugs.

In C++, bool is predefined *integer* type (not an enumeration type), with implicit conversion between non-zero values and a literal true, and between zero values and false. A C program with bool defined as shown above can be compiled in C++ simply by removing the typedef.

Even in C it is better not to use the implicit conversion of integer to Boolean, but rather to use explicit equality and inequality operators:

```
if (a+b == 2) ...              /* This version is clearer than */     C
if (a+b- 2) ...                /* ...this version. */
if (a+b != 0) ...              /* This version is clearer than */
if (!(a+b)) ...                /* ...this version. */
```

Finally, C supports Boolean algebra using short-circuit operators which we will discuss in Section 6.2.

4.5 * Subtypes

In the previous sections we have discussed integer types which allow computations to be performed on the large range of values that can be represented in a memory word, and enumeration types which work with smaller ranges but do not allow arithmetic computation to be done. However, in many cases we would like to do computations on smaller ranges of integers. For example, there should be some way of detecting errors such as:

```
Temperature: Integer;
Temperature := -280;          -- Below absolute zero!

Compass_Heading: Integer;
Compass_Heading := 365;       -- Compass shows 0..359 degrees!
```

Suppose we try to define a new class of types:

```
type Temperatures is Integer range -273 .. 10000;    -- Not Ada!
type Headings is Integer range 0 .. 359;             -- Not Ada!
```

This will solve the problem of checking errors caused by values outside the range of the type, but the question remains: are these two different types or not? If they are, then:

```
Temperature * Compass_Heading
```

is a valid arithmetic expression on an integer type; if not, type conversion must be used.

In practice, both of these interpretations are useful. Computation concerning the physical world tends to involve calculations among values of many ranges. On the other hand, indices into tables or serial numbers do not require computation between types: it makes sense to ask for the next index into a table, but not to add a table index to a serial number. Ada provides two separate facilities for these two classes of type definition.

A *subtype* is a restriction on an existing type. Discrete (integer and enumeration) types can have a *range constraint*.

```
subtype Temperatures is Integer range -273 .. 10000;
Temperature: Temperatures;

subtype Headings is Integer range 0 .. 359;
Compass_Heading: Headings;
```

The type of a value of a subtype S is still that of the underlying *base* type
T; here, the base type of both Temperatures and Headings is Integer. The
type is determined at *compile-time*. The value of a subtype has the same
representation as that of the base type and is acceptable wherever a value of
the base type is needed:

```
Temperature * Compass_Heading
```

is a valid expression, but the statements:

```
Temperature := -280;
Compass_Heading := 365;
```

cause errors because the values are not within the ranges of the subtypes.
Violations of the range of a subtype are checked at *run-time*.

Subtypes can be defined on any type that can have its set of values
restricted in a meaningful way:

```
subtype Upper_Case is Character range 'A' .. 'Z';
U: Upper_Case;
C: Character;
```

```
U := 'a';            -- Error, out of range
C := U;              -- Always OK
U := C;              -- May cause an error
```

Subtypes are essential in defining arrays as will be discussed in Section 5.4.
In addition, a named subtype can be used to simplify many statements:

```
if C in Upper_Case then ...        -- Range check
for C1 in Upper_Case loop ...      -- Loop bounds
```

4.6 * Derived types

The second interpretation of the relation between two similar types is that
they represent separate types that cannot be used together. In Ada, such
types are called *derived* types and are indicated by the word new in the
definition:

```
type Derived_Character is new Character;
C:  Character;
D:  Derived_Character;

C := D;                               -- Error, types are different
```

When one type is derived from another type (called its *parent* type), it inherits a *copy* of the set of values and a *copy* of the set of operations, but the types remain distinct. However, it is always possible to explicitly convert between types that are derived from one another:

```
D := Derived_Character(C);            -- Type conversion
C := Character(D);                    -- Type conversion
```

It is even possible to specify a different representation for the derived types; type conversion will then convert between the two representations (Section 5.8).

A derived type may include a restriction on the range of values of the parent type:

```
type Upper_Case is new Character range 'A' .. 'Z';
U: Upper_Case;
C: Character;

C := Character(U);        -- Always valid
U := Upper_Case(C);       -- May cause an error
```

Ada 83 derived types implement a weak version of inheritance, which is a central concept of object-oriented languages (see Chapter 14). The revised language Ada 95 implements true inheritance by extending the concept of derived types; we will return to study them in great detail.

Integer types

Suppose that we have defined the following type:

```
type Altitudes is new Integer range 0 .. 60000;
```

This definition works correctly when we program a flight simulation on a 32-bit workstation. What happens when we transfer the program to a 16-bit controller in our aircraft avionics? Sixteen bits can represent signed integers only up to the value 32,767. Thus the derived type would be in error (as would a subtype or a direct use of Integer), violating the portability of programs which is a central goal of the Ada language.

To solve this problem, it is possible to derive an *integer* type without explicitly specifying the underlying parent type:

```
type Altitudes is range 0 .. 60000;
```

The compiler is required to choose a representation that is appropriate for the requested range—Integer on a 32-bit computer and Long_Integer on a 16-bit computer. This unique feature makes it easy to write numeric programs in Ada that are portable between computers with different word lengths.

The drawback of integer types is that each definition creates a new type and we can't write calculations that use different types without type conversions:

```
I: Integer;
A: Altitude;

A := I;                    -- Error, different types
A := Altitude(I);          -- OK, type conversion
```

Thus there is an unavoidable tension between:

- Subtypes are potentially unsafe because mixed expressions may be written and portability is hard to achieve.

- Derived types are safe and portable, but may make a program difficult to read because of extensive type conversions.

4.7 Expressions

An expression may be as simple as a literal (24, 'x', True) or a variable, or it may be a complex composition involving operations (including calls to system- or user-defined functions). When an expression is *evaluated* it produces a *value*.

Expressions occur in many places in a program: assignment statements, Boolean expressions in if-statements, limits of for-loops, parameters of procedures, etc. We first discuss the expression by itself and then the assignment statement.

The value of a literal is what it denotes; for example, the value of 24 is the integer represented by the bit string 0001 1000. The value of a variable V is the contents of the memory cell it denotes. Note the potential for confusion in the statement:

       V1 := V2;

V2 is an *expression* whose value is the contents of a certain memory cell. V1 is the *address* of a memory cell into which the value of V2 will be placed.

More complex expressions are created from a function or an operator and a set of parameters or operands. The distinction is mostly syntactical: a function with parameters is written in prefix notation sin(x), while an operator with operands is written in infix notation a+b. Since the operands themselves can be expressions, expressions of arbitrary complexity can be created:

       a + sin(b) * ((c – d) / (e + 34))

When written in prefix notation, the order of evaluation is clearly defined except for the order of evaluation of the parameters of a single function:

       max(sin(cos(x)), cos(sin(y)))

It is possible to write programs whose result depends on the order of evaluation of the parameters of a function (see Section 7.3), but such order dependencies should be avoided at all costs, since they are a source of obscure bugs when porting or even when modifying a program.

Infix notation brings its own problems, namely those of precedence and associativity. Almost all programming languages adhere to the mathematical standard of giving higher precedence to the multiplying operators ("*", "/") over the adding operators ("+", "– "), and other operators will have arbitrary precedences defined by the language. Two extremes are APL which does not define *any* precedences (not even for arithmetic or \tors), and C which defines 15 levels of precedence! Part of the difficulty c \arning a programming language is to get used to the style that results from the precedence rules.

An example of a non-intuitive precedence assignment occurs in Pascal. The Boolean operator and is considered to be a multiplying operator with high precedence, whereas in most other languages such as C it is given a precedence below the relational operators. The following statement:

       if a > b and b > c then ...   `Pascal`

is in error, because the expression is interpreted to be:

       if a > (b and b) > c then ...   `Pascal`

and the syntax is not correct.

The meaning of an infix expression also depends upon the *associativity* of the operators, namely how operators of identical precedence are grouped:

from left to right, or from right to left. In most cases, but not all, it does not matter (except for the possibility of overflow as discussed in Section 4.1). However, the value of an expression involving integer division can depend on associativity because of truncation:

```
int i = 6, j = 7, k = 3;
i = i * j / k;                    /* Is the result 12 or 14 ? */
```
C

In general, binary operators associate to the left so the above example is compiled as:

```
i = (i * j) / k;
```
C

while unary operators associate to the right: in C !++i is computed as if written !(++i).

All precedence and associativity problems can be easily solved using parentheses; they cost nothing, so use them whenever there is the slightest possibility of confusion.

While precedence and associativity are specified by the language, evaluation order is usually left to the implementation to enable optimizations to be done. For example, in the following expression:

```
(a + b) + c + (d + e)
```

it is not defined if a+b is computed before or after d+e, though c will be added to the *result* of a+b before the *result* of d+e. The order can be significant if an expression uses *side-effects*, that is, if the evaluation of a sub-expression calls a function that modifies a global variable.

Implementation

The implementation of an expression depends of course on the implementation of the operators used in the expression. Nevertheless, certain general principles are worth discussing.

Expressions are evaluated from the inside out; for example a*(b+c) is evaluated:[3]

```
load     R1,b
load     R2,c
add      R1,R2          Add b and c, result to R1
load     R2,a
mult     R1,R2          Multiply a and b+c, result to R1
```

---

[3]Note this order is not the only possible one; the optimizer might move the load of **a** to an earlier position or exchange the loads of **b** and **c**, without affecting the result of the computation.

It is possible to write an expression in a form which makes this evaluation order explicit:

b c + a *

Reading from left to right: the name of an operand means load the operand, and the symbol for an operator means apply the operator to the two most recent operands and replace all three (two operands and the operator) with the result. In this case, addition is applied to b and c; then multiplication is applied to the result and to a.

This form, called *reverse polish notation*[4] (*RPN*), may be used by the compiler: the expression is translated into RPN, and then the compiler emits instructions for each operand or operator as the RPN is read from left to right.

If the expression were more complex, say:

(a + b) * (c + d) * (e + f)

more registers would be needed to store the intermediate results: a+b, c+d, and so on. As the complexity increases, the number of registers will not suffice, and the compiler must allocate anonymous temporary variables in order to store the intermediate results. In terms of efficiency: up to a certain point, it is more efficient to increase the complexity of an expression rather than to use a sequence of assignment statements, so that unnecessary storing of intermediate results to memory can be avoided. However, the improvement quickly ceases because of the need to allocate temporary variables, and at some point the compiler may not even be able to handle the complex expression.

An optimizing compiler will be able to identify that the subexpression a+b in the following expression:

(a + b) * c + d * (a + b)

need only be evaluated once, but it is doubtful if a common subexpression would be identified in:

(a + b) * c + d * (b + a)

If the common subexpression is complex, it may be helpful to explicitly assign it to a variable rather than trust the optimizer.

Constant folding is another optimization. In the expression:

2.0 * 3.14159 * Radius

---

[4]Named for the Polish logician Lukasiewicz who was interested in a parenthesis-free logical calculus. The notation is *reversed* because he placed the operators before the operands.

the compiler will do the multiplication once at compile-time and store the result. There is no reason to lower the readability of a program by doing the constant folding yourself, though you may wish to assign a name to the computed value:

```
PI: constant := 3.14159;                                    [Ada]
Two_PI: constant := 2.0 * PI;
Circumference: Float := Two_PI * Radius;
```

4.8 Assignment statements

The meaning of the assignment statement:

```
variable := expression;
```

is that the value of expression should be stored in the memory address denoted by variable. Note that the left-hand side of the statement may also be an expression, as long as that expression evaluates to an address:

```
a(i*(j+1)) := a(i*j);                                       [Ada]
```

An expression that can appear on the left-hand side of an assignment statement is called an *l-value*; a constant is of course not an l-value. All expressions produce a value and so can appear on the right-hand side of an assignment statement; they are called *r-values*. The language will usually not specify the order of evaluation of the expressions on the left- and right-hand sides of an assignment. If the order affects the result, the program will not be portable.

C defines the assignment statement itself as an expression. The value of:

```
variable = expression;
```

is the same as the value of the expression on the right-hand side:

```
int v1, v2, v3;                                             [C]
v1 = v2 = v3 = e;
```

means assign (the value of) e to v3, then assign the result to v2, then assign the result to v1 and ignore the final result.

In Ada assignments are statements, not expressions, and there is no multiple assignment. The multiple declaration:

```
V1, V2, V3: Integer := E;                                   [Ada]
```

is considered to be an abbreviation for:

```
V1: Integer := E;                                            Ada
V2: Integer := E;
V3: Integer := E;
```

and not an instance of multiple assignment.

While C programming style makes use of the fact that assignment is an expression, it probably should be avoided because it can be a source of obscure programming errors. A notorious class of bugs is due to confusion between the assignment ("=") and the equality operator ("=="). In the following statement:

```
if (i = j) ...                                               C
```

the programmer probably intended just to compare i and j, but i is inadvertently modified by the assignment. Some C compilers regard this as such bad style that they issue a warning message.

A useful feature in C is the combination of an operator with an assignment:

```
v += e;             /* This is short for ... */             Ada
v = v + e;          /*       this. */
```

Assignment operators are particularly important when the variable is complex, including array indexing, etc. The combination operator not only saves typing, but avoids the possibility of a bug if v is not written identically on both sides. Assignment operators are a stylistic device only, since an optimizing compiler can remove the second evaluation of v.

It is possible to prevent the assignment of a value to an object by declaring the object as a *constant*:

```
const int N = 8;              /* Constant in C */
N: constant Integer := 8;     -- Constant in Ada
```

Obviously a constant must be given an initial value.

There is a difference between a constant and a *static value*[5] which is known at compile-time:

```
procedure P(C: Character) is                                 Ada
    C1: constant Character := C;
    C2: constant Character := 'x';
```

---

[5] Called a *constant expression* in C++.

```
begin
    ...
    case C is
        when C1 =>                    -- Error, not static
        when C2 =>                    -- OK, static
        ...
    end case;
    ...
end P;
```

The local variable C1 is a constant object, meaning that its value cannot be changed *within* the procedure, even though its value will be different each time the procedure is called. On the other hand, the case statement selections must be known at compile time.

Unlike C, C++ considers constants to be static:

```
const int N = 8;                                              C++
int a[N];                 // OK in C++, not in C
```

Implementation

Once the expression on the right-hand side of an assignment statement has been evaluated, one instruction is needed to store the value of the expression in a memory location. If the left-hand side is complex (array indexing, etc.), additional instructions will be needed to compute the memory address that it specifies.

If the right-hand side is more than one word long, several instructions will be needed to store the value, unless the computer has a *block copy* operation which can copy a sequence of memory words given: the source starting address, the target starting address and the number of words to copy.

4.9 Exercises

1. Read your compiler documentation and list the precisions used for the different integer types.

2. Write $200 + 55 = 255$ and $100 - 150 = -50$ in two's complement notation.

3. Let a take on all values in the ranges 50..56 and $-56..50$, and let b be either 7 or -7. What are the possible quotients q and remainders r when a is divided by b? Use both definitions of remainder (denoted

rem and mod in Ada), and display the results in graphical form. Hint: if rem is used, r will have the sign of a; if mod is used, r will have the sign of b.

4. What happens if you execute the following C program on a computer which stores short int values in 8 bits and int values in 16 bits?

```
short int i;                                                          C
int j = 280;
for (i = 0; i < j; i++) printf("Hello world");
```

5. If a non-standard representation of an enumeration type is used, how would you implement the Ada attribute T'Succ(V)?

6. What will the following program print? Why?

```
int i = 2;                                                           C
int j = 5;
if (i & j) printf("Hello world");
if (i && j) printf("Goodbye world");
```

7. What is the value of i after executing the following statements?

```
int i = 0;                                                           C
int a[2] = {10,11};
i = a[i++];
```

8. C and C++ do not have an exponentiation operator; why?

9. Show how modular types in Ada 95 and unsigned integer types in C can be used to represent sets. How portable is your solution? Compare with the set type in Pascal.

5 Composite Data Types

From the beginning, programming languages have provided support for composite data types. Arrays are used to model vectors and matrices in mathematical models of the real world. Records are used in business data processing to model the forms and files that collect a variety of data into a single unit.

As with any type, we must describe the set of values of composite types and the operations on these values. In the case of composite types: how are they constructed from elementary values, and what operations can be used to access components of the composite value? The predefined operations on composite types are relatively limited, and most operations must be explicitly programmed from operations on the components of the composite type.

Since arrays are a specialization of records, we begin the discussion with records (called *structures* in C).

5.1 Records

A value of a record type is composed of a set of values of other types called *components* (Ada), *members* (C) or *fields* (Pascal). Within the type declaration, each field has a name and a type. The following declaration in C shows a structure with four components: one of type string, one of a user-defined enumeration type and two of integer type:

```
typedef enum {Black, Blue, Green, Red, White} Colors;

typedef struct {
    char      model[20];
    Colors    color;
    int       speed;
    int       fuel;
} Car_Data;
```

C

The equivalent declaration in Ada is:

```Ada
type Colors is (Black, Blue, Green, Red, White);
```

```Ada
type Car_Data is
    record
        Model:      String(1..20);
        Color:      Colors:
        Speed:      Integer;
        Fuel:       Integer;
    end record;
```

Once a record type has been defined, objects (variables and constants) of the type can be declared. Assignment is possible between variables of the same record type:

```C
Car_Data c1, c2;
c1 = c2;
```

and in Ada (but not in C) it is also possible to check equality of values of the type:

```Ada
C1, C2, C3:  Car_Data;
if C1 = C2 then
    C1 = C3;
end if;
```

Since a type is a set of values, you would think that it is always possible to denote a *value* of a record type. Surprisingly, this is not possible in general; for example, C permits record values only in initializations. In Ada, however, it is possible to construct a value of a record type, called an *aggregate*, simply by supplying a value of the correct type for each field. The association of a value with a field may be by position within the record, or by name of the field:

```Ada
if C1 = ("Peugeot", Blue, 98, 23) then ...
C1 := ("Peugeot", Red, C2.Speed, C3.Fuel);
C2 := (Model=>"Peugeot", Speed=>76,
        Fuel=>46, Color=>White);
```

This is extremely important because the compiler will report an error if you forget to include a value for a field; if you use individual assignments, it is easy to forget one of the fields:

C1.Model := "Peugeot"; Ada

                     -- Forgot C1.Color

C1.Speed := C2.Speed;
C1.Fuel := C3.Fuel;

Individual fields of a record can be *selected* using a period and the field name:

c1.speed = c1.fuel * x; C

Once selected, a field of a record is a normal variable or value of the field type, and all operations appropriate to that type are applicable.

The names of record fields are local to the type definition and can be reused in other definitions:

```
typedef struct {                                      C
        float  speed;          /* Reuse field name */
} Performance;

Performance p;
Car_Data c;
p.speed = (float) c.speed;     /* Same name, different field */
```

Single records as such are not very useful; the importance of records is apparent only when they form part of more sophisticated data structures such as arrays of records, or dynamic structures that are created with pointers (Section 8.2).

Implementation

A record value is represented by a sufficient number of   ıory words to include all of its fields. The layout of the record Car_L...a is shown in Figure 5.1. The fields are normally laid out in order of their appearance in the record type definition.

Accessing a specific field is very efficient because each field is placed at an offset from the beginning of the record which is constant and known at compile-time. Most computers have addressing modes that enable a constant to be added to an address register while the instruction is decoded. Once the address of the beginning of the record has been loaded into a register, subsequent accesses of fields do not require additional instructions:

```
load       R1,&C1          Address of record
load       R2,20(R1)       Load second field
load       R3,24(R1)       Load third field
```

Figure 5.1 Implementation of a record

Since a field may need an amount of memory that is not a multiple of the word size, the compiler may *pad* the record to ensure that each field is on a word boundary, because accesses not on a word boundary are much less efficient. On a 16-bit computer, the following type definition:

```
typedef struct {                                                    C
        char  f1;               /* 1 byte, skip 1 byte */
        int   f2;               /* 2 bytes */
        char  f3;               /* 1 byte, skip 1 byte */
        int   f4;               /* 2 bytes */
};
```

may cause four words to be allocated to each record variable so that fields of type int are word-aligned, whereas:

```
typedef struct {                                                    C
        int   f2;               /* 2 bytes */
        int   f4;               /* 2 bytes */
        char  f1;               /* 1 byte */
        char  f3;               /* 1 byte */
};
```

would require only three words. When using a compiler that packs fields tightly, you may be able to improve efficiency by adding dummy fields to pad out fields to word boundaries. See also Section 5.8 for ways of explicitly mapping fields. In any case, *never* assume a specific record layout, as that will make your program totally non-portable.

5.2 Arrays

An array is a record all of whose fields are of the same type. Furthermore, these fields (called *elements* or *components*) are not named by identifiers but by position within the array. The power of the array data type comes from the ability to efficiently access an element by using an *index*. Since all the elements are of the same type, it is possible to compute the location of a specific element by multiplying the index by the size of an element. Using indices it is easy to search through an array for a specific element, or to sort or otherwise rearrange the elements.

The index type in Ada may be any discrete type, that is any type on which "counting" is possible; these are integer types and enumeration types (including Character and Boolean):

```
type Heat is (Off, Low, Medium, High);                          Ada
type Temperatures is array(Heat) of Float;
Temp: Temperatures;
```

C restricts the index type to integers; you specify *how many* components you want:

```
#define Max 4                                                    C
float temp[Max];
```

and the indices are implicitly from 0 to one less than the number of components, in this case from 0 to 3. C++ allows any constant expression to be used for the array count, which improves readability:

```
const int last = 3;                                             C++
float temp[last+1];
```

The array component may be of any type:

```
typedef struct {...} Car_Data;                                  C
Car_Data database[100];
```

In Ada (but not in C) the operations of assignment and equality checking may be done on arrays:

```
type A_Type is array(0..9) of Integer;                          Ada
A, B, C: A_Type;

if A = B then A := C; end if;
```

As with records, array values called aggregates exist in Ada with an extensive range of syntactic options:

```
A := (1,2,3,4,5,6,7,8,9,10);                                    Ada
A := (0..4 => 1, 5..9 => 2);        -- Half one's, half two's
A := (others => 0);                 -- All zeros
```

In C, array aggregates are limited to initial values.

The most important array operation is *indexing*, which selects an element of an array. The index value, which may be an arbitrary expression of the array index type, is written following the array name:

```
type Char_Array is array(Character range 'a' .. 'z') of Boolean;      Ada
A: Char_Array := (others => False);
C: Character := 'z';
```

```
A(C) := A('a') and A('b');
```

Another way of understanding arrays is to consider them to be a function from the index type to the element type. Ada (like Fortran but unlike Pascal and C) encourages this view by using the same syntax for function calls and for array indexing. That is, without looking at the declaration you cannot know whether A(I) is a call to a function or an indexing operation on an array. The advantage to this common syntax is that a data structure may be initially implemented as an array, and later on if a more complex data structure is needed, the array can be replaced by a function without modifying the array accesses. The use of brackets rather than parentheses in Pascal and C is mostly for the convenience of the compiler.

Records and arrays may be nested arbitrarily in order to construct complex data structures. To access an elementary component of such a structure, field selection and element indexing must be done one after the other until the component is reached:

```
typedef int A[10];          /* Array type */                        C
typedef struct {            /* Record type */
    A       a;              /* Array within record */
    char    b;
    }   Rec;
```

```
Rec     r[10];              /* Array of records of arrays of int */
int     i,j,k;
```

```
k = r[i+1].a[j-1];          /* Index, then select, then index */
                            /* Final result is an integer value */
```

Note that partial selecting and indexing in a complex data structure yields values that are themselves arrays or records:

```
r                           Array of record of array of integer      C
r[i]                        Record of array of integer
```

r[i].a   Array of integer
r[i].a[j]   Integer

and these values can be used in assignment statements, etc.

5.3 Arrays and type checking

Probably the most common cause of difficult bugs is indexing that exceeds array limits:

```
int a[10];                                    C
for (i = 0; i <= 10; i++)
    a[i] = 2*i;
```

The loop will also be executed for i=10 but the last element of the array is a[9].

The reason that this type of bug is so common is that index expressions can be arbitrary expressions, but valid indices fall within the range defined in the array declaration. The slightest mistake can cause the index to receive a value that is outside this narrow range. The reason that the resulting bug is so disastrous is that an assignment to a[i] if i is out of range causes some *unrelated* memory location to be modified, perhaps even in the operating system area. Even if hardware protection restricts the modification to data within your own program, the bug will be difficult to find because the *symptoms* will be in the wrong place, namely in unrelated statements that use the modified memory rather than in the statement that caused the modification.

To demonstrate: if a numerical mistake causes a variable speed to receive the value 20 instead of 30:

```
int x = 10, y = 50;                           C
speed = (x + y) / 3;              /* Compute average ! */
```

the symptom is the incorrect value of speed, and the cause (division by 3 instead of 2) is in a statement that calculates speed. The symptom is directly related to the mistake, and by using breakpoints or watchpoints you can quickly locate the problem. In the following example:

```
int a[10];                                    C
int speed;

for (i = 0; i <= 10; i++)
    a[i] = 2*i;
```

speed is a victim of the fact that it was arbitrarily declared just after a and
thus modified in a totally unrelated statement. You can trace the computation
of speed for days without finding the bug.

The solution to these problems is to check indexing operation on arrays
to ensure that the bounds are respected. Any attempt to exceed the array
bounds is considered to be a violation of type checking. The first language
to propose index checking was Pascal:

```
type A_Type = array[0..9] of Integer;                                    Pascal
A: A_Type;
A[10] := 20;                         (* Error *)
```

With array type checking, the bug is caught *immediately* where it occurs and
not after it has "smeared" some unrelated memory location; an entire class
of difficult bugs is removed from programs. More precisely: such errors
become compile-time errors instead of run-time errors.

Of course you don't get something for nothing, and there are two problems
with array type checking. The first is that there is a run-time cost to the
checks which we will discuss in a later section. The second problem has to
do with an inconsistency between the way we work with arrays and the way
that type checking works. Consider the following example:

```
type A_Type = array[0..9] of Real;       (* Array types *)          Pascal
type B_Type = array[0..8] of Real;

A: A_Type;                                (* Array variables *)
B: B_Type;

procedure Sort(var P: A_Type);            (* Array parameter *)

sort(A);                                  (* OK *)
sort(B);                                  (* Error! *)
```

The two array type declarations define distinct types. The type of the actual
parameter to a procedure must match the type of the formal parameter, so
it seems that two different Sort procedures are needed, one for each type.
This is inconsistent with our intuitive concept of arrays and array operations,
because the detailed programming of procedures like Sort does not depend on
the number of elements there are in an array; the array bounds should simply
be additional parameters. Note that this problem does not occur in Fortran
or C simply because those languages do not have array parameters! They
simply pass the address of the start of the array and it is the responsibility
of the programmer to correctly define and use the array bounds.

The Ada language has an elegant solution to this problem.[1] The type of an array in Ada is determined solely by its *signature*, that is the type of the index and the type of the element. Such a type is called an *unconstrained array type*. To actually declare an array, an *index constraint* must be appended to the type:[2]

```
type A_Type is array(Integer range <>) of Float;                    Ada
                        -- Unconstrained array type declaration
```

```
A: A_Type(0..9);            -- Array with index constraint
B: A_Type(0..8);            -- Array with index constraint
```

The signature of A_Type is a one-dimensional array with Integer indices and Float components; the index bounds are *not* part of the signature.

As in Pascal, indexing operations are fully checked:

```
A(9) := 20.5;              -- OK, index range is 0..9        Ada
B(9) := 20.5;              -- Error, index range is 0..8
```

The importance of unconstrained arrays is apparent when we look at procedure parameters. Since the type of (unconstrained) array parameters is determined by the signature only, we can call a procedure with any actual parameter of that type regardless of its index constraint:

```
procedure Sort(P: in out A_Type);                           Ada
                        -- Unconstrained array type parameter
```

```
Sort(A);                -- Type of A is A_Type
Sort(B);                -- Type of B is also A_Type
```

The question now arises: how can the Sort procedure access the array bounds? In Pascal, the bounds were part of the type and so were also known within the procedure. In Ada, the constraint of the actual array parameter is automatically passed to the procedure at run-time, and can be accessed using functions called *attributes*. Given any array A:

- A'First is the index of the first element in A.

- A'Last is the index of the last element in A.

- A'Length is the number of elements in A.

---

[1] The Pascal standard defines *conformant array parameters* whose bounds are implicitly passed to a procedure, but we will focus on the Ada solution which introduces a new generalized concept not limited to array parameters.

[2] The symbol "<>" is read "box".

- A'Range is equivalent to A'First..A'Last.

For example:

```
procedure Sort(P: in out A_Type) is                    Ada
begin
    for I in P'Range loop
        for J in I+1 .. P'Last loop
    ...
    end Sort;
```

The use of array attributes enables the programmer to write software that is extremely robust to modifications: any change in the array bounds is automatically reflected in the attributes.

To summarize: array type checking is a powerful tool for improving the reliability of programs; however, the definition of the array bounds should not be part of the static definition of a type.

5.4 * Array subtypes in Ada

The subtypes that we discussed in Section 4.5 were defined by appending a *range constraint* to a discrete type (integer or enumeration). Similarly, an array subtype may be declared by appending an *index constraint* to an unconstrained array type:

```
type A_Type is array(Integer range <>) of Float;
subtype Line is A_Type(1..80);
L, L1, L2: Line;
```

A value of this named subtype may be used as an actual parameter corresponding to a formal parameter of the underlying unconstrained type:

```
Sort(L);
```

In any case, the unconstrained formal parameter of Sort is dynamically constrained by the actual parameter each time the procedure is called.

The discussion of subtypes in Section 4.5 is applicable here. Arrays of different subtypes of the same type can be assigned to each other (provided that they have the same number of elements), but arrays of different types cannot be assigned to each other without an explicit type conversion. The definition of a named subtype is just a convenience.

Ada has powerful constructs called *slices* and *sliding*, which enable partial arrays to be assigned:

```
    L1(10..15) := L2(20..25);
```

which assigns a slice of one array to another, sliding the indices until they match. The type signatures are checked at compile-time, while the constraints are checked at run-time and can be dynamic:

```
    L1(I..J) := (I*K..M+2);
```

The difficulties with array type definitions in Pascal led the designers of Ada to generalize the solution for arrays to the elegant concept of subtypes: separate the static type specification from the constraint which can be dynamic.

5.5 String type

Basically strings are simply arrays of characters, but additional language support is required for programming convenience. The first requirement is to have a special syntax for strings, otherwise working with arrays of characters would be too tedious. Both of the following declarations are valid but of course the first form is much more convenient:

```
    char s[] = "Hello world";                                    C
    char s[] = {'H','e','l','l','o',' ','w','o','r','l','d', '\0'};
```

Next we have to find some way of dealing with string length. The above example already shows that the compiler can determine the size of a string without having the programmer specify it explicitly. C uses a convention on the representation of strings, namely that the first zero byte encountered terminates the string. String processing in C typically contains a while-loop of the form:

```
    while (s[i++] != '\0') ...                                   C
```

The main drawback to this method is that if the terminating zero is somehow missing, memory can be smeared just like any statement that causes array bounds to be exceeded:[3]

```
    char s[11] = "Hello world";      /* No room for zero byte */   C
    char t[11];
    strcpy(t, s);                    /* Copy s to t. How long is s? */
```

---

[3]This particular error would be caught in C++ which does not ignore extra members in an initialization.

Other disadvantages of this method are:

- String operations require dynamic allocation and deallocation of memory which is relatively inefficient.

- Calls to string library functions require that the string length be recalculated.

- The zero byte cannot be part of the string.

An alternative solution used by some dialects of Pascal is to include an explicit length byte as the implicit zero'th character of a string whose maximum length is specified when it is declared:

```
S: String[10];                                    Pascal
S := 'Hello world';        (* Needs 11 bytes *)
writeln(S);
S := 'Hello';
writeln(S);
```

The first output of the program will be "Hello worl" because the string will be truncated to fit the declared length. The second output will be "Hello" because the writeln statement takes the implicit length into account. Unfortunately, this solution is also flawed because it is possible to directly access the hidden length byte and smear memory:

```
s[0] := 15;                                       Pascal
```

In Ada there is a predefined unconstrained array type called String whose definition is:[4]

```
type String is array(Positive range <>) of Character;      Ada
```

Each string must be of fixed length and declared with a constraint:

```
S: String(1..80);                                 Ada
```

Unlike C where all string processing is done using library procedures like strcpy, Ada includes operators on strings such as concatenation "&", equality and relational operators like "<". Type checking is strictly enforced, so a certain amount of gymnastics with attributes is needed to make everything work out:

---

[4]Using predefined subtype Positive is Integer range 1..Integer'First.

```
S1: constant String := "Hello";                              Ada
S2: constant String := "world";
T: String(1 .. S1'Length + 1 + S2'Length) := S1 & ' ' & S2;
Put(T);                              -- Will print Hello world
```

The exact length of T must be computed before the assignment is done! Fortunately, Ada supports array attributes and a construct for creating subarrays (called slices) that make it possible to do such computations in a portable manner.

Ada 83 provides the framework for defining strings whose length is not fixed, but not the necessary library subprograms for string processing. To improve portability, Ada 95 defines standard libraries for all three categories of strings: fixed, varying (as in Pascal) and dynamic (as in C).

5.6 Multi-dimensional arrays

Multi-dimensional matrices are extensively used in mathematical models of the physical world, and multi-dimensional arrays have appeared in programming languages since Fortran. There are actually two ways of defining multi-dimensional arrays: directly and as complex structures. We will limit the discussion to two-dimensional arrays; the generalization to higher dimensions is immediate.

A two-dimensional array can be directly defined in Ada by giving two index types separated by a comma:

```
type Two is                                                  Ada
    array(Character range <>, Integer range <>) of Integer;
T: Two('A'..'Z', 1..10);
I: Integer;
C: Character;

T('X', I*3) := T(C, 6);
```

As the example shows, the two dimensions need not be of the same type. Selecting an array element is done by giving both indices.

The second method of defining a two-dimensional array is to define a type that is an array of arrays:

```
type I_Array is array(1..10) of Integer;                     Ada
type Array_of_Array is array (Character range <>) of I_Array;
T: Array_of_Array('A'..'Z');
```

```
I: Integer;
C: Character;
```

```
T('X')(I*3) := T(C)(6);
```

The advantage of this method is that by using one index operation, the elements of the second dimension (which are themselves arrays) can be accessed:

```
T('X') := T('Y');                    -- Assign 10-element arrays        Ada
```

The disadvantage is that the elements of the second dimension must be constrained before they can be used to define the second dimension.

In C, only the second method is available and of course only for integer indices:

```
int a[10][20];                                                          C
a[1] = a[2];                    /* Assign 20-element arrays */
```

Pascal does not distinguish between a two-dimensional array and an array of arrays; since the bounds are considered to be part of the array type this causes no difficulties.

5.7 Array implementation

Arrays are represented by placing the array elements in sequence in memory. Given an array A the address of A(I) is (Figure 5.2):

$$addr(A) + size(element) * (i - A'First)$$

For example: the address of A(4) is $20 + 4 * (4 - 1) = 32$.

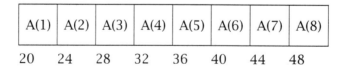

Figure 5.2 Implementation of array indexing

The generated machine code is:

```
load        R1,I              Get index
sub         R1,A'First        Subtract lower bound
multi       R1,size           Multiply by size -> offset
add         R1,&A             Add array addr. -> element addr.
load        R2,(R1)           Load contents
```

It may surprise you to learn how many instructions are needed for each array access!

There are many optimizations that can be done to improve this code. First note that if A'First is zero, we save the subtraction of the index of the first element; this explains why the designers of C specified that indices always start at zero. Even if A'First is not zero but is known at compile time, the address calculation can be rearranged as follows:

$$(addr(A) - size(element) * A' First) + (size(element) * i)$$

The first expression in parentheses can be computed at compile-time saving the run-time subtraction. This expression will be known at compile-time in a direct use of an array:

```
A: A_Type(1..10);                                          [Ada]
A(I) := A(J);
```

but not if the array is a parameter:

```
procedure Sort(A: A_Type) is                               [Ada]
begin
    ...
    A(A'First+I) := A(J);
    ...
end Sort;
```

The main obstacle to efficient array operations is the multiplication by the size of the array element. Fortunately, most arrays are of simple data types like characters or integers whose size is a power of two. In this case, the costly multiplication operation can be replaced by an efficient shift, since shift left by n is equivalent to multiplication by 2^n. If you have an array of records, you can squeeze out more efficiency (at the cost of extra memory) by padding the records to a power of two. Note that the portability of the program is not affected, but the *improvement* in efficiency is not portable: another compiler might lay out the record in a different manner.

C programmers can sometimes improve the efficiency of a program with arrays by explicitly coding access to array elements using pointers rather than indices. Given definitions such as:

```
typedef struct {                                                    C
    ...
    int field;
} Rec;
Rec a[100];
```

it may be more efficient (depending on the quality of the compiler's optimizer) to access the array using a pointer:

```
Rec* ptr;                                                           C
```

```
for (ptr = &a; ptr < &a+100*sizeof(Rec); ptr += sizeof(Rec))
    ... ptr-> field ... ;
```

than using an indexing operation:

```
for (i = 0; i < 100; i++)                                           C
    ... a[i].field ... ;
```

However, this style of coding is extremely error-prone, as well as hard to read, and should be avoided except when absolutely necessary.

A possible way of copying strings in C is to use:

```
while (*s1++ = *s2++)                                               C
    ;
```

where there is a null statement before the semicolon. If the computer has block-copy instructions which move the contents of a block of memory cells to another address, a language like Ada which allows array assignment would be more efficient. In general, C programmers should use library functions which are likely to be implemented more efficiently than the naive implementation shown above.

Multi-dimensional arrays can be very inefficient because each additional dimension requires an extra multiplication to compute the index. When programming with multi-dimensional arrays, you must also be aware of the layout of the data. Except for Fortran, all languages store a two-dimensional array as a sequence of rows. The layout of:

```
type T is array(1..3, 1..5) of Integer;                            Ada
```

is shown in Figure 5.3. This layout is consistent with the similarity between a two-dimensional array and an array of arrays. If you wish to compute a value for every element of a two-dimensional array, make sure that the last index is in the inner loop:

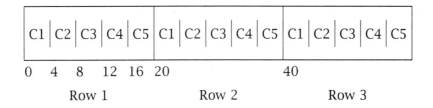

Figure 5.3 Implementation of a multi-dimensional array

```c
int matrix[100][200];
```
C

```c
for (i = 0; i < 100; i++)
    for (j = 0; j < 200; j++)
        m[i][j] = ...;
```

The reason is that operating systems that use paging are vastly more efficient if successive memory accesses are close together.

If you wish to squeeze the best performance out of a program in C, you can ignore the two-dimensional structure of the array and pretend that the array is one-dimensional:

```c
for (i = 0; i < 100*200; i++)
    m[0][i] = ...;
```
C

Needless to say, this is not recommended and should be carefully documented if used.

Array type checking requires that the index be checked against the bounds before each array access. The overhead to this check is high: two comparisons and jumps. Compilers for languages like Ada have to invest significant effort to optimize the instructions for array processing. The main technique is to utilize available information. In the following example:

```ada
for I in A'Range loop
    if A(I) = Key then ...
```
Ada

the index I will take on exactly the permitted values of the array so no checking is required. In general, the optimizer will perform best if all variables are declared with the tightest possible constraints.

When arrays are passed as parameters in a type-checking language:

```
type A_Type is array(Integer range <>) of Integer;        [Ada]
procedure Sort(A: A_Type) is ...
```

the bounds must also be implicitly passed in a data structure called a *dope vector* (Figure 5.4). The dope vector contains the upper and lower bounds,

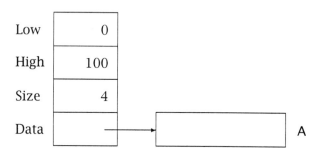

Figure 5.4 Dope vector

the size of an element and the address of the start of the array. As we have seen, this is exactly the information needed to compute an array indexing operation.

5.8   * Representation specification

This book repeatedly stresses the importance of viewing a program as an abstract model of the real world. Nevertheless, many programs such as operating systems, communications packages and embedded software require the ability to manipulate data at the physical level of their representation in memory.

Bitwise computation

C contains Boolean operators which compute on individual bits of *integer* values: "&" (and), "|" (or), "∧" (xor), "~" (not).

The Boolean operators in Ada: and, or, xor, not can also be applied to arrays of Boolean:

```
type Bool_Array is array(0..31) of Boolean;              [Ada]
B1: Bool_Array := (0..15 => True, 16..31 => False);
B2: Bool_Array := (0..15 => False, 16..31 => True);

B1 := B1 or B2;
```

However, just declaring a Boolean array does not ensure that it is represented as a bit string; in fact, a Boolean value is usually represented as a full integer. The addition of the directive:

> pragma Pack(Bool_Array);   `Ada`

requests the compiler to pack the values of the array as densely as possible. Since only one bit is needed for a Boolean value, the 32 elements of the array can be stored in one 32-bit word. While this does provide the required functionality, it does lack some of the flexibility of C, in particular the ability to use octal or hexadecimal constants like 0xf00f0ff0 in Boolean computations. Ada does provide a notation for such constants, but they are integer values and not arrays of Boolean and so cannot be used in bitwise computation.

These problems are solved in Ada 95: modular types (Section 4.1) can be used for bitwise computation:

> type Unsigned_Byte is mod 256;   `Ada`
> U1, U2: Unsigned_Byte;
>
> U1 := U1 and U2;

Subword fields

Hardware registers are usually composed of several subword fields. Classically, the way to access such fields is to use shift and mask; the statement:

> field = (i >> 4) & 0x7;   `C`

extracts the three-bit field located four bits from the right of the word i. This programming style is dangerous because it is very easy to make mistakes in specifying the shift counts and masks. In addition, the slightest change in the layout of a word can require massive modification of the program.

An elegant solution to this problem was first introduced by Pascal: use ordinary records, but pack the fields into a single word.[5] An ordinary field access Rec.Field is automatically translated by the compiler into the correct shift and mask.

In Pascal, the mapping was implicit; other languages have a notation for explicit mapping. C allows bit-field specifiers on a structure field (provided that the fields are of integer type):

---

[5]The motivation for this came from the CDC 6000 series computers that were used in the first Pascal implementation. These computers, intended for numerical calculations, used a 60 bit word and had no instructions for subword access except shift and mask.

```c
typedef struct {
    int       : 3;      /* Padding */
    int f1    : 1;
    int f2    : 2;
    int       : 3;      /* Padding */
    int f3    : 2;
    int       : 4;      /* Padding */
    int f4    : 1;
} reg;
```

and then ordinary assignment statements can be used, even though the fields are part of a word (Figure 5.5) and the assignment is implemented by the compiler using shift and mask:

```c
reg r;
int i;

i = r.f2;
r.f3 = i;
```

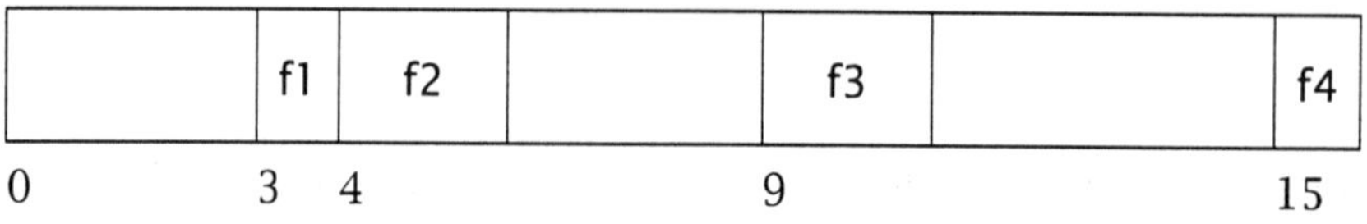

```
|         | f1 | f2 |          |   f3   |          | f4 |
0         3    4                9                   15
```

Figure 5.5 Subword record fields

Ada insists that type declarations be abstract; *representation specifications* use a different notation and are written separately from the type declaration. Given the record type declaration:

```ada
type Heat is (Off, Low, Medium, High);

type Reg is
    record
        F1: Boolean;
        F2: Heat;
        F3: Heat;
        F4: Boolean;
    end record;
```

a record specification can be appended:

```
for Reg use
    record
        F1 at 0 range 3..3;
        F2 at 0 range 4..5;
        F3 at 1 range 1..2;
        F4 at 1 range 7..7;
    end record;
```

Ada

The at clause specifies the byte within the record and range specifies the bit range assigned to the field, where we know that one bit is sufficient for a Boolean value and two bits are sufficient for a Heat value. Note that padding is not necessary because exact positions are specified.

Once the bit specifiers in C and representation specifications in Ada are correctly programmed, all subsequent accesses are ensured to be free of bugs.

Big endians and little endians

Conventionally, memory addresses start at zero and increase. Unfortunately, computer architectures differ in the way multibyte values are stored in memory. Let us assume that each byte can be separately addressed and that each word takes four bytes. How is the integer 0x04030201 to be stored? The word can be stored so that the most significant byte is first, an order called *big endian*, or so that the least significant byte has the lowest address, called *little endian*. Figure 5.6 shows the numbering of the bytes for the two options.

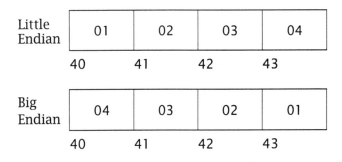

Figure 5.6 Big endian and little endian

This aspect of the computer architecture is handled by the compiler and is totally transparent to the programmer who writes abstractly using records.

However, when representation specifications are used, the differences between the two conventions can cause a program to be non-portable. In Ada 95, the bit ordering of a word can be specified by the programmer, so a program using representation specifications can be ported by changing only one statement.

Derived types and representation specifications in Ada

A derived type in Ada (Section 4.6) is defined as a new type whose values and operators are a copy of those of the parent type. A derived type may have a representation that is different from the parent type. For example, once an ordinary type Unpacked_Register is defined:

```
type Unpacked_Register is                              Ada
    record
        ...
    end record;
```

a new type may be derived and a representation specification associated with the derived type:

```
type Packed_Register is new Unpacked_Register;         Ada

for Packed_Register use
    record
        ...
    end record;
```

Type conversion (which is allowed between any types that are derived from each other) causes a change of representation, namely, packing and unpacking the subword fields of the record to ordinary variables:

```
U: Unpacked_Register;                                  Ada
P: Packed_Register;

U := Unpacked_Register(P);
P := Packed_Register(U);
```

This facility can contribute to the reliability of programs, because once the representation specification is correctly written, the rest of the program can be completely abstract.

5.9 Exercises

1. Does your compiler pack record fields or align them on word boundaries?

2. Does your computer have a block-copy instruction, and does your compiler use it for array and record assignments?

3. Pascal contains the construct with which opens the scope of a record so that the field names can be used directly:

   ```
   type Rec =                              Pascal
       record
           Field1: Integer;
           Field2: Integer;
       end;
   R: Rec;

   with R do Field1 := Field2;      (* OK, direct visibility *)
   ```

   What are the advantages and disadvantages of the construct? Study the Ada renames construct and show how some of the same functionality can be obtained. Compare the two constructs.

4. Explain the error message that you get if you try to assign one array to another in C:

   ```
   int a1[10], a2[10];                     C
   a1 = a2;
   ```

5. Write sort procedures in Ada and C, and compare them. Make sure that you use attributes in the Ada procedure so that the procedure will work on arrays with arbitrary indices.

6. Which optimizations does your compiler do on array indexing operations?

7. Icon has associative arrays called tables, where a string can be used as an array index:

   ```
   count["begin"] = 8;
   ```

   Implement associative arrays in Ada or C.

8. Are the following two types the same?

```
type Array_Type_1 is array(1..100) of Float;          Ada
type Array_Type_2 is array(1..100) of Float;
```

Ada and C++ use *name equivalence*: every type declaration declares a
new type, so two types are declared. Under *structural equivalence* (used
in Algol 68), type declarations that look alike define the same type.
What are the advantages and disadvantages of the two approaches?

9. An anonymous array (without a named type) can be defined in Ada. In
   the following example, is the assignment legal? Why?

```
A1, A2: array(1..10) of Integer;                      Ada
A1 := A2;
```

6

Control Structures

Control statements are used to modify the order of execution. There are two classes of well-structured control statements: choice statements (if and case) which select one alternative from two or more possible execution sequences, and loop statements (for and while) which repeatedly execute a series of statements.

6.1 switch-/case-statements

A choice statement is used to select one of several possible paths for the computation to pursue (Figure 6.1).[1] The generalized choice statement is

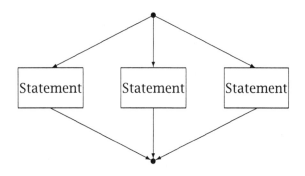

Figure 6.1 Choice statement

called a switch-statement in C and a case-statement in other languages. A switch-statement is composed of an expression and a statement for each

---

[1]Throughout this chapter we will use the term "statement" to describe a path of the computation. This should be interpreted to include a *compound statement* which is a sequence of one or more statements.

possible value of the expression:

```
switch (expression) {                                    C
    case value_1:
        statement_1;
        break;
    case value_2:
        statement_2;
        break;

    ...

}
```

The expression is evaluated and the result of the expression is used to
select a statement to execute; in terms of Figure 6.1, the selected statement
represents a path. This requires that there be *exactly* one **case** alternative for
each possible value of the expression. If the expression is of integer type,
this is impossible since it is not practical to write a statement for each 32-bit
integer value. In Pascal the **case**-statement is usable only for types which
have a small number of values, while C and Ada provide a default alternative,
so that the **case**-statement can be used even for types like **Character** that
have hundreds of values:

```
default:                                                 C
    default_statement;
    break;
```

If the value of the expression is not explicitly listed, the default statement
is executed. C actually assumes an empty default statement if the **default**
alternative is missing. This option should not be used because the reader
of the program has no way of knowing if an empty default statement is
intended, or if the programmer has simply forgotten to provide the necessary
statements.

In many cases, the statement for two or more alternatives is identical. C
has no direct way of expressing this (see below); in Ada there is an extensive
set of syntactical constructions for grouping alternatives:

```
C: Character;                                            Ada
case C is
    when 'A' .. 'Z'               => statement_1;
    when '0' .. '9'               => statement_2;
    when '+' | '-' | '*' | '/'    => statement_3;
    when others                   => statement_4;
end case;
```

In Ada the alternatives are introduced by the reserved keyword when, and the default alternative is called others. A case alternative may contain a range of values value_1..value_2, or it may contain a set of values separated by "|".

The break-*statement in C*

In C you must explicitly terminate each case alternative with the break-statement, otherwise the computation will "fall-through" to the next case alternative. A valid use of fall-through is to mimic the multiple-alternative construct in Ada:

```
char c;                                                    C
switch (c) {
    case 'A':   case 'B':   ...   case 'Z':
        statement_1;
        break;
    case '0':   ...   case '9':
        statement_2;
        break;
    case '+':   case '-':   case '*':   case '/':
        statement_3;
        break;
    default:
        statement_4;
        break;
}
```

Since each value must be explicitly written, the switch-statement in C is rather less convenient than the case-statement in Ada.

Fall-through should not be used in ordinary programming:

```
switch (e) {                                               C
    case value_1:
        statement_1;            /* After statement_1, */
    case value_2:
        statement_2;            /*    fall through to statement_2. */
        break;
}
```

Referring to Figure 6.1, the switch-statement is intended to be used to choose one of a set of possible paths. Fall-through is confusing because the end of a path loops back to the beginning of the tree of choices. Furthermore,

no semantic importance should be attributed to the sequence in which the
choices are written (though the order may be significant in terms of efficiency). Maintainers of the program should be free to rearrange existing
choices, or to insert new choices, without fear of introducing a bug. This
program is also difficult to test and debug: if a bug is traced to statement_2,
it is difficult to know if the statement was reached by direct selection or by
fall-through. Rather than using fall-through, common code should be placed
in a procedure:

```
switch (e) {                                                              C
    case value_1:
        statement_1;
        common_code();
        break;
    case value_2:
        common_code();
        break;
}
```

Implementation

The simplest way of compiling a case statement is as a sequence of tests:

```
        compute    R1,expr              Compute expression
        jump_eq    R1,#value_1,L1
        jump_eq    R1,#value_2,L2
        ...                             Other values
        default_statement               Instructions for default
        jump       End_Case

L1:     statement_1                     Instructions for statement_1
        jump       End_Case
L2:     statement_2                     Instructions for statement_2
        jump       End_Case
        ...                             Instructions for other statements
End_Case:
```

In terms of efficiency, it is apparent that the closer an alternative is to the
top of the statement, the more efficient it is to choose it; you can reorder
the alternatives to take advantage of this fact (provided that you don't use
fall-through!).

Certain case statements can be optimized to use jump tables. If the set of values of the expression form a short contiguous sequence, then the following code can be used (where we assume that the expression can take values from 0 to 3):

```
        compute    R1,expr
        mult       R1,#len_of_addr    expression*length_of_addr
        add        R1,&table          Start of table
        jump       (R1)               Jump to address in R1

    table:                            Jump table
        addr(L1)
        addr(L2)
        addr(L3)
        addr(L4)

L1:     statement_1
        jump       End_Case
L2:     statement_2
        jump       End_Case
L3:     statement_3
        jump       End_Case
L4:     statement_4
End_Case:
```

The value of the expression is used as an index into a table of addresses of statements, and the jump instruction jumps to the address contained in the register. In terms of efficiency, the overhead of a jump-table implementation is fixed and small for *all* choices.

It is imperative that the value of the expression be within the expected range (here 0 to 3), otherwise an invalid address will be computed and the computation will jump to a location that might not even be a valid instruction! In Ada, the expression can often be checked at compilation time:

```
    type Status is (Off, Warm_Up, On, Automatic);        Ada
    S: Status;
    case S is ...                -- There are exactly four values
```

In other cases, a run-time check will be needed to ensure that the value is within range. Jump tables are even compatible with a default alternative, provided that the explicit choices are contiguous. The compiler simply inserts the run-time check before attempting to use the jump table; if the check fails, the computation continues with the default alternative.

The choice of implementation is usually left to the compiler and there is no way of knowing which one is used without examining the machine code. The documentation of an optimizing compiler may inform its users under what circumstances it will compile into a jump table. Even if you take this knowledge into account when programming, your program is still portable, because the case-statement is portable; however, a different compiler may implement it in a different manner, so the improvement in efficiency is not portable.

6.2 if-statements

An if-statement is a special case of a case- or switch-statement where the expression is of Boolean type. Since Boolean types have only two possible values, an if-statement chooses between two possible paths. if-statements are probably the most frequently used control structures; the reason is that relational operators are extensively used and they return values of Boolean type:

```
if (x > y)                                          C
    statement-1;
else
    statement-2;
```

As we discussed in Section 4.4, C does not have a Boolean type. Instead, integer values are used with the convention that zero is false and non-zero is true.

A common mistake is to use an if-statement to create a Boolean value:

```
if X > Y then                                      Ada
    Result = True;
else
    Result = False;
end if;
```

instead of using a simple assignment statement:

```
Result := X > Y;                                   Ada
```

Remember that values and variables of Boolean type are first-class objects: in C they are just integers, and in Ada they are a distinct type but no different from any other enumeration type. The fact that Boolean types have a special status in if-statements does not otherwise restrict them.

Nested if-*statements*

The alternatives of an if-statement are themselves statements; in particular, they can also be if-statements:

```
if (x1 > y1)                                      C
    if (x2 > y2)
        statement-1;
    else
        statement-2;
else
    if (x3 > y3)
        statement-3;
    else
        statement-4;
```

It is best not to nest control structures (especially if-statements) too deeply, three or four levels at most. The reason is that it becomes difficult to follow the logic of the various paths. Furthermore, the indentation of the source code is only a guide: if you omit an else, the statement may still be syntactically valid even though the processing is no longer correct.

Another potential problem is that of the dangling else:

```
if (x1 > y1)                                      C
    if (x2 > y2)
        statement-1;
    else
        statement-2;
```

As implied by the indentation, the language definition associates the else with the inner-most if-statement. If you want to associate it with the outer if-statement, brackets must be used:

```
if (x1 > y1) {                                    C
    if (x2 > y2)
        statement-1;
}
else
    statement-2;
```

Nested if-statements can define a full binary tree of choices (Figure 6.2(a)), or any arbitrary sub-tree. In many cases, however, what is needed is to

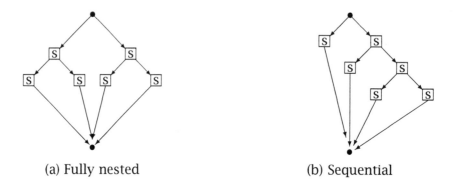

(a) Fully nested   (b) Sequential

Figure 6.2 if-statements

choose one of a sequence of outcomes (Figure 6.2(b)). If the selection is done on the basis of an expression, a switch-statement can be used. Otherwise, if the selection is done on the basis of a sequence of relational expressions, a sequence of nested if-statements is needed. In this case, it is conventional not to indent the statements:

```
if (x > y) {                                                  C
    ...
} else if (x > z) {
    ...
} else if (y < z) {
    ...
} else {
    ...
}
```

Explicit end if

The syntax of the if-statement in C (and Pascal) requires that each alternative be a single statement. If the alternative consists of a sequence of statements, they must be grouped into a single *compound* statement using braces ({, }) in C and (begin, end) in Pascal. The problem with this syntax is that if the terminating bracket is omitted, the compilation will continue without noticing the mistake. At best, the missing bracket will be noticed at the end of the compilation; at worst, a missing *opening* bracket will balance out the bracket count and an obscure run-time bug will be introduced.

This problem can be alleviated by explicitly terminating the if-statement. If the terminating bracket is omitted, it will be flagged as soon as another construct (a loop or procedure) is terminated with a different bracket. The if-statement syntax in Ada is:

```
if expression then                                    Ada
    statement-list-1;
else
    statement-list-2;
end if;
```

The problem with this construct is that in the case of a sequence of conditions (Figure 6.2(b)), there will be a confusing sequence of end if's at the end. To avoid this, a special construct is used; elsif introduces another condition and statement, but not another if-statement so no addition termination is required:

```
if x > y then                                         Ada
    . . .
elsif x > z then
    . . .
elsif y > z then
    . . .
else
    . . .
end if;
```

Implementation

The implementation of an if-statement is straightforward:

```
        compute    R1,expression
        jump_eq    R1,L1               False is represented as 0
        statement-1
        jump       L2
L1:     statement-2
L2:
```

Note that the False alternative is slightly more efficient than the True alternative since the latter executes an extra jump instruction.

On the surface it would seem that a condition of the form:

> if (!expression) ...   `C`

would require an extra instruction to negate the value. However, compilers are smart enough just to change the initial jump_false instruction to jump_true.

Short circuit and full evaluation

Suppose that the expression in an if-statement is not just a simple relational expression, but a compound expression:

> if (x > y) and (y > z) and (z < 57) then...   `Ada`

There are two possible implementations of this statement. The first, called *full evaluation*, evaluates each of the components, then takes the Boolean and of the components and jumps according to the result. The second implementation, called *short-circuit evaluation*, evaluates the components one-by-one: if any component evaluates to False, a jump is executed to the False alternative since the entire expression must obviously be False. A similar situation occurs if the expression is a compound or-expression: if any component is True, the entire expression is obviously True.

The choice between the two implementations can usually be left to the compiler. Short-circuit evaluation will in general require fewer instructions to be executed. However, these instructions include many jumps and on a computer with a large instruction cache (see Section 1.7), it may be more efficient to compute all the components and only jump after the full evaluation.

Pascal specifies full evaluation because it was originally developed for a computer with a large cache. Other languages have two sets of operators: one for (full) evaluation of Boolean values and the other for short-circuit evaluation. For example, in Ada, and is used for fully evaluated Boolean operations on Boolean and modular types, while and then specifies short-circuit evaluation:

> if (x > y) and then (y > z) and then (z < 57) then...   `Ada`

Similarly, or else is the short-circuit equivalent of or.

C contains three logical operators: "!" (not), "&&" (and), and "||" (or). Since C lacks a true Boolean type, these operators take integer operands and are defined in accordance with the interpretation described in Section 4.4. For example, a && b is equal to one if both operands are non-zero. Both "&&" and "||" use short-circuit evaluation. Also, be sure not to confuse these operators with the bitwise operators (Section 5.8).

In terms of programming style, Ada programmers should choose one style (either full evaluation or short circuit) for an entire program, using the other style only if necessary; C programmers always use the short-circuit operators.

Short-circuit evaluation is essential when the ability to evaluate one relation in a compound expression depends on a previous relation:

if (a /= 0) and then (b/a > 25) then ... | Ada |

Such situations are also common when pointers (Chapter 8) are used:

if (ptr /= null) and then (ptr.value = key) then ... | Ada |

6.3 Loop statements

Loop statements are the most difficult statements to program: they are prone to bugs especially at the boundaries of the loop, that is, the first and last executions of the loop body. Furthermore, an inefficient program is almost certainly spending most of its time in loops, so it is critical that their implementation be fully understood.

The structure of a loop statement is shown in Figure 6.3. A loop statement

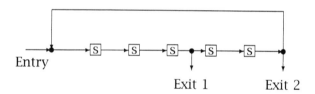

Figure 6.3 Loop statements

has an *entry* point,[2] a sequence of statements that compose the loop, and one or more *exit* points. Since we (usually) want our loop statements to terminate, an exit point will have a *condition* associated with it, which decides if the exit should be taken, or if the execution of the loop should be continued. Loop statements are distinguished by the number, type and placement of the exit conditions. We will begin by discussing loops with arbitrary exit conditions, called while-statements, and in the next section discuss a specialization called for-statements.

The most common type of loop has its single exit point at the beginning of the loop, that is at its entry point. This is called a while-statement:

---

[2]We will not even consider the possibility of jumping into a loop!

```
while (s[i].data != key)                                             C
    i++;
```

The while-statement is straightforward and reliable. Because the condition
is checked at the beginning of the loop, we know that the loop body will be
executed in its entirety a number of times that depends on the condition. If
the exit condition is initially False, the loop body will not be executed and
this simplifies the programming of boundary conditions:

```
while (count > 0)                                                    C
    process(s[count].data);
```

If there is no data in the array, the loop will exit immediately.

In many cases, however, the exit from a loop is naturally written at the
end of the loop. This is common when a variable must be initialized before
any processing is done. Pascal has the repeat-statement:

```
repeat                                                          Pascal
    read(v);
    put_in_table(v)
until v = end_value;
```

The Pascal repeat terminates when the exit condition is True. Do not confuse
it with the C do-statement, which terminates when the exit condition is False:

```
do {                                                                C
    v = get();
    put_in_table(v);
} while (v != end_value);
```

A pure approach to structured programming requires that all loops exit
only at the beginning or the end of the loop. This makes a program much
easier to analyze and verify, but in practice, exits from within a loop are
commonly needed, especially when an error is detected:

```
while not found do                                             Pascal
    begin
    (* Long computation *)
    (* Error detected, terminate *)
    (* Long computation *)
    end
```

Pascal, which has no way of exiting from within a loop, uses the following
unsatisfactory solution: set the exit condition and use an if-statement to skip
the remainder of the loop body:

```
while not found do                                    [Pascal]
    begin
    (* Long computation *)
    if error_detected then found := True
    else
        begin
        (* Long computation *)
        end
    end
```

In C, the break-statement can be used:

```
while (!found) {                                      [C]
    /* Long computation */
    if (error_detected()) break;
    /* Long computation */
}
```

Ada has the usual while-statement, as well as an exit-statement which is used to exit from an arbitrary location within the loop; the common occurrence of an if-statement together with an exit-statement can be conveniently expressed using a when-clause:

```
while not Found loop                                  [Ada]
    -- Long computation
    exit when error_detected;
    -- Long computation
end loop;
```

An operating system or real-time system is not intended to terminate, so there must be a way of indicating non-terminating loops. In Ada, this is directly expressed by a loop-statement with no exit condition:

```
loop                                                  [Ada]
    ...
end loop;
```

Other languages require you to write an ordinary loop with an artificial exit condition that ensures that the loop does not terminate:

```
while (1==1) {                                         [C]
    ...
}
```

Implementation

The implementation of a while-loop:

```
while (expression)                                              C
    statement;
```

is as follows:

```
L1:    compute     R1,expr
       jump_zero    R1,L2          Skip statement if false
       statement                   Loop body
       jump         L1             Jump to check for termination
L2:
```

Note that there are *two* jump instructions in the implementation of a while-statement! Surprisingly, if the loop exit is at the end of the loop, only one jump instruction is needed:

```
do {                                                            C
    statement;
} while (expression);
```

compiles to:

```
L1:    statement
       compute     expr
       jump_nz     L1              Not zero is true
```

Even though the while-loop is a very clear construct, the efficiency of the loop can be improved by changing it to a do-loop. Exiting a loop in the middle requires two jumps just like a while-statement.

6.4 for-statements

Very often, we know the number of iterations that a loop requires: either it is a constant known when the program is written, or it is computed before the beginning of the loop. Counting loops can be programmed as follows:

```
int i;                    /* Loop index */                     C
int low, high;            /* Loop limits */
```

```
    i = low;                    /* Initialize index*/
    while (i <= high) {         /* Evaluate exit expression */
        statement;
        i++;                    /* Increment index */
    };
```

Since this paradigm is so common, all (imperative) programming languages supply a for-statement to simplify programming. In C the syntax is:

```
    int i;                      /* Loop index */           C
    int low, high;             /* Loop limits */

    for (i = low; i <= high; i++) {
        statement;
    }
```

The syntax in Ada is similar, except that the declaration and incrementation of the loop variable is implicit:

```
    Low, High: Integer;                                    Ada

    for I in Low .. High loop
        statement;
    end loop;
```

Later in this section we will discuss the reasons for these differences.

for-statements are notorious for the bugs that they can introduce at the boundary values. The loop is executed for each of the values from low to high; thus the total number of iterations is $high - low + 1$. However, if the value of low is strictly greater than the value of high, the loop is executed zero times. If you wish to execute a loop exactly N times, the for-statement will be:

```
    for I in 1..N loop ...                                 Ada
```

and the number of iterations is $N - 1 + 1 = N$. In C, because arrays are required to start from index zero, ordinary counting loops are usually written:

```
    for (i = 0; i < n; i++) ...                            C
```

Since $i < n$ is the same as $i <= (n - 1)$, the loop is executed $(n - 1) - 0 + 1 = n$ times as required.

Generalized for-*statements*

Even though all imperative languages contain a for-statement, they differ greatly in the additional features that are provided. Two extremes are Ada and C.

Ada takes the point of view that a for-loop should be used *only* for loops with a fixed number of iterations, and that this number can be computed before starting the loop. The rationale for this point of view is: (1) most loops are in fact this simple, (2) other constructions can easily be explicitly programmed, and (3) for-loops are difficult enough to test and verify as it is. Ada even lacks the classic generalization: incrementing the loop variable by values other than 1 (or -1). In Algol, iteration over a sequence of odd numbers can be written:

```
for I := 1 to N step 2 do ...                    Algol
```

while in Ada we have to explicitly program:

```
for I in 1 .. (N+1)/2 loop                        Ada
   I1 = 2*I-1;

   ...

end loop;
```

In C, all three elements of the for-statement can be arbitrary expressions:

```
for (i = j*k;   (i < n) && (j+k > m);   i += 2*j) ...        C
```

The definition of C specifies that:

```
for (expression_1; expression_2; expression_3) statement;    C
```

is equivalent to:

```
expression_1;                                     C
   while (expression_2) {
       statement;
       expression_3;
   }
```

In Ada, expressions are also permitted for the loop limits, but these are evaluated only once at the loop entry. That is:

```
for I in expression_1 .. expression_2 loop        Ada
    statement;
end loop
```

is equivalent to:

```
I = expression_1;                                    Ada
Temp = expression_2;
while (I < Temp) loop
    statement;
    I := I + 1;
end loop;
```

If the body of the loop modifies the value of a variable used in computing expression_2, the upper limit of the Ada loop will not be modified. Compare this with the definition of the C for-loop above which re-evaluates the value of expression_2 on each iteration.

The generalizations in C are not just syntactic sugaring because of the possibility of side-effects, that is, statements within the loop that modify expression_2 and expression_3. Side-effects should be avoided for the following reasons:

- Side-effects make the loop difficult to fully verify and test.

- Side-effects adversely affect the readability and maintainability of the program.

- Side-effects make the loop much less efficient because expression_2 and expression_3 must be re-evaluated on each iteration. If side-effects are not used, an optimizing compiler will be able to move these evaluations outside the loop.

Implementation

for-statements are common sources of inefficiencies in programs because slight differences in language definition, or small changes in the use of the statement, can have significant consequences. In many cases, the optimizer can solve the problems, but it is better to be aware of and avoid problems, rather than to trust the optimizer. In this section, we will describe the implementation in greater detail at the register level.

In Ada, the loop:

```
for I in expression_1 .. expression_2 loop            Ada
    statement;
end loop;
```

compiles to:

```
        compute    R1,expr_1
        store      R1,I                Lower bound to index
        compute    R2,expr_2
        store      R2,High             Upper bound to index
L1:     load       R1,I                Load index
        load       R2,High             Load upper bound
        jump_gt    R1,R2,L2            Terminate loop if greater
        statement                      Loop body
        load       R1,I                Increment index
        incr       R1
        store      R1,I
        jump       L1
L2:
```

An obvious optimization is to dedicate a register to the index variable I and, if possible, another register to High:

```
        compute    R1,expr_1           Lower bound to register
        compute    R2,expr_2           Upper bound to register
L1:     jump_gt    R1,R2,L2            Terminate loop if greater
        statement
        incr       R1                  Increment index register
        jump       L1
L2:
```

Now consider a simple loop in C:

```
for (i = expression_1; expression_2; i++)
        statement;
```
C

This compiles to:

```
        compute    R1,expr_1
        store      R1,i                Lower bound to index
L1:     compute    R2,expr_2           Upper bound within loop !
        jump_gt    R1,R2,L2            Terminate loop if greater
        statement                      Loop body
        load       R1,i                Increment index
        incr       R1
        store      R1,i
        jump       L1
L2:
```

Note that expression_2, which may be very complicated, is now computed inside the loop. Also, expression_2 necessarily uses the value of the index variable i which is changed each iteration. Thus the optimizer must be able to identify the non-changing part of the evaluation of expression.2 in order to extract it from the loop.

Can the index variable be stored in a register for greater efficiency? The answer is "maybe" and depends on two properties of the loop. In Ada, the index variable is considered to be constant and cannot be modified by the programmer. In C, the index variable is a normal variable; it can be kept in a register only if there is no possibility that its current value will be needed except within the loop. Never use a global variable as an index variable because another procedure may read or modify its value:[3]

```
int i;                                                        C

void p2(void) {
    i = i + 5;
}

void p1(void) {
    for (i=0; i<100; i++)            /* Global index variable */
        p2();                        /* Side effect on index */
}
```

The second property that affects the ability to optimize the loop is the potential use of the index variable outside the loop. In Ada, the index variable is implicitly declared by the for-statement and is *not* accessible outside the loop. Thus no matter how the loop is exited, we do not have to save the value in the register. Consider the following loop which searches for a key value in an array a:

```
int a[100];                                                  C
int i, key;

key = get_key();
for (i = 0; i < 100; i++)
    if (a[i] == key) break;
process(i);
```

The variable i must contain the correct value regardless of which exit is taken. This can cause difficulty when trying to optimize the code. Note that in Ada, explicit coding is required to achieve the same effect because the index variable does not exist outside the scope of the loop:

---

[3]Also, in a multi-processing environment, another process may access the value.

```ada
Found: Integer := False;                                          Ada

for I in 1..100 loop
    if A(I) = Key then
        Found = I;
        exit;
    end if;
end loop;
```

The definition of the scope of loop indices in C++ has changed over the years, but the final definition is the same as in Ada: the index does not exist outside the scope of the loop:

```cpp
for (int i=0; i<100; i++) {                                       C++
    // Index variable is local to loop
}
```

In fact, any statement controlled by a condition (including if- and switch-statements) can have several declarations appear in the condition; their scope is limited to the controlled statements. This feature can contribute to the readability and reliability of a program by preventing unintended use of a temporary name.

6.5 Sentinels

The following section is not about programming languages as such; rather it is intended to show that a program can be improved by using better algorithms and programming techniques instead of fiddling with language details. The section is included because the topic of loop exit in a linear search is the subject of intense debate, and yet there exists a different algorithm that is simultaneously clear, reliable and efficient.

In the last example of the previous section (searching an array), there are three jump instructions in every execution of the loop: the conditional jump of the for-statement, the conditional jump of the if-statement and the jump from the end of the loop back to the beginning. The problem with this search is that we are checking two conditions at once: have we found the key, and have we reached the end of the array? By using a *sentinel*, we can reduce the two conditions to one. The idea is to extend the array by one extra place at the beginning of the array, and to store the key we are searching for in that place (Figure 6.4). Since we will necessarily find the key, either as an

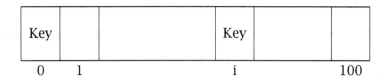

Figure 6.4 Sentinels

occurrence within the array or as the artificial occurrence, only one condition need be checked within the loop:

```ada
type A_Type is array(0..100) of Integer;                    Ada
        -- Extra place at zero for sentinel

function Find_Key(A: A_Type; Key: Integer)
        return Integer is
    I: Integer := 100;             -- Search from end
begin
    A[0] := Key;                   -- Store sentinel
    while A(I) /= Key loop
        I := I - 1;
    end loop;
    return I;
end Find_Key;
```

Upon return from the function, if I is zero then the Key does not exist in the array; otherwise, I contains the index of the occurrence. Not only is this code more efficient, but the loop is extremely simple and can be easily verified.

6.6 * Invariants

The formal definition of the semantics of loop statements is based on the concept of an *invariant*: a formula which remains true after every execution of the loop body. Consider a simplistic program for computing integer division of a by b to obtain the result y:

```c
y = 0;                                                      C
x = a;
```

```
while (x >= b) {              /* As long as b "goes into" x, */
    x -= b;                  /*   subtracting b means that */
    y++;                     /*   result must be incremented */
}
```

and consider the formula:

$$a = yb + x$$

where an italic letter denotes the value of the corresponding program variable. After the initialization statements, this is certainly true since $y = 0$ and $x = a$. Furthermore, at the end of the program the formula *defines* what it means for y to be the result of integer division a/b, provided that the remainder x is less than the divisor b.

What is not so obvious is that the formula remains true after every execution of the loop body. In this trivial program, that fact is easy to see by simple arithmetic, given the changes to the values of x and y in the loop body:

$$(y + 1)b + (x - b) = yb + b + x - b = yb + x = a$$

Thus the body of a loop statement transforms the state of a program from a state that satisfies the invariant to a different state that still satisfies the invariant.

Now note that for the loop to terminate, the Boolean condition in the while-statement must be False, that is the computation must be in a state such that $\neg(x \geq b)$ which is equivalent to $x < b$. Combining this formula with the invariant, we have shown that the program actually computes integer division.

More precisely, we have shown that *if* the program terminates, *then* the result is correct. This is called *partial correctness*. To prove *total correctness*, we must also show that the loop terminates.

This is done as follows. Since b is constant (and assumed positive!) during the execution of the program, what we have to show is that repeatedly decrementing x by b must eventually lead to a state in which $0 \leq x < b$. But (1) since x is repeatedly decremented, its value cannot stay indefinitely above that of b; (2) by the condition for terminating the loop and the computation in the loop body, x is never negative. These two facts imply that the loop must terminate.

Loop invariants in Eiffel

Eiffel supports the specification of assertions in general (see Section 11.5) and loop invariants in particular within the language:

```
from                                                        Eiffel
    y = 0; x = a;
invariant
    a = yb + x
variant
    x
until
    x < b
loop
    x := x - b;
    y := y + 1;
end
```

The from-clause establishes the initial condition, the until-clause gives the condition to terminate the loop, and the statements between loop and end form the loop body. The invariant-clause states the loop invariant and the variant-clause states the expression that will decrease (but stay non-negative) with each iteration of the loop. The correctness of the invariant is checked after each execution of the loop body.

6.7 goto-statements

In the original definition of Fortran there was only one structured control statement: the do-statement which is similar to the for-statement. All additional control used conditional or unconditional jumps to labels, called goto-statements:

```
          if (a .eq. b) goto 12                             Fortran
          ...
          goto 5
   4      ...
          ...
   12     ...
          ...
   5      ...
          if (x .gt. y) goto 4
```

In 1968, E. W. Dijkstra wrote a famous letter entitled "goto Considered Harmful" which launched a debate on structured programming. The main thrust of the "anti-goto" argument is that arbitrary jumps are not structured and create *spaghetti code*, that is, code whose possible threads of execution are so intertwined that it becomes impossible to understand or test the code. The "pro-goto" argument is that real programs often require control structures that are more general than those offered by structured statements, and that forcing programmers to use them results in artificial and complex code.

In retrospect, this debate was far too emotional and drawn-out because the basic principles are quite simple and are no longer seriously disputed. Furthermore, modern dialects of Fortran include more advanced control statements so that the goto-statement is no longer dominant.

It can be mathematically proven that if- and while-statements are sufficient to express any needed control structure. These statements are also easy to understand and use. Various syntactic extensions such as for-statements are well understood and if used properly pose no difficulty in understanding or maintaining a program. So why do programming languages (including Ada which was designed with reliability as the highest priority) retain the goto-statement?

The reason is that there are several well-defined situations where use of a goto-statement may be preferable. Firstly, many loops do not naturally terminate at their entry point as required by the while-statement. Attempting to force all loops into while-statements can lead to obscure code. With modern languages, the flexibility of exit- and break-statements means that goto-statements are usually unnecessary for this purpose. Nevertheless, the goto-statement still exists and can occasionally be useful. Note that both C and Ada limit the goto-statement by requiring that the label be in the same procedure.

A second situation that can be easily programmed using a goto-statement is an escape from a deeply nested computation. Suppose that deep within a series of procedure calls an error is detected that invalidates the entire computation. The natural way to program this requirement is to display an error message and terminate or reset the entire computation. However, this requires returning from many procedures, all of which have to know that an error has occurred. It is easier and more understandable just to goto a statement in the main program.

The C language has no means of dealing with this situation (not even with goto-statements which are limited to a single procedure), so facilities of the operating system must be used to handle serious errors. Ada, C++ and Eiffel have a language construct called *exceptions* (see Chapter 11) which directly solves this problem. Thus most of the uses of goto-statements have been superseded by improved language design.

Assigned goto-*statements*

Fortran includes a construct called an *assigned* goto-statement. A label variable can be defined and a label value assigned to the variable. When a jump is made to the label variable, the actual target of the jump is the current value of the label variable:

```
     assign 5 to Label                                    Fortran
     ...
     if (x .gt. y) assign 6 to Label
   5 ...
   6 ...
     goto Label
```

The problem, of course, is that the assignment of the label value could have been made millions of instructions before the goto is executed and it is practically impossible to verify or debug such code.

While assigned goto-statements do not exist in other languages, it is quite easy to simulate such a construct by defining many small subprograms and passing around pointers to the subprograms. You will find it difficult to relate a particular call with the pointer assignment that connected it to a specific subprogram. Thus pointers to subprograms should only be used in highly structured situations such as tables used by interpreters or callback mechanisms.

6.8 Exercises

1. Does your compiler implement all case-/switch-statements the same way, or does it try to choose an optimal implementation for each statement?

2. Simulate a Pascal repeat-statement in Ada and C.

3. The original definition of Fortran specified that a loop is executed at least one time even if the value of low is greater than the value of high! What could motivate this design?

4. The sequential search in C:

```
     while (s[i].data != key)                                  C
         i++;
```

might be written as follows:

```
while (s[i++].data != key)                              C
    ;                            /* Null statement */
```

What is the difference between the two computations?

5. Suppose that Ada did allow an index variable to exist after the scope of the loop. Show how optimization of a loop would be affected.

6. Compare the code generated for a search implemented using a break- or exit-statement with the code generated for a sentinel search.

7. Write a sentinel search using do-while rather than while. Is it more efficient?

8. Why did we put the sentinel at the beginning of the array rather than at the end?

9. (Scholten) The game of Go is played with stones of two colors, black and white. Suppose that you have a can with an unknown mixture of stones and that you execute the following algorithm:

```
while Stones_Left_in_Can loop                           Ada
    Remove_Two_Stones(S1, S2);
    if Color(S1) = Color(S2) then
        Add_Black_Stone;
    else
        Add_White_Stone;
    end if;
end loop;
```

Show that the loop terminates by identifying a value which is always decreasing but always non-negative. Can you say anything about the color of the last stone to be removed? (Hint: write a loop invariant on the number of white stones.)

7 Subprograms

7.1 Subprograms: procedures and functions

A *subprogram* is a segment of a program that can be invoked from elsewhere within the program. Subprograms are used for various reasons:

- A segment of a program that must be executed at various stages within the computation can be written once as a subprogram and then repeatedly invoked. This saves memory and prevents the possibility of errors caused by copying the code from one place to another.

- A subprogram is a logical unit of program decomposition. Even if a segment is executed only once, it is useful to identify it in a subprogram for purposes of testing, documentation and readability.

- A subprogram can also be used as a physical unit of program decomposition, that is, as a unit of compilation. In Fortran, subprograms (called *subroutines*) are the only units of decomposition and compilation. Modern languages use the module, a group of declarations and subprograms, as the unit of physical decomposition (Chapter 13).

A subprogram consists of:

- A declaration which defines the interface to the subprogram. The subprogram declaration includes the name of the subprogram, the list of parameters (if any)[1] and the type of the value returned (if any).

- Local declarations which are accessible only within the body of the subprogram.

---

[1] As a point of syntax, subprograms without parameters are usually declared without a parameter list (Ada, Pascal) or with an empty list (C++). C uses the explicit keyword void to indicate an absence of parameters.

- A sequence of executable statements.

The local declarations and the executable statements form the *body* of the subprogram.

Subprograms that return a value are called *functions*; those that do not are called *procedures*. C does not have a separate syntax for procedures; instead you must write a function that returns void which is a type with no values:

> void proc(int a, float b);   `C`

Such a function has the same properties as a procedure in other languages, so we will use the term procedure even when discussing C.

A procedure is invoked by a *call* statement. In Fortran, there is a special syntax:

> call proc(x,y)   `Fortran`

while in other languages you simply write the name of the procedure followed by the actual parameters:

> proc(x,y);   `C`

The semantics of a procedure call is as follows: the current sequence of instructions is suspended; the sequence of instructions within the procedure body is executed; upon completing the procedure body, the execution continues with the first statement following the procedure call. This description ignores parameter passing and scopes which will be the subject of extensive discussion in the next sections.

Since a function returns a value, the function declaration must specify the type of the returned value. In C, the type of a function precedes the function declaration:

> int func(int a, float b);   `C`

while Ada uses a distinctive syntax for functions:

> function Func(A: Integer; B: Float) return Integer;   `Ada`

A function call appears not as a statement, but as an element of an *expression*:

> a = x + func(r,s) + y;   `C`

The result type of the function must be consistent with the type expected in the expression. Note that C does implicit type conversions in many cases, while in Ada the result type must exactly match the context. The meaning of a function call is similar to that of a procedure call: the evaluation of the expression is suspended; the instructions of the function body are executed; the returned value is then used to continue the evaluation of the expression.

The term function is actually very inappropriate to use in the context of ordinary programming languages. When used in mathematics, a function is just a mapping from one set of values to another. To use the technical term, a mathematical function is *referentially transparent*, because its "computation" is transparent to the point at which it is "called". If you have a value 3.6 and you ask for the value of sin(3.6), you will get the same unique result every time that the function appears in an equation. In programming, a function can perform an arbitrary computation including input-output or modification of global data structures:

```
int x,y,z;                                                          C
int func(void)
{
    y = get();              /* Modifies a global variable */
    return x*y;             /* Value based on global variable */
}

z = x + func(void) + y;
```

If the optimizer rearranged the order of the computation so that x+y were computed before the function call, a different result will be obtained, because the function modifies the value of y.

Since all C subprograms are functions, C programming style extensively uses return values in non-mathematical situations like input-output subprograms. This is acceptable provided that the possible difficulties with order dependencies and optimization are understood. Programming language research has developed exciting languages that are based on the mathematically correct concept of functions (see Chapter 16).

7.2 Parameters

In the previous section, we defined subprograms as segments of code that may be repeatedly invoked. Almost always, each invocation will require that the code in the subprogram body be executed using different data. The way to influence the execution of a subprogram body is to "pass" it the data that it needs. Data is passed to a subprogram in the form of a sequence of values called *parameters*. The concept is taken from mathematics where a function is given a sequence of *arguments*:[2] $\sin(2\pi r)$.

There are two concepts that must be clearly distinguished:

- A *formal parameter* is a declaration that appears in the declaration of the subprogram. The computation in the body of the subprogram is written in terms of formal parameters.

- An *actual parameter* is a value that the calling program sends to the subprogram.

In the following example:

C

```
int i, j;
char a;
void p(int a, char b)
{
    i = a + (int) b;
}

p(i, a);
p(i+j, 'x');
```

the formal parameters of the subprogram p are a and b, while the actual parameters of the first call are i and a, and of the second call, i+j and 'x'.

There are several important points that can be noted from the example. The first is that since the actual parameters are values, they can be constants or expressions, and not just variables. In fact, even when a variable is used as a parameter, what we really mean is "the current value stored in the variable". Secondly, the *name space* of each subprogram is distinct. The fact that the first formal parameter is called a is not relevant to the rest of the program, and it could be renamed, provided, of course, that all occurrences of the formal parameter in the subprogram body are renamed. The variable a declared outside the subprogram is totally independent from the variable of the same name declared within the subprogram. In Section 7.7, we will explore in great detail the relationship between variables declared in different subprograms.

---

[2]Mathematical terminology uses *argument* for the value passed to a function, while *parameter* is usually used for values that are constant for a specific problem! We will, of course, use the programming terminology.

Named parameter associations

Normally the actual parameters in a subprogram call are just listed and the matching with the formal parameters is done by position:

```ada
procedure Proc(First: Integer; Second: Character);
Proc(24, 'X');
```
Ada

However, in Ada it is possible to use named association in the call, where each actual parameter is preceded by the name of the formal parameter. The order of declaration of the parameters need not be followed:

```ada
Proc(Second => 'X', First => 24);
```
Ada

This is commonly used together with default parameters, where parameters that are not explicitly written receive the default values given in the subprogram declaration:

```ada
procedure Proc(First: Integer := 0; Second: Character := '*');
Proc(Second => 'X');
```
Ada

Named association and default parameters are commonly used in the command languages of operating systems, where each command may have dozens of options and normally only a few parameters need to be explicitly changed. However, there are dangers with this programming style. The use of default parameters can make a program hard to read because calls whose syntax is different actually call the same subprogram. Named associations are problematic because they bind the subprogram declaration and the calls more tightly than is usually needed. If you use only positional parameters in calling subprograms from a library, you could buy a competing library and just recompile or link:

```ada
X := Proc_1(Y) + Proc_2(Z);
```
Ada

However, if you use named parameters, then you might have to do extensive modifications to your program to conform to the new parameter names:

```ada
X := Proc_1(Parm => Y) + Proc_2(Parm => Z);
```
Ada

7.3 Passing parameters to a subprogram

The definition of the mechanism for passing parameters is one of the most delicate and important aspects of the specification of a programming language. Mistakes in parameter passing are a major source of difficult bugs, so we will go into great detail in the following description.

Let us start from the definition we gave above: the value of the actual parameter is passed to the formal parameter. The formal parameter is just a variable declared within the subprogram, so the obvious mechanism is to copy the value of the actual parameter into the memory location allocated to the formal parameter. This mechanism is called *copy-in semantics* or *call-by-value*. Figure 7.1 demonstrates copy-in semantics, given the procedure

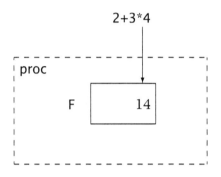

Figure 7.1 Copy-in semantics

definition:

```
procedure Proc(F: in Integer) is                                    Ada
begin
   ...;
end Proc;
```

and the call:

```
Proc(2+3*4);                                                        Ada
```

The advantages of copy-in semantics are:

- Copy-in is the safest mechanism for parameter passing. Since only a copy of the actual parameter is passed, the subprogram cannot cause any damage to the actual parameter, which of course "belongs" to the calling program. If the subprogram modifies the formal parameter, only the copy is modified and not the original.

- Actual parameters can be constants, variables or expressions.

- Copy-in can be extremely efficient because once the initial overhead of the copy is done, all accesses to the formal parameter are to the local copy. As we shall see in Section 7.7, accesses to local variables are extremely efficient.

If copy-in semantics is so good, why are there other mechanisms? The reason is that we will often want to modify the actual parameter despite the fact that such modification is "unsafe":

- A function can only return a single result, so if the result of a computation is more complex, we may want to return several results. The way to do so is to provide a procedure with several actual parameters which can be assigned the results of the computation. Note that this situation can often be avoided by defining a function that returns a record as a result.

- Similarly, the purpose of the computation in the subprogram may be to modify data that is passed to it rather than to compute a result. This is common when a subprogram is maintaining a data structure. For example, a subprogram to sort an array does not compute a value; its only task is to modify the actual parameter. There is no point in sorting a copy of the actual parameter!

- A parameter may be so big that it is inefficient to copy. If copy-in is used for an array of 50,000 integers, there may simply not be enough memory available to make a copy, or the overhead of the copy may be excessive.

The first two situations can easily be solved using *copy-out semantics*. The actual parameter must be a variable, and the subprogram is passed the address of the actual parameter which it saves. A temporary local variable is used for the formal parameter, and a value must be assigned to the formal parameter[3] at least once during the execution of the subprogram. When the execution of the subprogram is completed, the value is copied into the variable pointed to by the saved address. Figure 7.2 shows copy-out semantics for the following subprogram:

---

[3]Ada 83 does not allow the subprogram to read the contents of the formal parameter. The more common definition of copy-out semantics, which is followed in Ada 95, allows normal computation on the (uninitialized) local variable.

```ada
procedure Proc(F: out Integer) is                                    Ada
begin
    F := 2+3*4;                        -- Assign to copy-out parameter
end Proc;


A: Integer;
Proc(A);                              -- Call procedure with variable
```

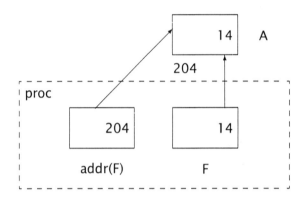

Figure 7.2 Copy-out semantics

When modification of the actual parameter is needed as in sort, *copy-in/out semantics* can be used: the actual parameter is copied into the subprogram when it is called and the final value is copied back upon completion.

However, copy-based parameter passing mechanisms cannot solve the efficiency problem caused by large parameters. The solution, which is known as *call-by-reference* or *reference semantics*, is to pass the address of the actual parameter and to access the parameter indirectly (Figure 7.3). Calling the subprogram is efficient because only a small, fixed-sized pointer is passed for each parameter; however, accessing the parameter can be inefficient because of the indirection.

In order to access the actual parameter, its address must be loaded and then an additional instruction is needed to load the value. Note that when using reference (or copy-out) semantics, the actual parameter must be a variable, not an expression, because a value will be assigned to it.

Another problem with call-by-reference is that it may result in *aliasing*: a situation in which the same variable is known by more than one name. In the following example, within the function f the variable global is also known by the alias *parm:

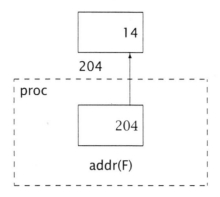

Figure 7.3 Reference semantics

```
int global = 4;                                       C
int a[10];

int f(int *parm)
{
    *parm = 5;                 /* Same variable as "global" */
    return 6;
}

x = a[global] + f(&global);
```

In the example, if the expression is evaluated in the order in which it is written, its value is a[4]+6, but because of aliasing, the value of the expression may be 6+a[5] if the compiler chooses to evaluate the function call before the array indexing. Aliasing is an important cause of non-portable behavior.

The real disadvantage of call-by-reference is that the mechanism is inherently unsafe. Suppose that for some reason the subprogram thinks that the actual parameter is an array whereas in fact it is just a single integer. This can cause an arbitrary amount of memory to be smeared, since the subprogram is working on the actual parameter, and not just on a local copy. This type of bug is extremely common, because the subprogram will typically have been written by a different programmer than the one calling the subprogram and misunderstandings always occur.

Safety of parameter passing can be improved by insisting on strong type checking which ensures that the types of the formal and actual parameters are compatible. Nevertheless, there is still room for misunderstanding between the programmer who wrote the subprogram and the programmer whose data is being modified. Thus we have an excellent parameter passing mechanism that is not always efficient enough (copy-in semantics), together with mechanisms that are necessary but unsafe (copy-out and reference semantics). The choice is complicated by constraints placed on the programmer by various programming languages. We will now describe the parameter passing mechanisms of several languages in detail.

Parameters in C and C++

C has only one parameter-passing mechanism, copy-in:

```
int i = 4;                  /* Global variables */         C

void proc(int i, float f)
{
    i = i + (int) f;        /* Local "i" */
}

proc(j, 45.0);              /* Function call */
```

In proc, the variable i that is modified is a local copy and not the global i.

In order to obtain the functionality of reference or copy-out semantics, a C programmer must resort to explicit use of pointers:

```
int i = 4;                  /* Global variables */         C

void proc(int *i, float f)
{
    *i = *i + (int) f;      /* Indirect access */
}

proc(&i, 45.0);             /* Address operator needed */
```

After executing proc, the value of the global variable i will be modified. The requirement that pointers be used for reference semantics is unfortunate, because beginning programmers must learn this relatively advanced concept at an early stage of their studies.

C++ has corrected this problem so that true call-by-reference is available using *reference parameters*:

```
int i = 4;                    // Global variables            C++
```

```
void proc(int & i, float f)
{
    i = i + (int) f;          // By reference access
}
```

```
proc(i, 45.0);                // No address operator needed
```

Note that the programming style is natural and does not use pointers artificially. This improvement in the parameter passing mechanism is so important that it justifies using C++ as a replacement for C.

You will often want to use pointers in C or references in C++ to pass large data structures. Of course, unlike copy-in parameters, there is a danger of accidental modification of the actual parameter. Read-only access to a parameter can be specified by declaring them const:

```
void proc(const Car_Data & d)
{
    d.fuel = 25;              // Error, cannot modify const
}
```

const declarations should be used whenever possible both to clarify the meaning of parameters to readers of the program, and to catch potential bugs.

Another problem with parameters in C is that arrays cannot be parameters. If an array must be passed, the address of the first element of the array is passed, and the procedure has the responsibility for correctly accessing the array. As a convenience, using an array name as a parameter is automatically considered to be the use of a pointer to the first element:

```
int b[50];                    /* Array variable */          C
```

```
void proc(int a[])            /* "Array parameter" */
{
    a[100] = a[200];          /* How many components ? */
}
```

```
proc(&b[0]);                  /* Address of first element */
proc(b);                      /* Address of first element */
```

C programmers quickly get used to this but it is a source of confusion and bugs. The problem is that since the parameter is actually a pointer to a single element, *any* pointer to a variable of a similar type is accepted:

```
int i;                                                              C
void proc(int a[]);              /* "Array parameter" */
proc(&i);                        /* Any pointer to integer is OK !! */
```

Finally, in C no type checking is done between files so that it is possible to declare:

```
void proc(float f) { ... }       /* Procedure definition */          C
```

in one file and:

```
void proc(int i);                /* Procedure declaration */         C
proc(100);
```

in another file, and then spend a month looking for the bug.

The C++ language requires that parameter type checking be performed. However, the language does not require that implementations include a library facility as in Ada (see Section 13.3) that can ensure type checking across separately compiled files. C++ compilers implement type checking by cooperation with the linker: parameter types are encoded in the external name of the subprogram (a process called *name mangling*), and the linker will make sure that calls are linked only to subprograms with the correct parameter signature.[4] Unfortunately, this method cannot catch all type mismatches.

Parameters in Pascal

In Pascal, parameters are passed by value unless reference semantics is explicitly requested:

```
procedure proc(P_Input: Integer; var P_Output: Integer);        Pascal
```

The keyword var indicates that the following parameter is called by reference, otherwise call-by-value is used even if the parameter is very large. Parameters can be of any type including arrays, records or other complex data structures. The one limitation is that the result type of a function must be a scalar. The types of actual parameters are checked against the types of the formal parameters.

As we discussed in Section 5.3, there is a serious problem in Pascal because the array bounds are considered part of the type. The Pascal standard defines *conformant array parameters* to solve this problem.

---

[4]For details, see Section 7.2c of the Annotated Reference Manual.

Parameters in Ada

Ada takes a novel approach in defining parameter passing in terms of intended use rather than in terms of the implementation mechanism. For each parameter you must explicitly choose one of three possible *modes*:

in The parameter may be read but not written (default).

out The parameter may be written but not read.

in out The parameter may be both read and written.

For example:

```
procedure Put_Key(Key: in Key_Type);            Ada
procedure Get_Key(Key: out Key_Type);
procedure Sort_Keys(Keys: in out Key_Array);
```

In the first procedure, the parameter Key must be read so that it can be "put" into a data structure (or output device). In the second, a value is obtained from a data structure and upon completion of the procedure, the value is assigned to the parameter. The array Keys to be sorted must be passed as in out, because sorting involves both reading and writing the data of the array.

Ada restricts parameters of a function to be of mode in only. This does not make Ada functions referentially transparent because there is still no restriction on accessing global variables, but it can help the optimizer to improve the efficiency of expression evaluation.

Despite the fact that the modes are not defined in terms of implementation mechanisms, the Ada language does specify some requirements on the implementation. Parameters of elementary type (numbers, enumerations and pointers) must be implemented by copy semantics: copy-in for in parameters, copy-out for out parameters, and copy-in/out for in out parameters. The implementation of modes for composite parameters (arrays and records) is not specified, and a compiler may choose whichever mechanism it prefers. This introduces the possibility that the correctness of an Ada program depends on the implementation-chosen mechanism, so such programs are simply not portable.[5]

Strong type checking is done between formal and actual parameters. The type of the actual parameter must be the same as that of the formal parameter; no implicit type conversion is ever performed. However, as we discussed

---

[5]Ada 95 requires that certain categories of parameters be passed by reference; these include task types and tagged types (Section 14.5).

in Section 5.3, the subtypes need not be identical as long as they are compatible; this allows an arbitrary array to be passed to an unconstrained formal parameter.

Parameters in Fortran

We will briefly touch on parameter passing in Fortran because it can cause spectacular bugs. Fortran can pass only scalar values; the interpretation of a formal parameter as an array is done by the called subroutine. Call-by-reference is used for all parameters. Furthermore, each subroutine is compiled independently and no checking is done for compatibility between the subroutine declaration and its call.

The language specifies that if a formal parameter is assigned to, the actual parameter must be a variable, but because of independent compilation this rule cannot be checked by the compiler. Consider the following example:

```
Subroutine Sub(X, Y)                                          Fortran
Real X,Y
X = Y
End

Call Sub(- 1.0, 4.6)
```

The subroutine has two parameters of type Real. Since reference semantics is used, Sub receives pointers to the two actual parameters and the assignment is done directly on the actual parameters (Figure 7.4). The result is that the

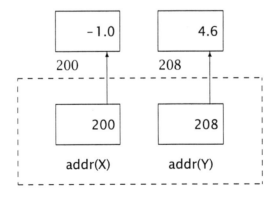

Figure 7.4 Smearing a constant in Fortran

memory location storing the value – 1.0 is modified! There is literally no way to "debug" this bug, since debuggers only allow you to examine and trace variables, not constants. The point of the story is that correct matching of actual and formal parameters is a cornerstone of reliable programming.

7.4 Block structure

A *block* is an entity consisting of declarations and executable statements. A similar definition was given for a subprogram body and it is more precise to say that a subprogram body *is* a block. Blocks in general and procedures in particular can be nested within one another. This section will discuss the relationships among nested blocks.

Block structure was first defined in the Algol language which includes both procedures and unnamed blocks. Pascal contains nested procedures but not unnamed blocks; C contains unnamed blocks but not nested procedures; and Ada returns to support both.

Unnamed blocks are useful for restricting the scope of variables by declaring them only when needed, instead of at the beginning of a subprogram. The trend in programming is to reduce the size of subprograms, so the use of unnamed blocks is less useful than it used to be.

Nested procedures can be used to group statements that are executed at more than one location within a subprogram, but refer to local variables and so cannot be external to the subprogram. Before modules and object-oriented programming were introduced, nested procedures were used to structure large programs, but this introduces complications and is not recommended.

The following is an example of a complete Ada program:

```
procedure Main is                              Ada
    Global: Integer;

    procedure Proc(Parm: in Integer) is
        Local: Integer;
    begin
        Global := Local + Parm;
    end Proc;

begin -- Main
    Global := 5;
    Proc(7);
    Proc(8);
end Main;
```

An Ada program is a *library* procedure, that is, a procedure that is not enclosed within any other entity and hence can be stored in the Ada library. The procedure begins with a procedure declaration for Main,[6] which serves as a definition of the interface to the procedure, in this case the external name of the program. Within the library procedure there are two declarations: a variable Global and a procedure Proc. Following the declarations is the sequence of executable statements for the main procedure. In other words, the procedure Main consists of a procedure declaration and a block. Similarly, the local procedure Proc consists of a procedure declaration (the procedure name and the parameters) and a block containing variable declarations and executable statements. Proc is said to be *local* to Main or *nested* within Main.

Each declaration has associated with it three properties:[7]

Scope The scope of a variable is the segment of the program within which it is defined.

Visibility A variable is visible within some subsegment of its scope if it can be directly accessed by name.

Lifetime The lifetime of a variable is the interval during the program's execution when memory is assigned to the variable.

Note that lifetime is a dynamic property of the run-time behavior of a program, while scope and visibility relate solely to the static program text.

Let us demonstrate these abstract definitions on the example above. The scope of a variable begins at the point of declaration and ends at the end of the block in which it is defined. The scope of Global includes the entire program while the scope of Local is limited to a single procedure. The formal parameter Parm is considered to be like a local variable and its scope is also limited to the procedure.[8]

The visibility of each variable in this example is identical to its scope: each variable can be directly accessed in its entire scope. Since the scope and visibility of the variable Local is limited to the local procedure, the following is not allowed:

```
begin -- Main                                          Ada
    Global := Local + 5;        -- Local is not in scope here
end Main;
```

However, the scope of Global includes the local procedure so the access within the procedure is correct:

---

[6]Unlike C, the main procedure need not be called main.

[7]To keep the discussion concrete, it will be given in terms of variables even though the concepts are more general.

[8]Ada allows named parameter associations, so this statement is not completely precise.

```
procedure Proc(Parm: in Integer) is          Ada
    Local: Integer;
begin
    Global := Local + Parm;          -- Global is in scope here
end Proc;
```

The lifetime of a variable is from the beginning of the execution of its block until the end of the execution of its block. The block of the procedure Main is the entire program so Global exists for the duration of the execution of the program. Such a variable is called *static*: once it is allocated it lives until the end of the program. The local variable has two lifetimes corresponding to the two calls to the local procedure. Since these intervals do not overlap, the variable may be allocated at a different location each time it is created. Local variables are called *automatic* because they are automatically allocated when the procedure is called (the block is entered), and released when the procedure returns (the block is left).

Hiding

Suppose that a variable name that is used in the main program is repeated in a declaration in a local procedure:

```
procedure Main is                            Ada
    Global: Integer;
    V: Integer;                      -- Declaration in Main

    procedure Proc(Parm: in Integer) is
        Local: Integer;
        V: Integer;                  -- Declaration in Proc
    begin
        Global := Local + Parm + V;  -- Which V is used ?
    end Proc;

begin -- Main
    Global := Global + V;            -- Which V is used ?
end Main;
```

In this case, the local declaration is said to *hide* the global declaration. Within the procedure, any reference to V is a reference to the locally declared variable. In technical terms, the scope of the global V extends from the point of declaration to the end of Main, but its visibility does not include local procedure Proc.[9]

Hiding of variable names by inner declarations is convenient in that the programmer can reuse natural names like Current_Key and not have to invent strange-sounding names. Furthermore, it is always possible to add a global variable without worrying that this will clash with some local variable name used by one of the programmers on your team. The disadvantage is that a variable name could be accidentally hidden, especially if large include-files are used to centralize global declarations, so it is probably better to avoid hiding variable names. However, there is no objection to reusing a name in different scopes since there is no way of accessing both variables simultaneously, regardless of whether the names are the same or different:

Ada

```
procedure Main is
    procedure Proc_1 is
        Index: Integer;              -- One scope

        ...
    end Proc_1;
    procedure Proc_2 is
        Index: Integer;              -- Non-overlapping scope

        ...
    end Proc_2;
    begin -- Main

        ...
    end Main;
```

Depth of nesting

There is no conceptual limit to the depth of nesting, though a compiler may arbitrarily limit the depth. Scope and visibility are determined by applying the rules given above: a variable's scope is from its point of declaration to the end of the block, and its visibility is the same unless hidden by an inner declaration. For example:

---

[9]In Ada (but not in Pascal) the hidden variable is accessible using the syntax Main.V. Similarly, in C++ (but not in C), ::V can be used to access a hidden global variable.

```
procedure Main is                                                    Ada
    Global: Integer;

    procedure Level_1 is
        Local: Integer;              -- Outer declaration of Local

        procedure Level_2 is
            Local: Integer;          -- Inner declaration of Local
        begin -- Level_2
            Local := Global;         -- Inner Local hides outer Local
        end Level_2;

    begin -- Level_1
        Local := Global;             -- Only outer Local in scope
        Level_2;
    end Level_1;

begin -- Main
    Level_1;
    Level_2;                         -- Error, procedure not in scope
end Main;
```

The scope of the variable Local defined in procedure Level_1 extends until the end of the procedure, but it is hidden within procedure Level_2 by the declaration of the same name.

The procedure declarations themselves are considered to have scope and visibility similar to variable declarations. Thus the scope of Level_2 is from its declaration in Level_1 until the end of Level_1. This means that Level_1 can *call* Level_2 even though it cannot access variables within Level_2. On the other hand, Main cannot call Level_2 directly, since it cannot access declarations that are local to Level_1.

Note the potential for confusion since the variable Local accessed by the statement in Level_1 is declared *further* away in the program text than the occurrence of Local enclosed within Level_2. If there were a lot of local procedures, it might be difficult to find the correct declaration. To prevent confusion, it is best to limit the depth of nesting to two or three levels below the main program.

Advantages and disadvantages of block structure

The advantage of block structure is that it provides an easy and efficient method of decomposing a procedure. If you avoid excessive nesting and hidden variables, block structure can be used to write reliable programs since related local procedures can be kept together. Block structuring is especially important when complex computations are being done:

```
procedure Proc(...) is                                    Ada
        -- Lots of declarations
begin
    -- Long computation 1
    if N < 0 then
            -- Long computation 2 version 1
    elsif N = 0 then
            -- Long computation 2 version 2
    else
            -- Long computation 2 version 3
    end if;
    -- Long computation 3
end Proc;
```

In this example, we would like to avoid writing Long computation 2 three times and instead make it an additional procedure with a single parameter:

```
procedure Proc(...) is                                    Ada
        -- Lots of declarations
        procedure Long_2(I: in Integer) is
        begin
            - Access declarations in Proc
        end Long_2;
begin
    -- Long computation 1
    if N < 0 then Long_2(1);
    elsif N = 0 then Long_2(2);
    else Long_2(3);
    end if;
    -- Long computation 3
end Proc;
```

However, it would be extremely difficult to make Long_2 an independent procedure because we might have to pass dozens of parameters so that it could access local variables. If Long_2 is nested, it needs just the one parameter, and the other declarations can be directly accessed according to normal scope and visibility rules.

The disadvantages of block structure become apparent when you try to program a large system in a language like standard Pascal that has no other means of program decomposition:

- Small procedures receive excessive "promotions". Suppose that a procedure to convert decimal digits to hexadecimal digits is used in many deeply-nested procedures. That utility procedure must be defined in some common ancestor. Practically, large block-structured programs tend to have many small utility procedures written at the highest level of declaration. This makes the program text awkward to work with because it is difficult to locate a specific procedure.

- Data security is compromised. Every procedure, even those declared deeply nested in the structure, can access global variables. In a large program being developed by a team, this makes it likely that errors made by one junior team member can cause obscure bugs. The situation is analogous to a company where every employee can freely examine the safe in the boss's office, but the boss has no right to examine the file cabinets of junior employees!

These problems are so serious that every commercial Pascal implementation defines a (non-standard) module structure to enable large projects to be constructed. In Chapter 13 we will discuss in detail constructs that are used for program decomposition in modern languages like Ada and C++. Nevertheless, block structure remains an important tool in the detailed programming of individual modules.

It is also important to understand block structure because programming languages are implemented using stack architecture, which directly supports block structure (Section 7.6).

7.5 Recursion

Most (imperative) programming is done using *iteration*, that is loops; however, *recursion*, the definition of an object or computation in terms of itself, is a more primitive mathematical concept, and is also a powerful, if often underused, programming technique. Here we will survey how to program recursive subprograms.

The most elementary example of recursion is the factorial function, defined mathematically as:

$$0! = 1$$
$$n! = n \times (n - 1)!$$

This definition translates immediately into a program that uses a recursive function:

```
int factorial(int n)                                      C
{
    if (n == 0) return 1;
    else return n * factorial(n - 1);
}
```

What properties are required to support recursion?

- The compiler must emit *pure code*. Since the same sequence of machine instructions are used to execute each call to factorial, the code must not modify itself.

- During run-time, it must be possible to allocate an arbitrary number of memory cells for the parameters and local variables.

The first requirement is fulfilled by all modern compilers. Self-modifying code is an artifact of older programming styles and is rarely used. Note that if a program is to be stored in read-only memory (ROM), by definition it cannot modify itself.

The second requirement arises from consideration of the lifetime of the local variables. In the example, the lifetime of the formal parameter n is from the moment that the procedure is called until it is completed. But before the procedure is completed, another call is made and that call requires that memory be allocated for the new formal parameter. To compute factorial(4), a memory location is allocated for 4, then 3 and so on, five locations altogether. The memory cannot be allocated before execution, because the amount depends on the run-time parameter to the function. Section 7.6 shows how this allocation requirement is directly supported by the stack architecture.

At this point, most programmers will note that the factorial function could be written just as easily and far more efficiently using iteration:

```
int factorial(int n)                                      C
{
    int i = n;
    result = 1;
    while (i != 0) {
        result = result * i;
        i--;
    }
    return result;
}
```

So why use recursion? The reason is that many algorithms can be elegantly and reliably written using recursion while an iterative solution is difficult to program and prone to bugs. Examples are the Quicksort algorithm for sorting and data structure algorithms based on trees. The language concepts discussed in Chapters 16 and 17 (functional and logic programming) use recursion exclusively instead of iteration. Even when using ordinary languages like C and Ada, recursion should probably be used more often than it is because of the concise, clear programs that result.

7.6 Stack architecture

A *stack* is a data structure that stores and retrieves data in a Last-In, First-Out (LIFO) order. LIFO constructions exist in the real world such as a stack of plates in a cafeteria, or a pile of newspapers in a store. A stack may be implemented using either an array or a list (Figure 7.5). The advantage of the

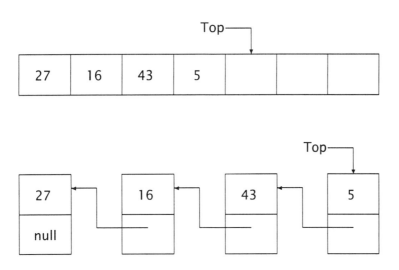

Figure 7.5 Stack implementation

list is that it is unbounded and its size is limited only by the total amount of available memory. Arrays are much more efficient and are implicitly used in the implementation of programming languages.

In addition to the array (or list), a stack contains an additional piece of data—the *top-of-stack pointer*. This is an index to the first available empty

position in a stack. Initially, a variable top will point to the first position in
the stack. The two possible operations on a stack are push and pop. push is
a procedure that receives an element as a parameter, which it places on the
top of the stack, incrementing top. pop is a function that returns the top
element in the stack, decrementing top to indicate that that position is the
new empty position.

The following C program implements a stack of integers as an array:

```
#define Stack_Size 100                                        C
int stack[Stack_Size];
int top = 0;

void push(int element)
{
    if (top == Stack_Size) /* Stack overflow, do something! */
    else stack[top++] = element;
}

int pop(void)
{
    if (top == 0) /* Stack underflow, do something! */
    else return stack[--top];
}
```

A stack can underflow if we try to pop from an empty stack, and it can
overflow if we try to push onto a full stack. Underflow is always due to a
programming error since you store something on a stack if and only if you
intend to retrieve it later on. Overflow can occur even in a correct program
if the amount of memory is not sufficient for the computation.

Stack allocation

How is a stack used in the implementation of a programming language? A
stack is used to store information related to a procedure call, including the
local variables and parameters that are automatically allocated upon entry
to the procedure and released upon exit. The reason that a stack is the
appropriate data structure is that procedures are entered and exited in a LIFO
order, and any accessible data belongs to a procedure that occurs earlier in
the chain of calls.

Consider a program with local procedures:

Ada

```
procedure Main is
    G: Integer;

    procedure Proc_1 is
        L1: Integer;
    begin ... end Proc_1;

    procedure Proc_2 is
        L2: Integer;
    begin ... end Proc_2;

begin
    Proc_1;
    Proc_2;
end Main;
```

When the Main begins executing, memory must be allocated for G. When Proc_1 is called, additional memory must be allocated for L1 without releasing the memory for G (Figure 7.6(a)).   The memory for L1 is released before

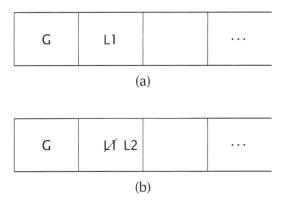

(a)

(b)

Figure 7.6 Allocating memory on a stack

memory is allocated for L2, since Proc_1 terminates before Proc_2 is called (Figure 7.6(b)). In general, no matter how procedures call each other, the first memory element to be released is the last one allocated, so memory for variables and parameters can be allocated on a stack.

Consider now nested procedures:

```ada
procedure Main is
   G: Integer;

   procedure Proc_1(P1: Integer) is
      L1: Integer;

      procedure Proc_2(P2: Integer) is
         L2: Integer;
      begin
         L2 = L1 + G + P2;
      end Proc_2;

   begin -- Proc_1
      Proc_2(P1);
   end Proc_1;

begin -- Main
   Proc_1(G);
end Main;
```

Proc_2 can only be called from within Proc_1. This means that Proc_1 has not terminated yet, so its memory has not been released and the memory assigned to L1 must still be allocated (Figure 7.7). Of course, Proc_2 terminates before Proc_1 which in turn terminates before Main, so memory can be freed using the pop operation on the stack.

Figure 7.7 Nested procedures

Activation records

The stack is actually used to support the entire procedure call and not just the allocation of local variables. The segment of the stack associated with each procedure is called the *activation record* for the procedure. In outline,[10], a procedure call is implemented as follows (see Figure 7.8):

---

[10]See Section 7.8 for more details.

1. The actual parameters are pushed onto the stack. They can be accessed as offsets from the start of the activation record.

2. The *return address* is pushed onto the stack. The return address is the address of the statement following the procedure call.

3. The top-of-stack index is incremented by the total amount of memory required to hold the local variables.

4. A jump is made to the procedure code.

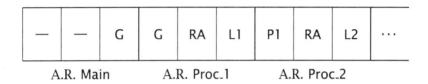

Figure 7.8 Activation records

Upon completion of the procedure the above steps are reversed:

1. The top-of-stack index is decremented by the amount of memory allocated for the local variables.

2. The return address is popped and the instruction pointer reset.

3. The top-of-stack index is decremented by the amount of memory allocated for the actual parameters.

While this code may seem complicated, it can actually be done very efficiently on most computers. The amount of memory needed for variables, parameters and call overhead is known at compile-time, and the above processing just requires modification of the stack index by a constant.

Accessing values on the stack

In a true stack, the only permissible operations are push and pop. The execution stack we have described is a more complex structure because we want to be able to efficiently access not only the most recent value pushed, but also all the local variables and all the parameters. One possibility would be to access these data relative to the top-of-stack index:

stack[top – 25]; $\boxed{\text{C}}$

However, the stack may hold other data besides that associated with a procedure call (such as temporary variables, see Section 4.7), so it is customary
to maintain an additional index called the *bottom pointer* which points to the
start of the activation record (see Section 7.7). Even if the top-of-stack index
varies during the execution of the procedure, all the data in the activation
record can be accessed at fixed offsets from the bottom pointer.

Parameters

There are two methods for implementing the passing of parameters. The
simpler method is just to push the parameters themselves (whether values
or references) onto the stack. This method is used in Pascal and Ada because
in those languages the number and type of each parameter is known at
compilation time. From this information, the offset of each parameter relative
to the beginning of the activation record can be computed at compile-time,
and each parameter can be accessed at this fixed offset from the bottom
pointer index:

```
load        R1,bottom-pointer
add         R1,#offset-of-parameter
load        R2,(R1)              Load value whose address is in R1
```

If the bottom pointer is kept in a register, this code can usually be collapsed
into a single instruction. When leaving the subprogram, *stack clean-up* is
done by having the subprogram reset the stack pointer so that the parameters
are effectively no longer on the stack.

There is a problem using this method in C, because C allows a procedure
to have a variable number of arguments:

void proc(int num_args, . . .); $\boxed{\text{C}}$

Since the subprogram does not know how many parameters there are, it
cannot clean-up the stack. The responsibility for stack clean-up is thus
shifted to the caller which does know how many parameters were passed.
This causes some memory overhead because the clean-up code is duplicated
at *every* call instead of being common to all calls.

When the number of parameters is not known, an alternative method
of parameter passing is to store the actual parameters in a separate block
of memory, and then to pass the address of this block on the stack. An
additional indirection is required to access a parameter, so this method is
less efficient than directly pushing parameters on the stack.

Note that it may not be possible to store a parameter directly on the stack. As you will recall, a formal parameter in Ada can be an unconstrained array type whose bounds are not known at compilation time:

procedure Proc(S: in String); | Ada |

Thus the actual parameter cannot be pushed directly onto the stack. Instead a dope vector (Section 5.4) which contains a pointer to the array parameter is placed on the stack.

Recursion

The stack architecture directly supports recursion because each call to a procedure automatically allocates a new copy of the local variables and parameters. For example, each recursive call of the function for factorial needs one memory word for the parameter and one memory word for the return address. The higher overhead of recursion relative to iteration comes from the extra instructions involved with the procedure entry and exit. Some compilers will attempt an optimization called *tail-recursion* or *last-call* optimization. If the only recursive call in a procedure is the last statement in the procedure, it is possible to automatically translate the recursion into iteration.

Stack size

If recursion is not used, the total stack usage can theoretically be computed before execution by adding the activation record requirements for each possible chain of procedure calls. Even in a complex program, it should not be hard to make a reasonable estimate of this figure. Add a few thousand spare words and you have computed a stack size that will probably not overflow.

However, if recursion is used, the stack size is theoretically unbounded at run-time:

i = get(); | C |
j = factorial(i);

In the Exercises, we describe Ackermann's function which is unconditionally guaranteed to overflow any stack you allocate! In practice, it is usually not difficult to make an estimate of stack size even when recursion is used. Suppose the size of an activation record is about 10 and the depth of recursion no more than a few hundred. Adding an extra 10K to the stack will more than suffice.

Readers who have studied data structures will know that recursion is convenient to use on tree-structured algorithms like Quicksort and priority queues. The depth of recursion in tree algorithms is roughly $\log_2$ of the size of the data structure. For practical programs this bounds the depth of recursion to 10 or 20 so there is very little danger of stack overflow.

Whether recursion is used or not, the nature of the system will dictate the treatment of potential stack overflow. A program might completely ignore the possibility and accept the fact that in extreme circumstances the program will crash. Another possibility is to check the stack size before each procedure call, but this might be too inefficient. A compromise solution would be to check the stack size periodically and take some action if it fell below some threshold, say 1000 words.

7.7   More on stack architecture

Accessing variables at intermediate levels

We have discussed how local variables are efficiently accessed at fixed offsets from the bottom pointer of an activation record. Global data, that is data declared in the main program, can also be accessed efficiently. The easiest way to see this is to imagine that global data is considered "local" to the main procedure; thus memory for the global data is allocated at the main procedure entry, that is, at the beginning of the program. Since this location is known at compile-time, or more exactly when the program is linked, the actual address of each element is known either directly or as an offset from a fixed location. In practice, global data is usually allocated separately (see Section 8.3), but in any case the addresses are fixed.

Variables at intermediate levels of nesting are more difficult to access:

```
procedure Main is                                        Ada
    G: Integer;

    procedure Proc_1 is
        L1: Integer;

        procedure Proc_2 is
            L2: Integer;
        begin L2 := L1 + G; end Proc_2;
```

```
procedure Proc_3 is
    L3: Integer;
begin L3 := L1 + G; Proc_2; end Proc_3;

begin -- Proc_1
    Proc_3;
end Proc_1;

begin -- Main
    Proc_1;
end Main;
```

We have seen that accessing the local variable L3 and the global variable G is easy and efficient, but how can L1 be accessed in Proc_3? The answer is that the value of the bottom pointer is stored at procedure entry and is used as a pointer to the activation record of the enclosing procedure Proc_1. The bottom pointer is stored at a known location and can be immediately loaded, so the overhead is an additional indirection.

If deeper nesting is used, each activation record contains a pointer to the previous one. These pointers to activation records form the *dynamic chain* (Figure 7.9). To access a *shallow variable* (one that is less deeply nested), instructions have to be executed to "climb" the dynamic chain. This potential inefficiency is the reason that accessing intermediate variables in deeply nested procedures is discouraged. Accessing the immediately previous level requires just one indirection and an occasional deep access should not cause any trouble, but a loop statement should not contain statements that reach far back in the chain.

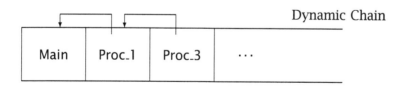

Figure 7.9 Dynamic chain

Calling shallow procedures

Accessing intermediate variables is actually more complicated than the discussion above would indicate because a procedure is allowed to call other procedures that are at the same level of nesting or lower. In the example, Proc_3 calls Proc_2. The activation record for Proc_2 will store the bottom pointer of Proc_3 so that it can be restored, but the variables of Proc_3 are *not* accessible in Proc_2 by the rules of scope.

Somehow the program must be able to identify the *static chain*, the link of activation records that defines the static context of the procedure according to the rules of scope, as opposed to the dynamic chain of procedure calls at execution time. As an extreme example, consider a recursive procedure: there may be dozens of activation records in the dynamic chain (one for each recursive call), but the static chain will consist only of the current record and the record for the main procedure.

One solution is to store the static level of nesting of each procedure in the activation record, because the compiler knows what level is needed for each access. In the example, if the main program is level 0, Proc_2 and Proc_3 are both at level 2. When searching up the dynamic chain, the level of nesting must decrease by one to be considered part of the static chain, thus the record for Proc_3 is skipped over and the next record, the one for Proc_1 at level 1, is used to obtain a bottom index.

Another solution is to explicitly include the static chain on the stack. Figure 7.10 shows the static chain just after Proc_3 calls Proc_2. Before the

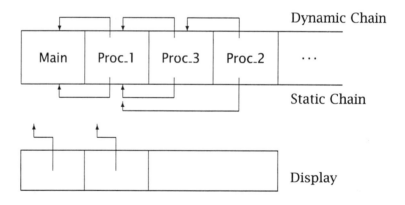

Figure 7.10 Variables at intermediate levels

call, the static chain is the same as the dynamic chain while after the call, the static chain is shorter and contains just the main procedure and Proc_2.

The advantage of using an explicit static chain is that a static chain is often shorter than a dynamic chain (again think of a recursive procedure as an extreme case). However, we still have to do the search for each access of an intermediate variable. A solution that can be more efficient is to use a *display* which is an array that holds the current static chain, indexed by the nesting level (Figure 7.10). Thus to access a variable at an intermediate level, the nesting level is used as an index to obtain a pointer to the correct activation record, then the bottom pointer is obtained from the record and finally the offset is added to obtain the variable address. The disadvantage of a display is that additional overhead is needed to update the display at procedure entry and exit.

The potential inefficiencies of accessing intermediate variables should not deter the use of nested procedures, but programmers should carefully consider such factors as the depth of nesting and the trade-offs between using parameters as opposed to direct access to variables.

7.8 * Implementation on the 8086

To give a more concrete idea of how a stack architecture is implemented, we describe the actual machine code for procedure entry and exit on the Intel 8086 series of processors. The example program is:

```
procedure Main is                                    Ada
    Global: Integer;

    procedure Proc(Parm: in Integer) is
        Local1, Local2: Integer;
    begin
        Local2 := Global + Parm + Local1;
    end Proc;

begin
    Proc(15);
end Main;
```

The 8086 has built-in push and pop instructions which assume that the stack grows from higher to lower addresses. Two registers are dedicated to stack operations: the sp register which points to the "top" element in the stack, and the bp register which is the bottom pointer that identifies the location of the start of the activation record.

To call the procedure the parameter is pushed onto the stack and the call instruction executed:[11]

---

[11] The extra mov instruction is there because stack operations work only to and from registers, in this case ax.

```
mov        ax,#15              Load value of parameter
push       ax                  Store parameter on stack
call       Proc                Call the procedure
```

Figure 7.11 shows the stack after executing these instructions—the parameter and the return address have been pushed onto the stack.

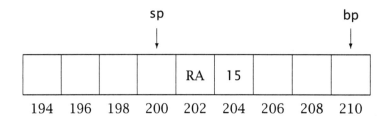

Figure 7.11 Stack before procedure entry

The next instructions are part of the code of the procedure and are executed at procedure entry; they store the old bottom pointer (the dynamic link), set up the new bottom pointer and allocate memory for the local variable by decrementing the stack pointer:

```
push       bp                  Save the old dynamic pointer
mov        bp,sp               Set the new dynamic pointer
sub        sp,#4               Allocate the local variables
```

The stack now appears as shown in Figure 7.12.

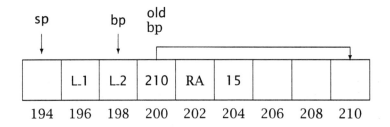

Figure 7.12 Stack after procedure entry

Now the body of the procedure can be executed:

```
mov      ax,ds:[38]      Load the variable Global
add      ax,[bp+06]      Add the parameter Parm
add      ax,[bp-02]      Add the variable Local1
mov      ax,[bp]         Store in the variable Local2
```

Global variables are accessed as offsets from a special area of memory pointed to by the ds (data segment) register. The parameter Parm which is "lower" down in the stack than the start of the activation record is accessed at a *positive* offset from bp. The local variables which are "higher" up in the stack are accessed at a *negative* offset from bp. What is important to note is that since the 8086 processor has registers and addressing modes designed for common stack-oriented computations, all these variables can be accessed in a single instruction.

Procedure exit must reverse the effects of the procedure call:

```
mov      sp,bp      Release all local variables
pop      bp         Restore the old dynamic pointer
ret      2          Return and release parameters
```

The stack pointer is reset to the value of the bottom pointer thus effectively releasing memory allocated for the local variables. Then the old dynamic pointer is popped from the stack so that bp now points at the previous activation record. The only remaining tasks are to return from the procedure using the return address, and to release the memory allocated for the parameters. The ret instruction performs both of these tasks; the operand of the instruction indicates how many bytes of parameter memory must be popped from the stack. To summarize: procedure exit and entry require just three short instructions each, and access to local and global variables and to parameters is efficient.

7.9 Exercises

1. Does your Ada compiler use value or reference semantics to pass arrays and records?

2. Show how last-call optimization is implemented. Can last-call optimization be done on the factorial function?

3. McCarthy's function is defined by the following recursive function:

```
function M(I: Integer) return Integer is          [Ada]
begin
    if I > 100 then return I-10;
    else return M(M(I+11));
end M;
```

(a) Write a program for McCarthy's function and compute M(I) for $80 \leq I \leq 110$.

(b) Simulate by hand the computation for M(91) showing the growth of the stack.

(c) Write an iterative program for McCarthy's function.

4. Ackermann's function is defined by the following recursive function:

```
function A(M, N: Natural) return Natural is       [Ada]
begin
    if M = 0 then return N + 1;
    elsif N = 0 then return A(M - 1, 1);
    else return A(M - 1, A(M, N - 1));
end A;
```

(a) Write a program for Ackermann's function and check that A(0,0)=1, A(1,1)=3, A(2,2)=7, A(3,3)=61.

(b) Simulate by hand the computation for A(2,2)=7 showing the growth of the stack.

(c) Try to compute A(4,4) and describe what happens. Try the computation using several compilers. Make sure you save your files before doing this!

(d) Write a non-recursive program for Ackermann's function.[12]

5. How are variables of intermediate scope accessed on an 8086?

6. There is a parameter passing mechanism called *call-by-name* in which each access of a formal parameter causes the actual parameter to be re-evaluated. This mechanism was first used in Algol but does not exist in most ordinary programming languages. What was the motivation for call-by-name in Algol and how was it implemented?

---

[12]Solutions can be found in: Z. Manna. *Mathematical Theory of Computation*. McGraw-Hill, 1974, p. 201 and p. 235.

PART III

Advanced Concepts

8
Pointers

8.1 Pointer types

A variable is nothing more than a convenient notation for referring to the address of a memory location. A variable name is static and determined at compile-time: distinct names refer to distinct locations and there is no way to "compute" a name except in limited contexts such as array indexing. A value of *pointer type* is an address; a pointer variable contains the address of another variable or constant. The object pointed *to* is called the *designated object*. Pointers are used for computing with the address of a memory location rather than with the contents of the location.

The following example:

```
int i = 4;
int *ptr = &i;
```
[C]

produces the result shown in Figure 8.1. ptr is itself a variable with its own memory location (284), but its contents are the address (320) of another variable i.

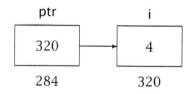

Figure 8.1 Pointer variable and designated variable

The syntax of the declaration is rather confusing because the asterisk "*" refers to the type int and not to the variable ptr. The correct way of reading

the declaration is: "ptr is of type pointer to int". The unary operator "&"
returns the address of its following operand.[1]

The value of the variable i can of course be accessed by using its name
in an expression such as i+1, but it can also be accessed by *dereferencing*
the pointer, using the syntax *ptr. When you dereference a pointer you are
asking not for the contents of the pointer variable ptr, but the contents of the
memory location pointed *to* by the address in ptr, that is for the designated
object.

Typed pointers

The addresses in the example are written like integers, but an address is *not*
an integer. The form of an address will depend on the computer architecture.
For example, the Intel 8086 computer uses two 16-bit words which are combined to form a 20-bit address. Nevertheless, it is a reasonable assumption
that all pointers are represented the same way.

In programming, it is more useful and safer to use typed pointers that are
declared to point to a specific type, such as int in the example above. The
designated object *ptr is required to be an integer, and after dereferencing
it can be used in any context in which an integer is required such as:

```
int a[10];                                                              C
a[*ptr] = a[(*ptr)+5];         /* Deference and index */
a[i] = 2 * *ptr;               /* Dereference and multiply */
```

It is important to distinguish between a pointer variable and the designated
object, and to be very careful when assigning or comparing pointers:

```
int i1 = 10;                                                            C
int i2 = 20;
int *ptr1 = &i1;               /* ptr1 points to i1 */
int *ptr2 = &i2;               /* ptr2 points to i2 */

*ptr1 = *ptr2;                 /* Both variables have same value */
if (ptr1 == ptr2) ...          /* False, different pointers */
if (*ptr1 == *ptr2) ...        /* True, designated objects equal */
ptr1 = ptr2;                   /* Both point to i2 */
```

Figure 8.2(a) shows the variables after the first assignment statement: dereferencing is used so designated objects are assigned and i1 receives the
value 20. After executing the second assignment statement which assigns

---

[1]Do not confuse this operator with the use of "&" to indicate a reference parameter in C++.

pointers, not designated objects, the variable i1 is no longer accessible through a pointer as shown in Figure 8.2(b).

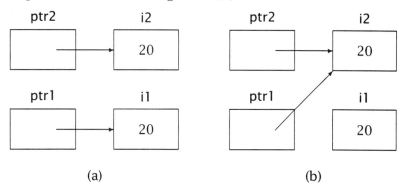

(a)　　　　　　　　　　　　　　　　(b)

Figure 8.2 Pointer assignment

It is also important to be aware of the difference between a constant pointer and a pointer to a constant designated object. Making a pointer constant does not protect the designated object from modification:

```
int i1, i2;                                                           C
int * const p1 = &i1;        /* Constant pointer */
const int * p2 = &i1;        /* Pointer to constant */
const int * const p3 = &i1;  /* Constant pointer to constant */

p1 = &i2;                    /* Error, pointer constant */
*p1 = 5;                     /* OK, designated obj. not constant */
p2 = &i2;                    /* OK, pointer not constant */
*p2 = 5;                     /* Error, designated obj. constant */
p3 = &i2;                    /* Error, pointer constant */
*p3 = 5;                     /* Error, designated obj. constant */
```

In C, a pointer to void is an untyped pointer. Any pointer can be implicitly converted to a pointer to void and conversely, though mixing typed pointer assignments will usually get you a warning message. Fortunately, C++ is much more careful about type checking. Typed pointers can be implicitly converted to void pointers but not conversely:

```
void    *void_ptr;          /* Untyped pointer */               C
int     *int_ptr;           /* Typed pointer */
char    *char_ptr;          /* Typed pointer */
```

```
void_ptr = int_ptr;          /* OK */
char_ptr = void_ptr;         /* OK in C, error in C++ */
char_ptr = int_ptr;          /* Warning in C, error in C++ */
```

Since no type checking in done in C, an arbitrary expression may be assigned to a pointer. There is no guarantee that the designated object is of the expected type; in fact, the value of a pointer might not even be an address assigned to the program. At best, this will cause the program to crash because of an addressing fault and you will get an appropriate message from the operating system. At worst, this can cause the operating system data to become corrupted. Mistakes with pointers are very difficult to debug because the absolute addresses that the debugger displays are hard to understand. The solution is stronger type checking on pointers as in Ada and C++.

Syntax

We depart from our usual custom of glossing over syntax because the syntax for dereferencing can be confusing and must be clearly understood. Dereferencing of pointers, indexing of arrays and selection within records are the means by which data within a data structure are accessed. Pascal has the clearest syntax because each of these three operations is denoted by a separate symbol which is written after the variable. In this example, Ptr is declared as a pointer to an array of records with an integer field:

```
type Rec_Type =                                                          Pascal
    record
        Field: Integer;
    end;
type Array_Type = array[1..100] of Rec_Type;
type Ptr_Type = ↑Array_Type;

    Ptr: Ptr_Type;
```

Then using the symbol (↑) which denotes dereferencing, each addition of a symbol goes one step deeper in the decomposition of the data structure:

```
Ptr                    (* Pointer to array of records with integer field *)
Ptr↑                   (* Array of records with integer field *)
Ptr↑[78]               (* Record with integer field *)
Ptr↑[78].Field         (* Integer *)
```

In C, the dereferencing symbol (*) is a prefix operator so that the above example would be written:

```
typedef struct {                                                    [C]
    int field;
} Rec_Type;
typedef Rec_Type Array_Type[100];

Array_Type *ptr;

ptr                 /* Pointer to array of records with integer field */
*ptr                /* Array of records with integer field */
(*ptr)[78]          /* Record with integer field */
(*ptr)[78].field    /* Integer */
```

where the parentheses are needed because array indexing has higher precedence than pointer dereferencing. In a complicated data structure it can be confusing to decipher a decomposition that uses dereferencing as a prefix, and indexing and selection as a suffix. Fortunately, the most common sequence of operations, dereferencing followed by selection, has a special elegant syntax. If ptr points to a record, then ptr->field is a shorthand for (*ptr).field.

The Ada syntax is based on the assumption that dereferencing is almost always followed by selection, so there is no need for a separate notation for dereferencing. You cannot tell if R.Field is simply the selection of a field of an ordinary record called R, or if R is a pointer to a record which is dereferenced before selection. While this can be confusing, it does have the advantage that a data structure can be changed from using records to using pointers to records, without otherwise modifying the program. On those occasions when pure dereferencing is needed, a rather awkward syntax is used, as shown by repeating the above example in Ada:

```
type Rec_Type is                                                    [Ada]
    record
        Field: Integer;
    end record;
type Array_Type is array(1..100) of Rec_Type;
type Ptr_Type is access Array_Type;

Ptr: Ptr_Type;

Ptr                 -- Pointer to array of records with integer field
Ptr.all             -- Array of records with integer field
```

```
Ptr.all[78]              -- Record with integer field
Ptr.all[78].Field       -- Integer
```

Note that Ada uses a keyword access, rather than a symbol, to denote pointers. The keyword all is used on those few occasions when deferencing without selection is required.

Implementation

The indirect access to data via pointers requires an additional instruction in the machine code. Let us compare a direct assignment statement with an indirect assignment; for example:

```
int i,j;
int *p = &i;
int *q = &j;
```
C

```
i = j;              /* Direct assignment */
*p = *q;            /* Indirect assignment */
```

The machine instructions for the direct assignment are:

```
load        R1,j
store       R1,i
```

while the instructions for the indirect assignment are:

```
load        R1,&q         Addr(designated object)
load        R2,(R1)       Load designated object
load        R3,&p         Addr(designated object)
store       R2,(R3)       Store to designated object
```

Some overhead is inevitable in indirection, but is usually not serious, because if a designated object is accessed repeatedly, the optimizer can ensure that the pointer is loaded only once. Given:

```
p->right = p->left;
```
C

once the address of p is loaded into a register, subsequent accesses can use the register:

```
load        R1,&p         Addr(designated object)
load        R2,left(R1)   Offset from start of record
store       R2,right(R1)  Offset from start of record
```

A potential source of inefficiency in indirect access to data via pointers is the size of the pointers themselves. In the early 1970's when C and Pascal were designed, computers usually had only 16K or 32K of main memory, and addresses could be stored in 16 bits. Now that personal computers and workstations are delivered with many megabytes of memory, pointers must be stored in 32 bits. In addition, because of memory management schemes based on caches and paging, arbitrary access to data through pointers can be much more expensive than access to arrays that are allocated in contiguous locations. The implication is that optimizing a data structure for efficiency is highly system-dependent, and should never be done without first using a profiler to measure execution times.

The typed pointers in Ada offer one possibility for optimization. The set of designated objects associated with a specific access type is called a *collection*, and you can specify its size:[2]

```
type Node_Ptr is access Node;                          Ada
for Node_Ptr'Storage_Size use 40_000;
```

Since the amount of memory requested for Nodes is less than 64K, the pointers can be stored in 16 bits relative to the start of the block of memory, thus saving both space in data structures and CPU time to load and store pointers.

* Aliased pointers in Ada 95

A pointer in C can be used to give an alias to an ordinary variable:

```
int i;                                                   C
int *ptr = &i;
```

Aliases are occasionally useful; for example, they can be used to construct compile-time linked structures. Since pointer-based structures can only be created at run-time in Ada 83, this can cause unnecessary overhead in both time and memory.

Ada 95 has added an aliasing facility, called *general access types*, but it is restricted so that it cannot create dangling pointers (see Section 8.3). A special syntax is needed both for the pointer declaration and for the aliased variable:

---

[2]Ada 95 has more sophisticated ways of controlling memory allocation; see the Language Reference Manual 13.11.

```
type Ptr is access all Integer;        -- Ptr can point to alias   [Ada]
I: aliased Integer;                     -- I can be aliased
P: Ptr := I'Access;                     -- Create the alias
```

The first line declares a type that can point to an aliased Integer variable, the second lines declares such a variable and the third line declares a pointer and initializes it with the variable's address. Such general access types and aliased variables can be components of arrays and records so that linked structures can be built without invoking the run-time memory manager.

* *Memory mapping*

Memory mapping is trivial in C because an arbitrary address may be assigned to a pointer:[3]

```
int * const reg = 0x4f00;        /* Address (in hex) */        [C]

*reg = 0x1f1f;                   /* Value to absolute location */
```

By using a constant pointer, we are assured that the address of the register will not be accidentally modified.

Ada uses the concept of representation specification to explicitly map an ordinary variable to an absolute address:

```
Reg: Integer;                                           [Ada]
for Reg use at 16#4f00#;        -- Address (in hex)

Reg := 16#1f1f#;                -- Value to absolute location
```

The advantage of the Ada method is that no explicit pointers are used.

8.2 Data structures

Pointers are used to implement dynamic data structures such as lists and trees. In addition to data elements, a node in the structure will contain one or more pointers which point to another node (Figure 8.3).

Nodes must be defined using recursive type definitions, that is, a record of type node must contain a pointer to its own type node. Languages have

---

[3]Recall that an address may not be a simple integer, so use of this construct introduces a machine-dependency.

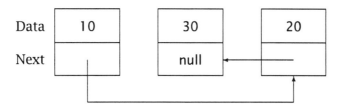

Figure 8.3 Dynamic data structure

provisions for declaring such types by allowing a partial declaration of the
record to supply a name for the record, followed by a declaration of the
pointer which refers to this name, followed by the full declaration of the
record which can now reference the pointer type. These three declarations
in Ada are:

```
type Node;                  -- Incomplete type declaration      Ada
type Ptr is access Node;    -- Pointer type declaration
type Node is                -- Complete the declaration
    record
        Data: Integer;      -- Data in the node
        Next: Ptr;          -- Pointer to next node
    end record;
```

The syntax in C requires the use of structure *tags*, which provide an alternative
syntax for record declarations:

```
typedef struct node *Ptr;   /* Pointer to (tagged) node */       C
typedef struct node {       /* Declaration of node structure */
    int     data;           /* Data in the node */
    Ptr     next;           /* Pointer to next node */
} node;
```

In C++, there is no need to use a typedef as struct defines both a structure
tag and a type name:

```
typedef struct node *Ptr;   /* Pointer to (tagged) node */      C++
struct node {               /* Declaration of node structure */
    int     data;           /* Data in the node */
    Ptr     next;           /* Pointer to next node */
};
```

Algorithms on these data structures use pointer variables to *traverse* the
structure. The following statement in C searches for a node whose data field

is key:

```
while (current->data != key)                                C
    current = current->next;
```

The analogous statement in Ada is (using implicit dereferencing):

```
while Current.Data /= Key loop                              Ada
    Current := Current.Next;
end loop;
```

Data structures are characterized by the number of pointers per node and the directions in which they point, as well as by the algorithms used to traverse and modify the structure. All the methods that you studied in a course on data structures can be directly programmed in C or Ada using records and pointers.

The null pointer

In Figure 8.3, the next field of the final element of the list does not point to anything. By convention, such a pointer is considered to have a special value called *null*, which is different from any valid pointer. The null value is denoted in Ada by a reserved word null. The search in the previous section would actually be programmed as follows so as not to run off the end of the list:

```
while (Current /= null) and then (Current.Data /= Key) loop   Ada
    Current := Current.Next;
end loop;
```

Note that it is essential that short-circuit evaluation be used (see Section 6.2). C uses the ordinary integer literal zero to indicate the null pointer:

```
while ((current != 0) && (current->data != key))            C
    current = current->next;
```

The zero literal is just a syntactic convention; if you use a debugger to examine a null pointer, the bit string *may or may not* be all zeros depending on your computer. To improve readability, a symbol NULL is defined in the C library:

```
while ((current != NULL) && (current->data != key))        C
    current = current->next;
```

When a variable such as an integer is first declared, its value is undefined. This does not cause too much difficulty because every possible bit string that might be stored in such a variable is a valid integer. However, pointers that are not null, and yet do not point to valid blocks of memory, can cause serious bugs. Therefore, Ada implicitly initializes every pointer variable to null. C implicitly initializes every *global* variable to zero; global pointer variables are initialized to null, but you have to take care to explicitly initialize local pointer variables.

One must be very careful not to dereference a null pointer, because the null value doesn't point to anything (or rather probably points to system data at address zero):

```
Current: Ptr := null;                                    Ada
Current := Current.Next;
```

In Ada this error causes an exception (see Chapter 11), but in C the result of attempting to dereference null is potentially catastrophic. Operating systems which protect programs from each other will be able to abort the program; without such protection, the dereference could interfere with another program or even crash the system.

Pointers to subprograms

In C a pointer can point to a function. This is extremely useful in two programming situations:

- Passing a function as a parameter.

- Creating a data structure which associates a procedure with a key or an index.

For example, one of the parameters of a numerical integration package will be the function to be integrated. This is easily programmed in C by creating a data type which is a pointer to a function; the function will receive a parameter of type float and return a value of type float:

```
typedef float (*Func)(float);                            C
```

The syntax is rather confusing because the name of the type is Func which is deep within the declaration, and because precedence in C requires the extra set of parentheses.

Once the type is declared, it can be used as the type of a formal parameter:

```
float integrate(Func f, float upper, float lower)                    C
{
    float u = f(upper);
    float l = f(lower);

    ...
}
```

Note that dereferencing is automatic when the function parameter is called, otherwise we would have to write (*f)(upper). Now, if a function of the appropriate signature is defined, it can be used as an actual parameter to the integrate subprogram:

```
float fun(float parm)                                                C
{
...           /* Definition of "fun" */
}
```

```
float x = integrate(fun, 1.0, 2.0);   /* "fun" as actual parameter */
```

Data structures with pointers to functions are used when creating *interpreters*, which are software programs that receive a sequence of codes and perform actions according to those codes. While a static interpreter can be implemented using a case-statement and ordinary procedure calls, a dynamic interpreter will have the association between codes and actions determined at run-time. Modern windowing systems use a similar programming technique: the programmer is required to provide a *callback* which is a procedure that provides the appropriate action for each event. This is a pointer to a subprogram that will be executed when a code is received indicating that an event has occurred:

```
typedef enum {Event1, ..., Event10} Events;                          C
typedef void (*Actions)(void);
        /* Pointer to procedure */
Actions action[10];
        /* Array of ptr's to procedures */
```

At run-time, a procedure is called to create the association between the event and the action:

```
void install(Events e, Actions a)                                    C
{
    action[e] = a;
}
```

Then when an event occurs, its code can be used to index and call the appropriate action:

```
action[e]();                                              C
```

Since Ada 83 does not have pointers to subprograms, this technique cannot be programmed without using non-standard features. When the language was designed, pointers to subprograms were left out because it was assumed that generics (see Section 10.3) would suffice for creating mathematical libraries, and the callback technique was not yet popular. Ada 95 has corrected this deficiency and allows pointers to subprograms. The declaration of a mathematical library function is as follows:

```
type Func is access function(X: Float) return Float;          Ada
        -- Pointer to function type
function Integrate(F: Func; Upper, Lower: Float);
        -- Parameter is a pointer to a function
```

and the callback is declared as follows:

```
type Events is (Event1, ..., Event10);                        Ada
type Actions is access procedure;
        -- Pointer to procedure type
Action: array(Events) of Actions;
        -- Array of pointers to procedures
```

Pointers and arrays

In the strongly typed framework of Ada, the only possible operations on pointers are assignment, equality and dereferencing. C, however, considers pointers to be implicit sequential addresses and arithmetic is possible on pointer values. This is most clearly seen in the relationship between pointers and arrays: pointers are considered to be the more primitive concept, while array accesses are defined in terms of pointers. In the following example:

```
int *ptr;              /* Pointer to integer */       C
int a[100];            /* Array of integer */

ptr = &a[0];           /* Explicitly address first element */
ptr = a;               /* Implicitly do the same thing */
```

the two assignment statements are equivalent because an array name is considered to be just a pointer to the first element of the array. Furthermore, if addition or subtraction is done on the pointer, the result is not the numerical result but the result of incrementing or decrementing the pointer by the size of the designated type. If an integer requires four bytes and p contains the address 344, then p+1 is not 345 but rather 348 which is the "next" integer. Accessing an element of an array is done by adding the index to the pointer and dereferencing, so that the two following expressions are equivalent:

```
*(ptr + i)
a[i]
```
[C]

Despite this equivalence, there is still an important distinction in C between an array and a pointer:

```
char s1[] = "Hello world";
char *s2 = "Hello world";
```
[C]

s1 is the location of a sequence of 12 bytes of memory containing the string, while the array s2 is a pointer variable containing the address of a similar sequence of bytes (Figure 8.4). However, s1[i] is the same as *(s2+i) for any i in range, because an array is automatically converted to a pointer when used.

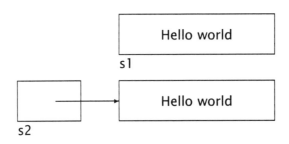

Figure 8.4 Array versus pointer in C

The problem with pointer arithmetic is that there is no guarantee that the result of the expression actually points to an element of the array. While it is relatively easy to understand indexing notation and be convinced of its correctness, pointer arithmetic should in general be avoided. It can be very useful for improving efficiency in loops if your optimizer is not good enough.

8.3 Memory allocation

During the execution of a program, memory is used to store both code and a variety of data structures such as the stack. While the allocation and release of memory is more properly discussed in the context of compilers and operating systems, it is appropriate to survey the topic here because the choice of language constructs and style can be profoundly affected by the implementation.

There are five types of memory that need to be allocated:

Code The machine instructions that are the result of the compilation of the program.

Constants Small constants like 2 and 'x' can often be included within an instruction, but memory must be allocated for large constants, in particular for floating point constants and strings.

Stack Stack memory is used mainly for activation records which contain parameters, variables and links. It is also used as a source of temporary variables when evaluating expressions.

Static Data Variables declared in the main program and elsewhere: in Ada, data declared directly within library packages; in C, data declared directly within a file or declared static in a block.

Heap The heap is the term used for the data area from which data is dynamically allocated by malloc in C and by new in Ada and C++.

Code and constants are similar in that they are fixed at compile-time and are not modified. Thus we will group the two types together in the following discussion. Note that code and constants can be allocated in read-only memory (ROM) if the system supports it. The stack was discussed in great detail in Section 7.6.

We mentioned there that static (global) data could be considered to be allocated at the beginning of the stack. However, static data are usually allocated separately. For example, on the Intel 8086, each area of data (called a *segment*) is limited to 64K bytes of memory. Thus a separate segment would be allocated for the stack in addition to one or more segments for static data.

Finally, we must allocate memory for the heap. A heap differs from a stack in that the allocation and deallocation can be very chaotic. The run-time system must employ sophisticated algorithms to ensure optimal use of the heap.

A program is usually allocated a single, contiguous area in memory which must be divided up to accommodate the required memory areas. Figure 8.5 shows the way that this is done. Since the code, constant and static data areas are fixed, they are allocated at the beginning of the memory. The two

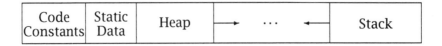

Figure 8.5 Memory allocation: code, data, stack and heap

variable-length areas, the heap and the stack, are allocated at opposite ends of the remaining memory.[4] This way if a program uses a large amount of stack during one phase of a computation and a large amount of heap during another, there is less chance that there will not be enough memory.

What is important to understand is that each allocation of memory on the stack or the heap (that is each procedure call and each execution of a storage allocator) can potentially fail for lack of memory. A well-designed program should gracefully recover from lack of memory, but this is not an easy situation to handle, because even more memory might be needed for the procedure which executes the recovery! Therefore it is recommended that lack of memory be signalled when a substantial reserve remains.

Allocation and deallocation

Imperative programming languages have explicit expressions or statements for allocating and deallocating memory. C uses malloc which is dangerous because no checking is done that the amount of memory returned is correct for the size of the designated object. sizeof should be used even though it is not required:

```
int *p = (int *) malloc(1);              /* Error */        C
int *p = (int *) malloc(sizeof(int));    /* Better */
```

Note that malloc returns an *untyped* pointer that should be explicitly converted to the required type.

The size of the block need not be given when memory is freed:

```
free(p);                                                     C
```

The allocated memory block includes a few extra words which are used to store the size of the block. The size is used in algorithms for heap management as described below.

---

[4]Note that the arrangement is symmetric in that the stack could grow up and the heap down instead of as shown.

C++ and Ada use a notation which clearly brings out the fact that a designated object of a specific type is being created. There is no danger of incompatibility between the type and size of the object:

```
typedef Node *Node_Ptr;
Node_Ptr *p = new Node;              // C++


type Node_Ptr is access Node;
P: Node_Ptr := new Node;             -- Ada
```

The delete operator frees memory in C++. Ada would prefer that you do not free memory allocated from the heap, because freeing memory is inherently dangerous (see below). Of course this is impractical, so a method for releasing memory is supplied called *unchecked deallocation*, named as such to remind you that any use is dangerous. Note that the memory freed is that of the designated object (the object that is pointed *to*) and not the memory used to store the pointer itself.

Dangling pointers

A serious danger with pointers is the possibility of creating *dangling pointers* when releasing a block of memory:

```
int *ptr1 = new int;                              C++
int *ptr2;


ptr2 = ptr1;                // Both point to the same block
result = delete ptr1;       // ptr2 now points to released block
```

After executing the first assignment statement, the allocated block of memory is pointed to by two pointers. When the memory is freed, the second pointer still retains a copy of the address but this address is now meaningless. In a complex data structure algorithm, a double reference of this type is quite easy to construct by mistake.

Dangling pointers can also be created in C and C++ without any explicit deallocation on the part of the programmer:

```
char *proc(int i)          /* Returns pointer to char */         C
{
    char c;                /* Local variable */
    return &c;             /* Pointer to local char */
}
```

The memory for c is implicitly allocated on the stack when the procedure is called and implicitly deallocated upon return, so the pointer value returned no longer points to a valid object. This is easy to see in a two-line procedure but may not be so easy to notice in a large program.

Ada tries to avoid dangling pointers:

- Pointers to objects (named variables, constants and parameters) are forbidden in Ada 83; in Ada 95, they are subject to the special alias construct whose rules prevent dangling pointers.

- Explicit allocation cannot be avoided, but it is given a name Unchecked Deallocation that is intended to warn the programmer of the dangers.

8.4 Algorithms for heap allocation

The heap manager is a component of the run-time system that allocates and releases memory. It does this by maintaining a list of *free* blocks. The list is searched when an allocation request is made, and a released block is relinked to the free list. The run-time system designer must make many choices such as the order in which the blocks are maintained, the data structure used, the order of search and so on.

The problem with heap allocation is *fragmentation*. In Figure 8.6, five blocks of memory have been allocated and the second and fourth have been released. Now even though there are 1000 bytes available, it is impossible to

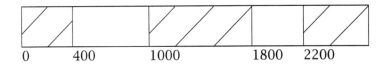

Figure 8.6 Heap fragmentation

successfully allocate more than 600 bytes because the memory is fragmented into small blocks. Even if the third block were released, it does not immediately follow that there will be enough memory, unless the heap manager has been designed so that it can merge adjacent free blocks.

In addition to merging, the heap manager can help prevent fragmentation by searching for an appropriate-sized block rather than simply taking the first available one, or by allocating large blocks from one area in the heap and small blocks in another. There is a clear trade-off between the sophistication of the head manager and the run-time overhead required.

The programmer should be aware of the heap algorithms used and can write a program that takes account of this knowledge.[5] Alternatively, it is possible to refrain from dependence of the heap algorithm by maintaining a cache of deallocated blocks. When a block is released, simply link it onto the cache. When a block is needed, the cache is checked first to avoid both the overhead and the fragmentation dangers of calling the heap manager.

Ada has a facility that allows the programmer to specify different heap sizes, one for each type of pointer. This can prevent fragmentation but runs the risk of one heap running out of memory while others have plenty of free blocks.

Virtual memory

There is one case where heap allocation is essentially risk-free and that is when *virtual memory* is being used. In a virtual memory system, the programmer receives an extremely large address space, so large that memory overflow is practically impossible. The operating system takes care of allocating the logical address space to physical memory as needed. When physical memory is exhausted, blocks of memory called *pages* are swapped to disk.

With virtual memory, the heap allocator can continue allocating from the heap almost forever, so no fragmentation problems are encountered. The only risk is the standard risk of virtual memory called *thrashing*, which occurs when the code and data required for a phase of a computation are spread over so many pages that there is not enough room for all of them in memory. So much time is spent swapping pages that the computation does not progress.

Garbage collection

The final problem with heap allocation is the creation of *garbage*:

```
int *ptr1 = new int;      // Allocate first block          C
int *ptr2 = new int;      // Allocate second block
ptr2 = ptr1;              // Now, second block inaccessible
```

Following the assignment statement, the second block of memory is accessible through either of the pointers, but there is no way to access the first block (Figure 8.7). This may not be a bug because memory you can't access, called garbage, can't hurt you. However, if memory continues to *leak*, that is if

---

[5]This is another case where the program can be portable, but its efficiency may be highly system-dependent.

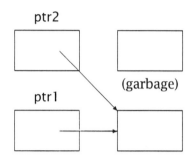

Figure 8.7 Creation of garbage

garbage creation continues, eventually the program will fail because of lack of memory. It is extremely difficult to locate the cause of memory leakage, because there is no direct connection between the cause and the symptom (lack of memory).

The obvious solution is not to create garbage in the first place by being careful to deallocate every block before it becomes inaccessible. Alternatively, the run-time system of a programming language may contain a *garbage collector*. The task of a garbage collector is to "recycle" garbage by identifying inaccessible memory blocks and returning them to the heap manager. There are two basic garbage collection algorithms: one maintains a count of the number of pointers currently pointing to each block and automatically deallocates the block when the count goes to zero. The other algorithm marks all accessible blocks and then collects unmarked (and hence inaccessible) blocks. The first algorithm is problematical because a group of blocks, all of which are garbage, may point at one another so the count may never decrease to zero. The second algorithm requires that the computation be interrupted for long periods of time, so that the marking and collecting can be done without interference from the computation. This of course is not acceptable in interactive systems.

Garbage collection is traditionally done in languages like Lisp and Icon which create large amounts of temporary data structures that quickly become garbage. Extensive research has been done into garbage collection, with emphasis on concurrent and incremental methods that will not disrupt an interactive or real-time computation. Eiffel is one of the few imperative languages that include garbage collectors in their run-time systems.

8.5 Exercises

1. How is a pointer represented on your computer? How is the null pointer represented on your computer?

2. Write an array algorithm in C using indexing and then change it to use explicit pointer manipulation. Compare the resulting machine instructions and then compare the run time of the two programs. Does optimization make a difference?

3. Show how sentinels can be used to make searching a list more efficient.

4. For an actual parameter of type pointer to function, why wasn't the addressing operator used:

   float x = integrate(&fun, 1.0, 2.0);   `C`

5. Show how dangling pointers can be used to break the type system.

6. Study the Ada 95 definition of *accessibility* and show how the rules prevent dangling pointers.

7. Write a program that uses a dynamic data structure such as a linked list. Modify the program to use a cache of nodes.

8. Study your compiler's documentation; what algorithms does the run-time system use for heap allocation? Is there any memory overhead when allocating from the heap, that is, are extra words allocated in addition to those you requested? If so, how many?

9. If you have access to a computer that uses virtual memory, see how long you can continue to allocate memory. What limit finally terminates allocation?

9

Real Numbers

9.1 Representations of real numbers

In Chapter 4 we discussed how integer types are used to represent a subset of the mathematical integers. Computation with integer types can cause overflow—a concept which has no meaning for mathematical integers—and the possibility of overflow means that the commutativity and associativity of arithmetical operations is not ensured during the computation.

Representation of real numbers on computers and computation with their representations are extremely problematical, to the point where a specialist should be consulted during the construction of critical programs. This chapter will explore the basic concepts of computation with real numbers; the superficial ease with which real-number computations can be written in a program must not obscure the underlying problems.

First of all let us note that decimal numbers cannot be accurately represented in binary notation. For example, 0.2 (one-fifth) has no exact representation as a binary number, only the repeating binary fraction:

$$0.0011001100110011\ldots$$

There are two solutions to this problem:

- Represent decimal numbers directly, for example by assigning four bits to each decimal numeral. This representation is called *binary-coded decimal* (*BCD*).

- Store binary numbers and accept the fact that some loss of accuracy will occur.

BCD wastes a certain amount of memory because four bits could represent 16 different values and not just the 10 needed for decimals. A more important disadvantage is that the representation is not "natural" and calculation with

BCD is much slower than with binary numbers. Thus the discussion will be
limited to binary representations; the reader interested in BCD computation
is referred to languages such as Cobol which support BCD numbers.

Fixed-point numbers

To simplify the following discussion, it will be given in terms of decimal
numbers, but the concepts are identical for binary numbers. Suppose that
we can represent seven digits, five before and two after the decimal point,
in one 32-bit memory word:

$$12345.67, \quad -1234.56, \quad 0.12$$

This representation is called *fixed-point*. The advantage of fixed-point numbers is that the *accuracy*, that is the absolute error, is fixed. If the above
numbers denote dollars and cents, then any error caused by the limited size
of a memory word is at most one cent. The disadvantage is that the *precision*,
that is the relative error which is the number of significant digits, is variable.
The first number uses all available seven digits of precision, while the last
uses only two. More importantly, the varying precision means that many
important numbers such as the $1,532,854.07$ that you won in the lottery,
or your $0.00572 income-tax refund, cannot be represented at all.

Fixed-point numbers are used in applications where total accuracy is essential. For example, accounting computations are usually done in fixed-point,
since the required precision is known in advance (say 12 or 16 digits) and
the account must balance to the last cent. Fixed-point numbers are also
used in control systems where sensors and actuators communicate with the
computer in fixed-length words or fields. For example, speed could be represented in a 10-bit field with range 0 to 102.3 km/hour; one bit will represent
0.1 km/hour.

Floating-point numbers

Scientists who have to deal in a wide range of numbers use a convenient
notation called *scientific notation*:

$$123.45 \times 10^3, \quad 1.2345 \times 10^{-8}, \quad -0.00012345 \times 10^7, \quad 12345000.0 \times 10^4$$

How can we use this concise notation on a computer? First note that there
are three items of information that have to be represented: the *sign*, the
mantissa (123.45 in the first number) and the *exponent*. On the surface it
would seem that there is no advantage to representing a number in scientific

notation, because of the varying precisions needed to represent the mantissa: five digits in the first and second numbers above, as opposed to eight digits for the other two.

The solution is to note that trailing zero digits of a mantissa greater than 1.0 (and leading zero digits of a mantissa less than 1.0) can be discarded in favor of changes in the value (not the precision!) of the exponent. More precisely, the mantissa can be multiplied or divided repeatedly by 10 until it is in a form that uses the maximum precision; each such operation requires that the exponent be decremented or incremented by 1, respectively. For example, the last two numbers can be written to use a five-digit mantissa:

$$-0.12345 \times 10^4, \quad 0.12345 \times 10^{12}$$

It is convenient for computation on a computer if every such number has this standard form, called *normalized* form, where the first non-zero digit is the "tenth's" digit. This also saves on space in the representation, because the decimal point is always in the same position and need not be explicitly represented. The representation is called *floating-point* because we require that the decimal point "float" left or right until the number can be represented with maximum precision.

What is the main disadvantage of computation with floating-point numbers? Consider 0.12345×10^{10} which is normalized floating-point for

$$1,234,500,000$$

and suppose that this is how the bank represented your deposit of

$$\$1,234,567,890$$

Your bank manager would be proud that the *relative error*:

$$\frac{67,890}{1,234,567,890}$$

is a very small fraction of one percent, but you would justifiably demand your $67,890, the *absolute error*.

In scientific calculations relative error is much more important than absolute error. In a program that controls the speed of a rocket, the requirement may be that the error be no more than 0.5% even though this translates into a few km/h during launch and a few hundred km/h nearing orbit. Floating-point computation is much more common than fixed-point, because relative accuracy is required more often than absolute accuracy. For this reason most computers have hardware that directly implements floating-point computation.

Representation of floating-point numbers

Floating-point numbers are stored as *binary* numbers in the normalized form we have described:

$$-0.101100111 \times 2^{15}$$

A typical implementation on a 32-bit computer would assign 1 bit to the sign, 23 bits to the mantissa and 8 bits to the exponent. Since it takes $\log_2 10 \approx 3.3$ bits to store one decimal digit, $23/3.3 \approx 7$ digits of precision are obtained. If more precision is needed, a 64-bit double word with a 52-bit mantissa can achieve about 15 digits of precision.

There is a "trick" that is used to represent more numbers than would otherwise be available. Since all floating-point numbers are normalized, and since the first digit of a normalized mantissa is necessarily 1, this first digit need not be explicitly represented.

The signed exponent is represented by *biasing* the exponent so that it is always positive, and the exponent is placed in the high-order bits of a word next to the sign bit. This makes comparisons easier because ordinary integer comparison may be done without extracting a signed two's-complement exponent field. For example, an 8-bit exponent field with values in the range 0..255 represents exponents in the range $-127..128$ with a bias of 127.

We can now decipher a bit string as a floating point number. The string:

$$1 \ \ 1000\,1000 \ \ 0110\,0000\,0000\,0000\,0000\,000$$

is deciphered as follows:

- The sign bit is 1 so the number is negative.

- The exponent is $1000\,1000 = 128 + 8 = 136$. Removing the bias gives

$$136 - 127 = 9$$

- The mantissa is $0.10110\ldots$ (note the hidden bit restored), which is

$$\frac{1}{2} + \frac{1}{8} + \frac{1}{16} = \frac{11}{16}$$

- Thus the number stored is $2^9 \times 11/16 = 352$.

Just as with integers, floating point overflow occurs when the result of the computation is too large:

$$(0.5 \times 10^{70}) \cdot (0.5 \times 10^{80}) = 0.25 \times 10^{150}$$

Since the largest exponent that can be represented is 128, the computation overflows.

Consider now the computation:

$$(0.5 \times 10^{-70}) \cdot (0.5 \times 10^{-80}) = 0.25 \times 10^{-150}$$

The computation is said to *underflow* because the result is too small to be represented. You may claim that such a number is so small that it might as well be zero, and a computer may choose to treat underflow by storing a zero result, but underflow does represent an error and should be either handled or accounted for.

9.2 Language support for real numbers

All programming languages have support for floating-point calculations. Variables can be declared to be of type float,[1] and floating-point literals are represented using a form similar to scientific notation:

```
float f1 = 7.456;
float f2 = -46.64E-3;
```
[C]

Note that the literals need not be in binary notation or in normalized form; the conversion is done by the compiler.

A minimum of 32 bits is needed for meaningful floating-point calculations. Often more precision is needed, and languages support declaration and computation with higher precisions. At a minimum *double-precision* variables using 64 bits are supported, and some computers or compilers will support even longer types. Double precision floating-point types are called double in C and Long_Float in Ada.

The notation for double-precision literals varies with the language. Fortran uses a separate notation, replacing the E that precedes the exponent with a D: -45.64D-3. C chooses to store *every* literal in double precision, allowing a suffix F if you want to specify single precision. Be careful if you are storing a large array of floating-point constants.

Ada introduces a new concept, *universal types*, to handle the varying precision of literals. A literal such as 0.2 is stored by the compiler in potentially infinite precision (recall that 0.2 cannot be exactly represented as a binary number). When a literal is actually used, it is converted into a constant of the correct precision:

---

[1]Pascal and Fortran use the name real.

```
PI_F:    constant Float          := 3.1415926535;          Ada
PI_L:    constant Long_Float     := 3.1415926535;
PI:      constant               := 3.1415926535;
F: Float       := PI;            -- Convert number to Float
L: Long_Float  := PI;           -- Convert number to Long_Float
```

The first two declarations declare constants of the named types. The third declaration for PI is called a *named number* and is of universal real type. When PI is actually used in the initializations, it is converted to the correct precision.

The four arithmetic operators (+, -, * and /) as well as equality and the relational operators are defined for floating-point types. Mathematical functions such the trigonometric functions may be defined within the language (Fortran and Pascal), or they be supplied by subprogram libraries (C and Ada).

Portability of floating-point

Programs that use floating-point can be difficult to port because different definitions are used for the type specifiers. There is nothing to prevent a compiler for C or Ada from using 64 bits to represent float (Float) and 128 bits to represent double (Long_Float). Both porting directions are problematical: when porting from an implementation which uses a high-precision representation of float to one which uses a low-precision representation, all float's must be converted to double's to retain the same level of precision. When porting from a low-precision to a high-precision implementation, the opposite modification may be needed, because using excess precision wastes execution time and memory.

An elementary partial solution is to declare and use an artificial floating-point type; then only a few lines need be changed when porting the program:

```
typedef double Real;            /* C */
subtype Real is Long_Float;     -- Ada
```

See Section 9.4 for Ada's comprehensive solution to the problem of portable computation with real numbers.

Hardware and software floating-point

Our discussion of the representation of floating-point numbers should have made it clear that arithmetic on these values is a complex task. The words must be decomposed, the exponent biases removed, the multiword arithmetic done, the result normalized and the result word composed. Most computers use special hardware for efficient execution of floating-point calculations.

A computer without the appropriate hardware can still execute floating-point calculations using a library of subprograms that *emulate* floating-point instructions. Attempting to execute a floating-point instruction will cause a "bad-instruction" interrupt which will be handled by calling the appropriate emulation. Needless to say this can be very inefficient, since there is the interrupt and subprogram overhead in addition to the floating-point computation.

If you think that your program may be extensively used on computers without floating-point hardware, it may be prudent to avoid floating-point computation altogether. Instead you can explicitly program fixed-point calculations where needed. For example, a financial program can do all its computation in terms of "cents" rather than fractions of dollars. Of course this runs the risk of overflow if the Integer or Long_Integer types are not represented with sufficient precision.

Mixed arithmetic

Mixed integer and real arithmetic is very common in mathematics: we write $A = 2\pi r$ and not $A = 2.0\pi r$. When computing, mixed integer and floating-point operations must be done with some care. The second form is preferable because 2.0 can be stored directly as a floating-point constant, whereas the literal 2 would have to be converted to a floating representation. While this is usually done automatically by the compiler, it is better to write exactly what you require.

Another potential source of difficulty is the distinction between integer division and floating-point division:

```
I: Integer := 7;                              Ada
J: Integer := I / 2;
K: Integer := Integer(Float(I) / 2.0);
```

The expression in the assignment to J calls for integer division; the result, of course, is 3. In the assignment to K, floating-point division is required: the result is 3.5 and it is converted to an integer by rounding to 4.

Languages even disagree on how to convert floating-point values to integer values. The same example in C:

```
int i = 7;                                    C
int j = i / 2;
int k = (int) ((float i) / 2.0);
```

assigns 3 to both j and k, because the floating-point value 3.5 is truncated rather than rounded!

C implicitly performs mixed arithmetic, converting integers to floating-point types if necessary and converting lower precision to higher precision. Also, values are implicitly converted upon assignment. Thus the above example could be written:

```
int k = i / 2.0;                                                    C
```

While the *promotion* of the integer i to floating-point is clear, programs will be more readable if explicit conversions are used on assignment statements (as opposed to initializations):

```
k = (int) i / 2.0;                                                  C
```

Ada forbids *all* mixed arithmetic; however, any value of a numeric type can be explicitly converted from a value of any other numeric type as shown above.

If efficiency is important, rearrange a mixed expression so that the computation is kept as simple as possible for as long as possible. For example (recalling that literals are considered **double** in C):

```
int i, j, k, l;                                                     C
float f = 2.2 * i * j * k * l;
```

would be done by converting i to double, performing the multiplication 2.2 * i and so on, with every integer being converted to double. Finally, the result would be converted to float for the assignment. It would be more efficient to write:

```
int i, j, k, l;                                                     C
float f = 2.2F * (i * j * k * l);
```

to ensure that the integer variables are first multiplied using fast integer instructions and that the literal be stored as float and not as double. Of course, these optimizations could introduce integer overflow which would not occur if the computation was done in double precision.

One way to improve the efficiency of any floating-point computation is to arrange the algorithm so that only part of the computation has to be done in double precision. For example, a physics problem can use single precision when computing the motion of two objects that are close to each other (so the distance between them can be precisely represented in relatively few digits); the program can then switch to double precision as the objects get further away from each other.

9.3 The three deadly sins

Every floating-point operation produces a result that is possibly incorrect in the least significant digit because of rounding errors. Programmers writing numerical software should be well-versed in the methods for estimating and controlling these errors. In these paragraphs, we will summarize three serious errors that can occur:

- Negligible addition

- Error magnification

- Loss of significance

Negligible addition occurs when adding or subtracting a number that is very small relative to the first operand. In five-digit decimal arithmetic:

$$0.1234 \times 10^3 + 0.1234 \times 10^{-4} = 0.1234 \times 10^3$$

It is unlikely that your high-school teacher taught you that $x + y = x$ for non-zero y, but that is what has occurred here!

Error magnification is the large absolute error that can occur in floating-point arithmetic even though the relative error is small. It is usually the result of multiplication or division. Consider the computation of $x \cdot x$:

$$0.1234 \times 10^3 \cdot 0.1234 \times 10^3 = 0.1522 \times 10^5$$

and suppose now that during the calculation of x, there had been a one-digit error, that is an absolute error of 0.1:

$$0.1235 \times 10^3 * 0.1235 \times 10^3 = 0.1525 \times 10^5$$

The error is now 30 which is 300 times the size of the error before the multiplication.

The most serious error is complete loss of significance caused by subtracting nearly equal numbers:

```
float f1 = 0.12342;
float f2 = 0.12346;
```
☐C

In mathematics, $f2 - f1 = 0.00004$ which is certainly representable as a four-digit floating-point number: 0.4000×10^{-4}. However, a program computing f2-f1 in four-digit floating-point will give the answer:

$$0.1235 \times 10^0 - 0.1234 \times 10^0 = 0.1000 \times 10^{-3}$$

which is not even close to being a reasonable answer.

Loss of significance is more common than might be supposed because equality calculations are usually implemented by subtracting and then comparing to zero. The following if-statement is thus totally unacceptable:

```
f1 = ... ;                                                    C
f2 = ... ;
if (f1 == f2) ...
```

The most innocent rearrangement of the expressions for f1 and f2, whether done by a programmer or by an optimizer, can cause a different branch of the if-statement to be taken. The correct way of checking equality in floating-point is to introduce a small error term:

```
#define Epsilon 10e-20                                        C

if ((fabs(f2 - f1)) < Epsilon) ...
```

and then compare the absolute value of the difference to the error term. For the same reason, there is no effective difference between <= and < in floating-point calculation.

Errors in floating-point calculations can often be reduced by rearrangement. Since addition associates to the left, the four-digit decimal computation:

$$1234.0 + 0.5678 + 0.5678 = 1234.0$$

is better if done:

$$0.5678 + 0.5678 + 1234.0 = 1235.0$$

to avoid negligible addition.

As another example, the arithmetic identity:

$$(x + y)(x - y) = x^2 - y^2$$

can be used to improve the accuracy of a computation:[2]

```
X, Y: Float_4;                                                Ada
Z: Float_7;

Z := Float_7( (X+Y)*(X-Y) );      -- This way ?
Z := Float_7( X*X - Y*Y );        -- or this way ?
```

---

[2]Float_4 and Float_7 are assumed to be types with four and seven digit precision, respectively.

If we let x = 1234.0 and y = 0.6, the correct value of this expression is 1522755.64. Evaluated to eight digits, the results are:

$$(1234.0 + 0.6) \cdot (1234.0 - 0.6) = 1235.0 \cdot 1233.0 = 1522755.0$$

and

$$(1234.0 \cdot 1234.0) - (0.6 \cdot 0.6) = 1522756.0 - 0.36 = 1522756.0$$

When $(x + y)(x - y)$ is evaluated, the small error resulting from the addition and subtraction is greatly modified by the magnification caused by the multiplication. By rearranging, the formula $x^2 - y^2$ avoids the negligible addition and subtraction and gives a more correct answer.

9.4 * Real types in Ada

Note: the technical definition of real types was significantly simplified in the revision of Ada from Ada 83 to Ada 95, so if you intend to study the details of this subject, it would be best to skip the older definition.

Floating-types in Ada

In Section 4.6 we described how an integer type can be declared to have a given range, while the implementation is chosen by the compiler:

    type Altitude is range 0 .. 60000;

Similar support for portability of floating-point computations is given by the declaration of arbitrary floating-point types:

    type F is digits 12;

This declaration requests 12 (decimal) digits of precision. On a 32-bit computer this will require double precision, while on a 64-bit computer single precision will suffice. Note that as with integer types, this declaration creates a new type which cannot be used in operations with other types without explicit conversions.

The Ada standard describes in great detail conforming implementations of such a declaration. Programs whose correctness depends only on the requirements of the standard, and not on any quirks of a particular implementation, are assured of easy porting from one Ada compiler to another, even to a compiler on an entirely different computer architecture.

Fixed-point types in Ada

A fixed-point type is declared as follows:

    type F is delta 0.1 range 0.0 .. 1.0;

In addition to a range, when writing a fixed-point type declaration you indicate the absolute error required by writing a fraction after the keyword delta.

Given delta D and a range R, an implementation is required to supply a set of numbers, called *model numbers*, at most D from one another which cover R. On a binary computer, the model numbers would be multiples of a power of two just below the value of D, in this case $1/16 = 0.0625$. The model numbers corresponding to the above declaration are:

$$0, \; 1/16, \; 2/16, \; \ldots, \; 14/16, \; 15/16$$

Note that even though 1.0 is specified as part of the range, that number is not one of the model numbers! The definition only requires that 1.0 be within 0.1 of a model number, and this requirement is fulfilled because $15/16 = 0.9375$ and $1.0 - 0.9375 < 0.1$.

There is a predefined type Duration which is used for measuring time intervals. Fixed-point is appropriate here because time will have an absolute error (say 0.0001 second) depending on the hardware of the computer.

For business data processing, Ada 95 defines *decimal fixed-point types*:

    type Cost is delta 0.01 digits 10;

Unlike ordinary fixed-point types which are represented by powers of two, these numbers are represented by powers of ten and so are suitable for exact decimal arithmetic. The type declared above can hold values up to $99,999,999.99$.

9.5   Exercises

1. What floating-point types exist on your computer? List the range and precision for each one. Is exponent bias used? Normalization? Hidden high-order bit? What infinite or other usual values exist?

2. Write a program that takes a floating-point number and prints the sign, mantissa and exponent (after removing any bias).

3. Write a program for infinite precision integer addition and multiplication.

4. Write a program to print the binary representation of a decimal fraction.

5. Write a program for BCD arithmetic.

6. Write a program to emulate floating-point addition and multiplication.

7. Declare various fixed-point types in Ada and check how values are represented. How is Duration represented?

8. In Ada there are limitations on fixed-point arithmetic. List and motivate each limitation.

10

Polymorphism

Polymorphism means "many-formed". Here we use the term to refer to facilities that enable the programmer to use a variable, value or subprogram in two or more different ways. Almost by definition polymorphism can be the source of bugs; it is difficult enough to understand a program where each name has one meaning, much less one where a name can have multiple meanings! Nevertheless, in many situations polymorphism is essential and can be safe if used carefully.

Polymorphism can be either static or dynamic. In static polymorphism, the multiple forms are resolved at compile time, and appropriate machine code generated. Examples are:

- Type conversion: a value is converted from one type to another.

- Overloading: the same name is used for two or more different objects or subprograms (including operators).

- Generics: a parameterized template of a subprogram is used to create several instances of a subprogram.

In dynamic polymorphism, the structural uncertainty is not resolved until run-time:

- Variant and unconstrained records: one variable can have values of different types.

- Run-time dispatching: the selection of a subprogram to call is done at run-time.

10.1 Type conversion

Type conversion is the operation of taking a value of one type and converting it to a value of another type. There are two variations: (1) translating a value

195

of one type to a valid value of the other, and (2) transferring the value as an uninterpreted bit string.

Conversion of numeric values, say floating-point to integer, involves executing instructions to rearrange the bits of the floating-point value so that they represent a suitable integer. In effect, type conversion is done by a function receiving a parameter of one type and returning a result of another type; the Ada syntax for type conversion is the same as that of a function:

```
I: Integer := 5;                                                          Ada
F: Float := Float(I);
```

while the C syntax can be confusing, especially when used in a complicated expression:

```
int i = 5;                                                                 C
float f = (float) i;
```

C++ retains the C syntax for compatibility but also introduces a functional syntax as in Ada for improved readability.

In addition, both C and C++ include implicit type conversion between types, primarily numerical types:

```
int i;                                                                     C
float f = i;
```

Explicit type conversions are safe because they are simply functions: if the predefined type conversion didn't exist, you could always write your own. Implicit type conversions are more problematical, because the reader of the program can never know if the conversion was intended or if it is an unintended oversight. Using integer values in a complicated floating-point expression should cause no problems, but other conversions should be explicitly written out.

The second form of type conversion simply allows the program to use the same bit string in two different ways. Unfortunately, C uses the same syntax for both forms of conversion: if it makes sense to do a type conversion, such as between numeric types or pointer types, a true conversion is done; otherwise, the bit string is transferred as it is.

In Ada, it is possible to do an *unchecked conversion* between any two types; the conversion treats the value as an uninterpreted bit string. Since this is inherently unsafe and renders all the hard-earned type checking invalid, unchecked conversion is discouraged and the syntax in Ada is designed to highlight its use. Uses of unchecked conversion will not be overlooked during a code inspection and the programmer will have to justify its use.

C++, while retaining C type conversion for compatibility, has defined a new set of *cast* operators:

dynamic_cast See Section 15.3.

static_cast An expression of type T1 can be statically cast to type T2, if T1 can be implicitly converted to T2 or conversely. static_cast would be used for type-safe conversions like float to int or conversely.

reinterpret_cast Unsafe type conversions.

const_cast Used to allow assignments to constant objects.

10.2 Overloading

Overloading is the use of the same name to denote different objects in a single scope. The use of the same name for variables in two different procedures (scopes) is not considered to be overloading, because the two variables do not exist simultaneously. The idea for overloading comes from the need to use mathematical and input-output libraries for variables of different types. In C, different names need to be used for the absolute value function on different types:

```
int    i  = abs(25);
double d  = fabs(1.57);
long   l  = labs(-25L);
```
C

In Ada and in C++, the same name can be used for two or more different subprograms provided that the *parameter signatures* are different. As long as the number and/or the types (but not just the names or modes) of the formal parameters are different, the compiler will be able to resolve any subprogram call by checking the number and types of the actual parameters:

```
function Sin(X: in Float) return Float;
function Sin(X: in Long_Float) return Long_Float;

F1, F2: Float;
L1, L2: Long_Float;

F1 := Sin(F2);
L1 := Sin(L2);
```
Ada

An interesting difference between the two languages is that Ada takes the function result type into account when searching for overloading, while C++ restricts itself to the formal parameters:

```
float      sin(float);                                                    C++
double     sin(double);           // Overloads sin
double     sin(float);            // Error, redefinition in a scope
```

Of particular interest is the possibility of overloading predefined operators like + and * in Ada:

```
function "+"(V1, V2: Vector) return Vector;                               Ada
```

Of course you have to supply the function to implement the overloaded operator for the new types. Note that the syntactic properties of the operator, in particular its precedence, are not changed. C++ has a similar facility for overloading:

```
Vector operator+(const Vector &, const Vector &);                        C++
```

This is just like a function declaration except for the use of the reserved keyword **operator**. Operator overloading should only be used for operations that are similar to the predefined meaning, so as not to confuse maintainers of the program.

If used carefully, overloading can reduce the size of the name space and ensure the portability of a program. It can even enhance the clarity of a program because artificial names like **fabs** are no longer needed. On the other hand, indiscriminate overloading can easily destroy readability by assigning too many meanings to the same name. Overloading should be restricted to subprograms that do the same sort of computation, so that the reader of a program can interpret the meaning just from the subprogram name.

10.3 Generics

Arrays, lists and trees are data structures that can store and retrieve data elements of arbitrary type. If it is necessary to store several types simultaneously, some form of dynamic polymorphism is needed. However, if we are working only with homogeneous data structures such as an array of integers, or a list of floating-point numbers, it is sufficient to use static polymorphism to create instances of a program template at compile time.

For example, consider a subprogram to sort an array. The type of the array element is used only in two places: when comparing elements and when swapping elements. The complex manipulation of indices is the same whatever the array element type:[1]

---

[1]This algorithm is called *selection sort*; it is much more efficient and no more difficult than

```ada
type Int_Array is array(Integer range <>) of Integer;          [Ada]

procedure Sort(A: Int_Array) is
    Temp, Min: Integer;
begin
    for I in A'First ..A'Last-1 loop
        Min := I;
        for J in I+1 .. A'Last loop
            if A(J) < A(Min) then Min := J; end if;
                                -- Compare elements using "<"
        end loop;
        Temp := A(I); A(I) := A(Min); A(Min) := Temp;
                                -- Swap elements using ":="
    end loop;
end Sort;
```

In fact, even the index type is irrelevant to the programming of the procedure, as long as a discrete type (such as characters or integers) is used.

To obtain a Sort procedure for some other element type such as **Character**, we could physically copy the code and make the necessary modifications, but this would introduce the possibility of errors. Furthermore, if we wish to modify the algorithm, we would have to do so in each copy separately. Ada defines a facility called *generics* that allows the programmer to define a template of a subprogram and then to create instances of the template for several types. While C lacks a similar facility, its absence is less serious because void pointers, the **sizeof** operator and pointers to functions can be used to program general, if unsafe, subprograms. Note that the use of generics does not ensure that any of the object code will be common to the instantiations; in fact, an implementation may choose to produce independent object code for each instantiation.

Here is a declaration of a *generic subprogram* with two *generic formal parameters*:

```ada
generic                                                        [Ada]
    type Item is (<>);
    type Item_Array is array(Integer range <>) of Item;
procedure Sort(A: Item_Array);
```

This generic declaration does *not* declare a procedure, only a template of a procedure. A procedure body must be supplied; the body will be written in

---

the *bubble sort* algorithm that you may have been taught. The idea is to search for the smallest element remaining in the unsorted part of the array and to move it to the front.

terms of the generic parameters:

```
procedure Sort(A: Item_Array) is                              [Ada]
    Temp, Min: Item;
begin
    ...                              -- Exactly as before
end Sort;
```

To get a (callable) procedure, you must *instantiate* the generic declaration, that is, create an instance by furnishing generic actual parameters:

```
type Int_Array is array(Integer range <>) of Integer;        [Ada]
type Char_Array is array(Integer range <>) of Character;

procedure Int_Sort(A: Int_Array) is new Sort(Integer, Int_Array);
procedure Char_Sort(A: Char_Array) is new Sort(Character, Char_Array);
```

These are actual procedure declarations; instead of a body following the is keyword, a new copy of the generic template is requested.

The generic parameters are *compile-time* parameters and are used by the compiler to generate the correct code for the instance. The parameters form a *contract* between the code of the generic procedure and the instantiation. The first parameter, Item, is declared with the notation (<>), which means that the instantiating program promises to supply a discrete type such as Integer or Character, and the code promises to use only operations valid on such types. Since every discrete type has the relational operators defined on its values, the procedure Sort is assured that "<" is valid. The second generic parameter Item_Array is a clause in the contract that says: whatever type was given for the first parameter, the second parameter must be an integer-indexed array of that type.

The contract model works both ways. An attempt to do an arithmetic operation such as "+" on values of type Item in the generic body is a compilation error, since there are discrete types such as Boolean for which arithmetic is not defined. Conversely, the generic procedure could not be instantiated with a record type because the procedure needs "<" which is not defined for records.

The motivation for the contract model is to allow programmers to use or reuse generic units with the certainty that they need not know how the generic body is implemented. Once the generic body compiles correctly, an instantiation can fail only if its actual parameters do not fit the contract. An instantiation will *not* cause a compile error in the body.

Templates in C++

In C++, generics are implemented with the *template* facility:

```
template <class Item_Array> void Sort(Item_Array parm)
{
        . . .
}
```

There is no need for explicit instantiation; a subprogram is created implicitly when the subprogram is used:

```
typedef int I_Array[100];
typedef char C_Array[100];
I_Array a;
C_Array c;

Sort(a);                        // Instantiate for int arrays
Sort(c);                        // Instantiate for char arrays
```

Explicit instantiation is an optional programmer-specified optimization; otherwise, the compiler decides exactly which instantiations need to be done. Templates can only be instantiated with types and values, or more generally with classes (see Chapter 14).

C++ does not use the contract model, so an instantiation can fail by causing a compilation error in the template definition. This makes it more difficult to supply templates as proprietary software components.

* Generic subprogram parameters in Ada

Ada allows generic parameters to be subprograms. The sort example can be written:

```
generic
    type Item is private;
    type Item_Array is array(Integer range <>) of Item;
    with function "<"(X, Y: in Item) return Boolean;
procedure Sort(A: Item_Array);
```

The contract is now extended to require that a Boolean function be supplied for the operator "<". Since the comparison operator is supplied, Item need no longer be restricted to discrete types for which the operator is predefined. The keyword private means that any type upon which assignment and equality are defined can be supplied during instantiation:

```
type Rec is record ... end record;
type Rec_Array is array(Integer range <>) of Rec;
function "<"(R1, R2: in Rec) return Boolean;

procedure Rec_Sort(A: Rec_Array) is new Sort(Rec, Rec_Array, "<");
```

Within the Sort subprogram, assignment is the usual bitwise assignment of
the record values, and when two records must be compared the function "<"
is called. This programmer-supplied function will decide if one record value
is smaller than another.

The contract model of Ada is very powerful: types, constants, variables,
pointers, arrays, subprograms and packages (in Ada 95) can be used as
generic parameters.

10.4 Variant records

Variant records are used when it is necessary to interpret a value in several
different ways at run-time. Common examples are:

- Messages in a communications system and parameter blocks in operating system calls. Usually, the first field of the record is a code whose
  value determines the number and types of the remaining fields in the
  record.

- Heterogeneous data structures, such as a tree which may contain nodes
  of various types.

To solve these types of problems, programming languages introduce a
new category of types called *variant records* which have *alternative* lists of
fields. Thus a variable may initially contain a value of one variant and later be
assigned a value of another variant with a completely different set of fields.
In addition to the alternative fields, there may be fields which are common
to all records of this type; such fields usually include a code which is used by
the program to determine which variant is actually being used. For example,
suppose that we wish to create a variant record whose fields may be either
an array or a record:

```
typedef int Arr[5];                                          [C]
typedef struct {
    float   f1;
    int     i1;
} Rec;
```

Let us first define a type that encodes the variant:

```
typedef enum {Record_Code, Array_Code} Codes;                    C
```

Now a *union type* in C can be used to create a variant record which can itself
be embedded into a structure that includes the common tag field:

```
typedef struct {                                                 C
    Codes code;                  /* Common tag field */
    union {                      /* Union with alternative fields */
        Arr a;                   /* Array alternative */
        Rec r;                   /* Record alternative */
    } data;
} S_Type;

S_Type s;
```

From a syntactical point of view, this is just ordinary nesting of records
and arrays within other records. The difference is in the implementation:
the field data is allocated enough memory to contain the larger of the array
field a or the record field r (Figure 10.1). Since enough memory is allocated

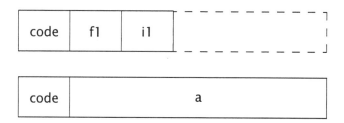

Figure 10.1 Variant records

to accommodate the largest possible field, variant records can be extremely
wasteful of memory if one alternative is very large and the others small:

```
union {                                                          C
    int a[1000];
    float f;
    char c;
};
```

At the cost of complicating the programming, the best solution in this case
is to use a pointer to the long fields.

The assumption underlying variant records is that exactly one of the fields of the union is meaningful at any one time, unlike an ordinary record where all fields exist simultaneously:

```
if (s.code == Array_Code)                                        C
    i = s.data.a[5];              /* Access first variant */
else
    i = s.data.r.i1;             /* Access second variant */
```

The main problem with variant records is that they can potentially cause serious bugs. It is possible to treat a value of one type as if it were a value of any other type (say to access a floating-point number as an integer), since the union construction enables the program to access the same bit string in different ways. In fact, Pascal programmers use variant records to do type conversion which is not directly supported in the language. In the above example, the situation is even worse because it is possible to access memory locations which have no meaning at all: the field **s.data.r** might be 8 bytes long to accommodate the two numbers, while the field **s.data.a** might be 20 bytes long to accommodate ten integers. If a valid record is stored in **s.data.r**, **s.data.a[5]** is meaningless.

Ada does not allow variant records to be used to break type checking. The "code" field that we used in the example is now a required field called the *discriminant*, and accesses to the variant fields are checked against the value of the discriminant. The discriminant appears as a "parameter" to the type:

```
type Codes is (Record_Code, Array_Code);                        Ada

type S_Type(Code: Codes) is
    record
        case Code is
            when Record_Code => R: Rec;
            when Array_Code => A: Arr;
        end case;
    end record;
```

and a record must be declared with a specific discriminant so that the compiler can know exactly how much memory to allocate:

```
S1: S_Type(Record_Code);                                        Ada
S2: S_Type(Array_Code);
```

Alternatively, a pointer to the variant record can be declared and the discriminant set at run-time:

```
type Ptr is access S_Type;                              Ada

P: Ptr := new S_Type(Record_Code);
I := P.R.I1;                        -- OK
I := P.A(5);                        -- Error
```

The first of the assignment statements is correct because the discriminant of the record P.all is Record_Code which ensures that the field R exists, while the second causes a run-time exception because the discriminant does not match the requested field.

The basic rule concerning discriminants in Ada is that they can be read but not written, so that the type checking cannot be bypassed. This also means that memory can be allocated exactly according to the variant chosen, rather than always allocating according to the largest variant.

* *Unconstrained records in Ada*

In addition to the constrained records whose variant is fixed when the variable is created, Ada allows the declaration of *unconstrained records* which allow a type-safe way of assigning values of different variants to a variable during the execution of a program:

```
S1, S2: S_Type;                    -- Unconstrained records

S1 := (Record_Code, 4.5);
S2 := (Array_Code, 1..10 => 17);
S1 := S2;                          -- Assign a different variant to S1
                                   -- S2 is larger than S1 !
```

Two rules ensure that the type checking is not broken:

- A default value must be given for the discriminant to ensure that initially the record has a valid discriminant:

  ```
  type S_Type(Code: Codes := Record_Code) is ...
  ```

- The discriminant field cannot be changed by itself. Only assignment of a valid value to the entire record is acceptable as shown in the example.

There are two possible implementations of unconstrained records. It is possible to create every variable with the maximum size needed to hold any variant. Alternatively, implicit heap allocation can be used so that when it is required to assign a large value to a variable, memory can be freed and reallocated. Most implementations choose the first method: it is both simpler and does not use implicit heap allocation which is undesirable in many applications.

10.5 Dynamic dispatching

Suppose that each variant of the record S_Type is to be processed by its own subprogram. A case-statement must be used to *dispatch* to the appropriate subprogram:

```
procedure Dispatch(S: S_Type) is                                    Ada
begin
    case S.Code is
        when Record_Code => Process_Rec(S);
        when Array_Code => Process_Array(S);
    end case;
end Dispatch;
```

Suppose now further that during modification of the program, it is necessary to add an additional variant to the record. The modifications to the program are not difficult: add a code to the type Codes, add an alternative to the case-statement in Dispatch, and add the new processing subprogram. As easy as these modifications are, they can be problematic in large systems because they require that the *source* code of existing, well-tested program components be modified and recompiled. Additionally, retesting is probably necessary to ensure that the modification of the global enumeration type does not have unintended side-effects.

The solution is to arrange for "dispatching" code to be part of the run-time system of the language, rather than explicitly programmed as shown above. This is called dynamic polymorphism, since it is now possible to call a general routine Process(S), and the binding of the call to a specific routine can be delayed until run-time when the current tag of S can be evaluated. This polymorphism is supported by *virtual functions* in C++ and by subprograms with *class-wide parameters* in Ada 95 (see Chapter 14).

10.6 Exercises

1. Why doesn't C++ use the result type to distinguish overloaded functions?

2. What problems does overloading pose for the linker?

3. In C++, the operators "++" and "--" can be both prefix and postfix. What are the implications for overloading and how does C++ cope with these operators?

4. Neither Ada nor C++ allows overloading to modify the precedence or associativity of an operator; why?

5. Write a template sort program in C++.

6. Write a generic sort program in Ada and use it to sort an array of records.

7. The first generic sort program defined the item type as (<>). Can Long_Integer be used in an instantiation of this procedure? How about Float?

8. Write a program that maintains a heterogeneous queue, that is, a queue whose nodes can contain values of more than one type. Each node will be a variant record with alternative fields for Boolean, integer and character values.

11 Exceptions

11.1 Exception handling requirements

A run-time error is called an *exception*. When programs were used only for offline computation, an appropriate response to an exception was simply to print an error message and terminate. However, the response to an exception in an interactive environment cannot be limited to notification, but must also include recovery to the point that the user can retry the computation or at least choose another option. Software that is used in embedded systems such as aircraft must perform error recovery without human intervention. Exception handling has not been routinely supported within programming languages until recently; rather, facilities supplied by the operating system have been used. This section will describe some of the exception handling mechanisms that exist in modern programming languages.

Error recovery does not come for free. There is always the cost of the extra data structures and algorithms needed to identify and handle the exceptions. In addition, it is often overlooked that exception handling code is itself a program component, and may contain bugs that can cause problems that are more serious than the original exception! It is also extremely difficult to identify error-causing situations and to test the exception handling code, because it may be difficult, if not impossible, to create the error situation.

What makes a good exception-handling facility?

- There should be very little overhead if no exception occurs.

- Exception handling should be both easy to use and safe.

The first requirement is more important than it may seem. Since we assume that exceptions generally *do not* occur, the overhead to the application should be minimal. Once an exception does occur, the overhead to process it is usually not an important consideration. The second requirement says that since exceptions occur infrequently, no great programming effort should be required to implement an exception handler; it goes without saying that the exception handler facility should not use constructs likely to cause bugs.

One warning to the programmer: an exception handler is *not* a replacement for an if-statement. If a situation is likely to arise, it is not an error and should be explicitly programmed. For example, a data structure such as a list or tree is very likely to be empty, and this situation should be explicitly checked using an if-statement:

> if Ptr.Next = null then ... else ...   Ada

On the other hand, stack overflow or floating-point underflow are very rare and almost certainly indicate a bug in the computation.

Elementary exception handling is defined in some languages by allowing the user to define a block of code to be executed before program termination. This is useful for cleaning up (closing files, etc.) before exiting the program. In C, the setjmp/longjmp facility enables the user to define additional points within the program that the exception handler can return to. This type of exception handling is sufficient for ensuring that the program gracefully exits or restarts, but is not flexible enough to enable detailed exception handling to be programmed.

Note that according to our definition of an exception as an unexpected, run-time fault, there are fewer "exceptions" in C than in a language such as Ada. Firstly, errors such as exceeding array bounds are not defined in the C language; they are simply *bugs* that cannot be "handled". Secondly, since C does not have a flexible exception-handling facility, every language facility that is requested through a subprogram returns a code indicating if the request was successful or not. Thus an Ada memory allocation new can cause an exception if there is not enough memory, while in C, malloc returns a code that must be explicitly tested. The implications for programming style are: in Ada new can be used routinely and exception handling designed separately, while in C you should write an *envelope* subprogram around malloc so that exception handling can be centrally designed and programmed, rather than allowing each team member to test (or forget to test) for lack of memory:

```
void* get_memory(int n)                                   C
{
    void* p = malloc(n);
    if (p == 0)                    /* Allocation failed */
        ...                        /* Do something or abort gracefully */
    return p;
}
```

11.2 Exceptions in PL/I

PL/I was the first language to include a facility for exception handling within
the language: the *on-unit*. An on-unit is a block of code that is executed when
an exception occurs; upon termination of the on-unit, the computation is
resumed. The problem with the PL/I on-unit is that it interferes with routine
computation. Suppose that an on-unit for floating-point underflow is in force.
Then *every* floating-point expression is potentially affected by the on-unit;
more exactly, every floating-point expression includes an implicit call to and
return from the on-unit. This makes it difficult to perform optimizations
such as maintaining values in registers or extracting common subexpressions.

11.3 Exceptions in Ada

Ada defines a very elegant exception handling mechanism which has served
as a model for other languages.

There are four predefined exceptions in Ada:

Constraint_Error Violation of a constraint such as an array indexing not in
bounds or a variant field selection not matching the discriminant.

Storage_Error Not enough memory.

Program_Error Violation of a language rule, for example, leaving a function
without executing a return-statement.

Tasking_Error Errors occurring during task communication (see Chapter 12).

Of course, Constraint_Error is by far the most common exception given the
strong type checking of Ada. In addition, the programmer can declare exceptions which are treated exactly like predefined exceptions.

When an exception occurs, in Ada terminology when an exception is *raised*,
a block of code called an *exception handler* is called. Unlike PL/I, executing
an exception handler *terminates* the enclosing procedure. Since the handler
does not return to the normal computation, there is no interference with
optimization. Unlike global error handlers in C, Ada exception handling
is extremely flexible since exception handlers can be associated with any
subprogram:

```
procedure Main is
    procedure Proc is
        P: Node_Ptr;
    begin
        P := new Node;           -- Exception may be raised
        Statement_1;             -- Skip if exception is raised
    exception
        when Storage_Error =>
            ...                  -- Exception handler
    end Proc;
begin
    Proc;
    Statement_2;                 -- Skip if exception is propagated
exception
    when Storage_Error =>
        ...                      -- Exception handler
end Main;
```

After the last executable statement of a subprogram, the keyword **exception** introduces a sequence of exception handlers—one for each distinct exception. When the exception is raised, execution of the statements in the procedure is abandoned and the statements of the exception handler are executed instead. When the exception handler is completed, the procedure terminates *normally*. In the example: the allocator may raise the exception Storage_Error, in which case Statement_1 is skipped and the exception handler is executed. Upon completion of the exception handler, the procedure terminates normally and the main program continues with Statement_2.

The semantics of exception handling allow the programmer great flexibility in defining exception handling:

- If an exception is not handled within the procedure, the procedure is abandoned and the exception is raised again at the point of call. In the absence of an exception handler in Proc, the exception would be reraised in Main, Statement_2 would be skipped and the exception handler in Main executed.

- If an exception is raised *during* the execution of the handler, the handler is abandoned and the exception is raised again at the point of call.

- The programmer can choose to raise the same or another exception at the point of call rather than allowing the procedure to terminate normally. For example, we might want to translate a predefined exception

such as Storage_Error to an application-defined exception. This is done
by using an explicit raise-statement in the exception handler:

```
exception
    when Storage_Error =>
        ...                      -- Exception handler, then
        raise Overflow;          --    raise Overflow in caller
```

A handler for others can be used to handle all exceptions that are not mentioned in previous handlers.

If there is no handler for an exception even in the main program, the exception is handled by the run-time system which usually aborts the execution
of the program with a message. It is good programming practice to ensure
that all exceptions are handled, at least at the level of the main program.

The definition of exceptions in Ada 83 did not allow the exception handler
access to any information about the exception. If more than one exception
is handled identically, there is no way even to know which one occurred:

```
exception
    when Ex_1 | Ex_2 | Ex_3 =>
        -- Which exception has occurred ?
```

Ada 95 allows an exception handler to have a parameter:

```
exception
    when Ex: others =>
```

Whenever an exception occurs, the parameter Ex will contain the identity of
the exception and predefined procedures enable the programmer to retrieve
information about the exception. This information can also be programmer-
defined (see the Language Reference Manual 11.4.1).

Implementation

The implementation of exception handlers is very efficient. A procedure that
contains exception handlers will have an extra field in its activation record
pointing to the handlers (Figure 11.1). It takes just one instruction during
procedure call to set up this field, and that is the only overhead there is if
no exception occurs. If an exception is raised, finding a handler may require
extensive computation to search the dynamic chain, but since exceptions
rarely happen this is not a problem. Recall our warning not to use exception
handlers as a replacement for a much more efficient if-statement.

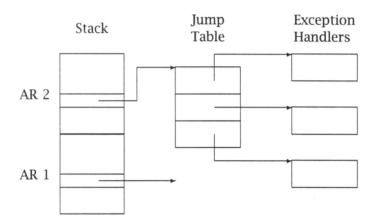

Figure 11.1 Implementation of exception handlers

11.4 Exceptions in C++

Exception handling in C++ is very similar to Ada in that an exception can be explicitly raised, handled by the appropriate handler (if any) and then the block (subprogram) is terminated. The differences are:

- Rather than attaching an exception handler to a subprogram, a special syntax is used to indicate a group of statements to which a handler applies.

- The exceptions are identified by a parameter type instead of by name. There is a special syntax equivalent to others for handling exceptions not explicitly mentioned.

- Exception families can be constructed using inheritance (Chapter 14).

- If an exception is not handled in Ada, a system-defined handler is invoked. In C++, the programmer can define a function terminate() which is called when an exception is not handled.

In the following example, the try block identifies the scope of a sequence of statements for which exception handlers (denoted by catch-blocks) are active. The throw-statement causes an exception to be raised; in this case it will be handled by the second catch-block since the string parameter of the throw-statement matches the char* parameter of the second catch-block:

```
    void proc()
    {
        ...                          // Exceptions not handled here
        try {
            ...
            throw "Invalid data";    // Raise exception
            ...
        }
        catch (int i) {
            ...                      // Exception handler
        }
        catch (char *s) {
            ...                      // Exception handler
        }
        catch (...) {                // Other exceptions
            ...                      // Exception handler
        }
    }
```

In both Ada and C++, it is possible that an exception handler is called upon to handle an exception which it cannot see, because the exception is declared in a package body (Ada), or the type is declared as private in a class (C++). If not handled by others (or ...), the exception will be reraised repeatedly until finally being processed as an unhandled exception. C++ has a way of preventing such unbounded behavior by specifying on a subprogram declaration exactly which exceptions it is willing to handle:

```
    void proc() throw (t1, t2, t2);
```

Such *exception specifications* mean that an unlisted exception, which is raised but not handled in proc (or any subprogram called by proc), immediately calls the globally defined function unexpected() rather than continuing the search for a handler. In large systems, this construct is useful to document the full interface to subprograms, including the exceptions that it will propagate.

11.5 Error handling in Eiffel

Assertions

Eiffel's approach to exception handling is based on the concept that you shouldn't make errors in the first place. Of course all programmers strive for this, the difference being that Eiffel includes support within the language for specifying the correctness of a program. This is based on the concept of *assertions*, which are logical formulas commonly used for formalizing a program but not part of the program itself (Section 2.2).

Every subprogram (called a *routine* in Eiffel) can have assertions associated with it. For example, a subprogram for computing the result and the remainder of integer division would be written as follows:

```
integer_division(dividend, divisor, result, remainder: INTEGER) is
    require
        divisor > 0
    do
        from
            result = 0; remainder = dividend;
        invariant
            dividend = result*divisor + remainder
        variant
            remainder
        until
            remainder < divisor
        loop
            remainder := remainder – divisor;
            result := result + 1;
        end
    ensure
        dividend = result*divisor + remainder;
        remainder < divisor
end
```

The require-clause is called the *precondition* which specifies what the subprogram expects to be true about the input data. The do-clause contains the executable statements that comprise the subprogram. The ensure-clause, called the *postcondition*, specifies what the subprogram promises will be true if the do-clause is executed on data that satisfies the precondition. In this case it is trivial to see that the postcondition is satisfied because it follows immediately from the invariant (Section 6.6) and the until-clause.

On a larger scale, you can attach an invariant to a class (Section 15.4). For example, a class that implements a stack using an array would include an invariant of the form:

```
invariant
    top >= 0;
    top < max;
```

All the subprograms of the class must ensure that the invariant is true when an object of the class is created and that every subprogram maintains the truth of the invariant. For example, the pop subprogram would have a precondition top>0, otherwise executing the statement:

```
top := top - 1
```

would falsify the invariant.

Enumeration types

Another use of invariants is to ensure type-safety that is achieved in other languages by the use of enumeration types. The Ada declarations:

```
type Heat is (Off, Low, Medium, High);          Ada
Dial: Heat;
```

would be written in Eiffel as an ordinary integer variable, with named constants:

```
Dial:       Integer;
Off:        Integer is 0;
Low:        Integer is 1;
Medium:     Integer is 2;
High:       Integer is 3;
```

An invariant will ensure that meaningless assignments are not done:

```
invariant
    Off <= Dial <= High
```

The latest version of Eiffel includes *unique constants* which are like enumeration names in that their actual values are assigned by the compiler. However, they are still integers so type safety must still be enforced using assertions: a postcondition should be attached to any subprogram that modifies variables whose values are to be limited to these constants.

Design by contract

Assertions are the basis of what Eiffel calls *design by contract*, meaning that the designer of the subprogram makes an implicit contract with the user of the subprogram: if you supply a state which satisfies the precondition, then I promise to transform the state so that it satisfies the postcondition. Similarly, a class maintains the truth of its invariants. If contracts are used throughout the system, then nothing can ever go wrong.

In practice, of course, the implementor of a subprogram may fail to fulfil the contract (either because the statements don't satisfy the assertions or because the wrong assertions were chosen). To support debugging and testing, an Eiffel implementation allows the user to request that assertions be checked upon subprogram entry and exit, so that the execution can be halted if an assertion is false.

Exceptions

Eiffel subprograms can have exception handlers:

```
proc is
    do
        ...                        -- Exception may be raised
    rescue
        ...                        -- Exception handler
    end;
```

When an exception occurs, the subprogram is deemed to have failed and the statements following the rescue-clause are executed. Unlike Ada, when the exception handler terminates the exception is raised again in the calling program. This is equivalent to terminating an Ada exception handler by a raise-statement, which reraises in the calling subprogram the same exception that caused the handler to be entered.

The motivation behind this design is that a subprogram is supposed to satisfy a postcondition (and/or a class invariant). If it fails, you may want to cause a notification to be sent, but you certainly *cannot* satisfy the postcondition and you have failed in the task that the calling subprogram expects you to do. In other words, if you know how to fix the problem and satisfy the postcondition, then the fix should be part of the subprogram! This is similar to our advice not to use exceptions as replacements for an if-statement.

To assist in fixing a failed computation, the exception handler may make some modification, and then ask the subprogram to try again from the beginning by including the keyword retry as the last statement of the handler. The subsequent execution may then either succeed or fail. The principle is that a successful subprogram execution must terminate normally and fulfil its postcondition; otherwise, the execution fails.

An Ada exception handler can be simulated in Eiffel as follows, though this goes against the philosophy of the language:

```
proc is
    local
        tried: Boolean;          -- Initialized to false;
    do
        if not tried then
            -- Regular processing
            -- Raise exception
        else
            -- "Exception handler"
        end
    rescue
        if not tried then
            tried := true;       -- Don't retry twice
            retry
        end
end;
```

11.6 Exercises

1. The package Ada.Exceptions in Ada 95 defines types and subprograms for associating information with exceptions. Compare these constructs with the C++ constructs throw and catch.

2. Show that it is possible for an Ada exception to be raised outside the scope of the exception. (Hint: see Chapter 13.) How can you handle an exception whose declaration is not in scope?

3. Show how exception specifications in C++:

    void proc() throw (t1, t2, t2);

   can be simulated using multiple catch-blocks.

4. Show how to simulate an Ada exception in Eiffel, that is the execution of the Eiffel exception handler will not reraise the exception in the calling subprogram.

5. Study the class EXCEPTIONS in Eiffel and compare it with Ada exception handlers.

12 Concurrency

12.1 What is concurrency?

Computers with multiple CPU's can execute a set of programs or program components in *parallel*. A computation can thus be completed in less *elapsed* (clock) time than on a computer with a single CPU, at the expense of additional CPU time for synchronization and communication. It is also possible for several programs to share a computer with a single CPU by switching the CPU so fast from one program to another that it appears that they are executing simultaneously. Even though CPU-switching does not implement true parallelism, it is convenient to design and program software for these systems as if the execution of the programs is actually in parallel. *Concurrency* is a term used for the simultaneous execution of more than one program without specifying if the computation is truly or only apparently parallel.

Concurrency is familiar to most programmers in one or more of these forms:

- *Multi-programming* operating systems enable more than one person to use the computer at the same time. Such *time-sharing* systems implemented on mainframe computers and minicomputers were for many years the only way of supplying computational facilities to a large community like a university.

- *Multi-tasking* operating systems enable components of a single program (or programs of a single user) to proceed concurrently. With the advent of personal computers, multi-programming computers are less common, but even a single person will often need multi-tasking to perform different tasks simultaneously, such as printing in the background while interactively writing a paper.

- *Embedded systems* in factories, transportation systems and medical facilities control sets of sensors and actuators in "real-time". These systems are characterized by the requirement that they perform relatively small amounts of computations at very frequent intervals: each sensor needs to be read and interpreted, then the program must decide upon an appropriate action, and finally items of data are formatted and sent to the actuators. To implement embedded systems, multi-tasking operating systems are used to coordinate among dozens of separate computations.

Designing and programming a concurrent system is extremely difficult, and entire textbooks are devoted to various aspects of the problem: system architecture, task scheduling, hardware interfaces, etc. This purpose of this section is to give an overview of *programming language* support for concurrency, which traditionally has been provided by hardware and operating system functions.

A *concurrent program* consists of one or more program components called *processes* that can potentially be executed in parallel. Concurrent programs have to deal with two problems:

Synchronization Even though the processes execute concurrently, occasionally one process will have to synchronize execution with other processes. The most important form of synchronization is mutual exclusion: two processes must not access the same resource (such as a disk or a shared table) simultaneously.

Communication Processes are not totally independent; they must send data to each other. For example, in a flight control program the process that reads the altitude sensor must send the result to the process that computes the autopilot algorithms.

12.2 Shared memory

The simplest model for concurrent programming is the *shared-memory* model (Figure 12.1). Two or more processes can access the same area in memory (though they may also have their own private memory). Suppose that we have two processes that are trying to update the same variable in shared-memory:[1]

```
procedure Main is                                    Ada
    N: Integer := 0;
    task T1;
    task T2;
```

---

[1]In Ada processes are called *tasks*.

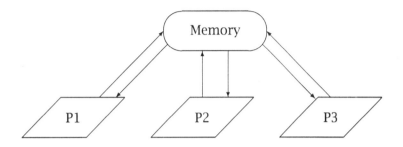

Figure 12.1 Shared-memory model for concurrency

```
task body T1 is
begin
    for I in 1..100 loop N := N + 1; end loop;
end T1;

task body T2 is
begin
    for I in 1..100 loop N := N + 1; end loop;
end T2;

begin
    null;
end Main;
```

Consider now the implementation of the assignment statement:

```
load       R1,N              Load from memory
add        R1,#1             Increment register
store      R1,N              Store to memory
```

If each execution of the loop body in T1 is completed before T2 executes its loop body, N will be incremented 200 times. However, each task may be executed on a separate computer with a separate set of registers. In this case, the following sequence of events may take place:

- T1 loads N into its register R1 (value is n).

- T2 loads N into its register R1 (value is n).

- T1 increments R1 (value is $n + 1$).

- T2 increments R1 (value is $n + 1$).

- T1 stores the contents of its R1 into N (value is $n + 1$).

- T2 stores the contents of its R1 into N (value is $n + 1$).

The result will be that the execution of the two loop bodies will only increment N by one. The final value of N can be anywhere between 100 and 200, depending on the relative speeds of the two processors.

It is important to realize that this can occur even on a computer that implements multi-tasking by sharing a single CPU. When the CPU is switched from one process to another, the registers that the blocked process used are saved and then restored when it is allowed to continue.

In the theory of concurrency, the execution of a concurrent program is defined as *any interleaving* of the *atomic instructions* of the tasks. An atomic instruction is simply one that cannot be "partially" executed or interrupted to allow another task to proceed. In the shared-memory model of concurrency, load from memory and store to memory are atomic instructions.

Within the framework of interleaved computations, languages and systems that support concurrency differ in the level of atomic instructions that are defined. The implementation of the instruction must ensure that it is executed atomically. In the case of shared-memory load and store, this is ensured by the memory interface hardware. Higher-level atomic instructions are implemented within the underlying run-time system, supported by special instructions in the CPU.

12.3   The mutual exclusion problem

The *mutual exclusion problem* for concurrent programs is a generalization of the above example. Each one of a set of tasks is assumed to have its computation divided into a *critical section* and a *non-critical section* which are executed repeatedly:

```
task body T_i is                                        Ada
begin
    loop
        Prologue;
        Critical_Section;
        Epilogue;
        Non_Critical_Section;
    end loop;
end T_i;
```

To solve the mutual exclusion problem, we must find sequences of code (called the *prologue* and the *epilogue*) such that the program satisfies the following requirements, which must hold for *all* interleavings of the instruction sequences of the set of tasks:

Mutual exclusion At most one task is executing its critical section at any time.

No deadlock There is always at least one task that is able to continue its execution.

Liveness If a task wishes to enter its critical section, *eventually* it will do so.

Fairness Access to the critical section is granted "fairly".

There are solutions to the mutual exclusion problem using just load and store as atomic instructions, but the solutions are complicated and beyond the scope of this book, and we refer the reader to textbooks on concurrent programming.

E.W. Dijkstra defined a higher-level synchronization abstraction called a *semaphore* that trivially solves the problem. A semaphore S is a variable which has an integer value; two *atomic* instructions are defined on semaphores:

```
Wait(S):    when S > 0 do S := S - 1;
Signal(S):  S := S + 1;
```

Wait(S) instruction blocks the process that executes it until the value of S is positive. Note that since the instruction is atomic, once the process checks that S is positive, it decrements S before any other process executes an instruction. Similarly, Signal(S) is executed atomically with no possibility of another process interrupting between the load and the store of S.

The mutual exclusion problem is solved as follows:

```
procedure Main is                                          Ada
    S: Semaphore := 1;
    task T_i;                        -- One of many
    task body T_i is
    begin
        loop
            Wait(S);
            Critical_Section;
            Signal(S);
            Non_Critical_Section;
        end loop;
    end T_i;
begin
    null;
end Main;
```

We leave it to the reader to check that this is a correct solution. Of course
the trivial solution is achieved by placing the burden on the implementor of
the run-time system.

12.4 Monitors and protected variables

The problem with the semaphore and similar facilities supplied by the operating system is that they are not structured. If you forget to match each Wait
with a Signal the program can lose synchronization or deadlock. To solve the
lack of structuring, a concept called *monitors* was defined and implemented
in several programming languages. A monitor is a grouping of data and
subprograms which has the following properties:

- The data can only be accessed by the subprograms of the monitor.

- At most one monitor subprogram can be executed at any one time. A
  process attempting to call a monitor procedure while another process
  is already executing within the monitor will cause the new process to
  be suspended.

Since all synchronization and communication is done within the monitor,
potential concurrency errors are limited to the programming of the monitor
itself; user processes cannot cause additional errors. The interface to a
monitor is similar to that of an operating system in that a process calls the
monitor to request and receive a service. Synchronization among processes

is automatically ensured. The disadvantage of the monitor is that it is a centralized facility.

The original concurrency model in Ada (described in Section 12.7 below) is quite sophisticated and it turned out to have too much overhead for simple mutual exclusion problems. To correct this, in Ada 95 a monitor-like facility was introduced called *protected variables*. For example, a semaphore can be simulated as a protected variable. This interface defines the two operations, but keeps the integer value of the semaphore *private*, which means that it is not accessible to the users of the semaphore:

Ada

```
protected type Semaphore is
    entry Wait;
    procedure Signal;
private
    Value: Integer := 1;
end Semaphore;
```

The implementation of the semaphore is:

Ada

```
protected body Semaphore is
    entry Wait when Value > 0 is
    begin
        Value := Value - 1;
    end Wait;
    procedure Signal is
    begin
        Value := Value + 1;
    end Signal;
end Semaphore;
```

The execution of both the entry and the procedure are mutually exclusive: at most one task will execute an operation of a protected variable at any time. An entry also has a *barrier*, which is a Boolean expression. A task trying to execute an entry will be blocked if the expression is false. Whenever a protected operation is completed, all barriers will be re-evaluated and a task whose barrier is now true will be allowed to execute. In the example, when Signal increments Value, the barrier on Wait will now be true and a blocked task will be allowed to execute the entry body.

12.5 Message passing

As computer hardware has become less expensive, *distributed programming* has become important. Programs are decomposed into concurrent components which are executed on separate computers. The shared-memory model is no longer appropriate; instead synchronization and communication are based on *synchronous message passing* (Figure 12.2). In this model, a commu-

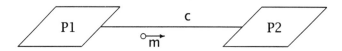

Figure 12.2 Concurrency by message passing (occam)

nications channel c can exist between any two processes. When one process sends a message m on the channel, the process is suspended until the other process is ready to receive. Symmetrically, a process that wishes to receive a message is suspended until the sending process is ready. This suspension is used to synchronize the processes.

The synchronous model of concurrency can be implemented within a programming language, or as an operating system service (pipes, sockets, etc.). Models differ in the ways that processes address each other and in the manner of message passing. We now describe three languages that chose radically different ways to implement synchronous concurrency.

12.6 occam

The synchronous message model was originally developed by C.A.R. Hoare in a formalism called *CSP* (Communicating Sequential Processes). The practical implementation is in the language occam[2] which was developed for programming the *transputer*—a hardware architecture for distributed processing.

In occam, addressing is fixed and message passing is one-way as shown in Figure 12.2. A *channel* has a name and may only be used for sending from one process and receiving on another:

---

[2]occam is a trademark of INMOS Groups of Companies. Note that the initial letter is not capitalized.

```
CHAN OF INT c :
PAR
    INT m :
    SEQ
        -- Create integer value m
        c ! m
    INT v :
    SEQ
        c ? v
        -- Use integer value in v
```

c is declared as a channel that can pass integers. The channel must be used in exactly two processes: one process contains output instructions (c!) and the other input instructions (c?).

The syntax of occam is interesting. In other languages, the "default" mode of execution is sequential execution of a group of statements and a special notation is used for parallelism. In occam, parallel and sequential computation are considered equally important, so you have to explicitly state using PAR and SEQ how each group of (indented) statements is to be executed.

Even though each channel connects exactly two processes, occam allows a process to simultaneously wait for communications on any one of several channels:

```
[10]CHAN OF INT c :            -- Array of channels
ALT i = 0 FOR 10
    c[i] ? v
    -- Use integer value in v
```

This process waits for communications on any of ten channels and the processing of the received value can depend on the channel index.

The advantage of point-to-point communications is that it is extremely efficient because all addressing information is "compiled-in". No run-time support is required other than to synchronize the processes and move the data; on a transputer this is done in hardware. Of course this efficiency is achieved at the cost of lack of flexibility.

12.7 Ada rendezvous

Ada tasks communicate with each other during a *rendezvous*. One task T1 is said to call an *entry* e in another task T2 (Figure 12.3). The called task must execute an accept-statement for the entry:

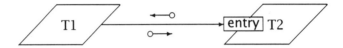

Figure 12.3 Ada tasks and entries

```
accept E(P1: in Integer; P2: out Integer) do
    ...
end E;
```

When a task executes an entry call and there is another task that has executed an accept-statement for the entry, a rendezvous takes place:

- The calling task passes in-parameters to the accepting task and then is blocked.

- The accepting task executes the statements in the accept body.

- The accepting task returns out-parameters to the calling task.

- The calling task is unblocked.

The definition of the rendezvous is symmetrical in that if a task executes an accept-statement and there is no waiting entry call, it will block until some task calls the entry for this accept-statement.

Thus addressing is only in one direction: the calling task must know the name of the accepting task, but the accepting task does not know the name of the calling task. The rationale for this design is to allow the implementation of *servers* which are processes that provide a specific service to any other process. The *client* task must of course know the name of the service it is requesting, while the server task will provide the service to any arbitrary task, and it has no need to know about the client.

A single rendezvous can involve message passing in two directions, because a typical service might be a request for an element from a data structure. The overhead of an additional interaction to return the result would be prohibitive.

The rendezvous mechanism is quite sophisticated: a task can wait simultaneously for different entry calls using the select-statement:

```
select
    accept E1 do ... end E1;
or
    accept E2 do ... end E2;
or
    accept E3 do ... end E3;
end select;
```

Select alternatives can have Boolean expressions called *guards* which enable the task to control which calls it is willing to accept. Timeouts (limiting the time spent waiting for a rendezvous) and polling (checking for an immediate rendezvous) can also be specified. Unlike the ALT construct in occam, an Ada select-statement cannot wait simultaneously on an arbitrary number of entries.

Note the basic difference between protected variables and rendezvous:

- The protected variable is a passive mechanism and its operations are executed by other tasks.

- An accept-statement is executed by the task in which it appears, that is, it performs computation on behalf of other tasks.

Rendezvous would be used to program a server if the server had significant processing to do in *addition* to communication with a client:

```
task Server is
begin
    loop
        select
            accept Put(I: in Item) do
                -- Save I in data structure
            end Put;
        or
            accept Get(I: out Item) do
                -- Retrieve I from data structure
            end Get;
        end select;
        -- Maintain data structure
    end loop;
end Server;
```

The server saves and retrieves items from a data structure, but after each operation it perform additional processing on the data structure, for example, logging the modifications. There is no reason to block other tasks while this time-consuming processing is being done.

The Ada concurrency mechanism is extremely flexible, but the flexibility is bought at the price of less efficient communication than with the occam point-to-point channels. On the other hand, it is practically impossible to implement a flexible server process in occam, since each additional client process needs a separate named channel, and this requires modification of the server code.

12.8   Linda

Linda is not a programming language as such but a model for concurrency that can be added to an existing programming language. Instead of one-way (Ada) or two-way (occam) addressing, Linda does not use any addressing between concurrent processes! Instead a process can choose to send a message to a global *Tuple Space*. The name is derived from the fact that each message is a tuple, that is a sequence of one or more values of possibly different types. For example:

    (True, 5.6, 'C', False)

is a 4-tuple consisting of values that are Boolean, float, character and again Boolean.

There are three operations that access the Tuple Space:

out Put a tuple in tuple space.

in Block until a matching tuple exists, then remove it (Figure 12.4).

read Block until a matching tuple exists (but do not remove it).

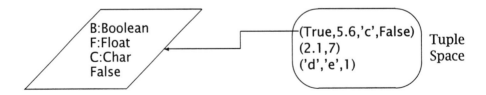

Figure 12.4 Linda tuple-space

Synchronization is achieved because the **in**- and **read**-commands must specify a tuple-signature: the number of elements and their types. Only if a tuple exists with a matching signature can the receive operation be executed; otherwise, the process is suspended. In addition, one or more elements of the tuple can be explicitly specified. If a value is given in the signature it must match the value at the same position of a tuple; if a type is given it can match any value of that type in the position. For example, all of the following statements will remove the first tuple in the Tuple Space of Figure 12.4:

```
in(True, 5.6, 'C', False)
in(B: Boolean, 5.6, 'C', False)
in(True, F: Float, 'C', B2: Boolean)
```

The second in-statement will return the value True in the formal parameter B; the third in-statement will return the values 5.6 in F and False in B2.

The Tuple Space can be used for dispatching computational jobs to processes that may reside on different computers. A tuple ("job", J, C) will indicate that job J should be assigned to computer C. Each computer will block waiting for a job:

```
in("job", J: Jobs, 4);          -- Computer 4 waits for a job
```

The dispatching task will "throw" jobs into the tuple space. The out-statement can also use a formal parameter to indicate that it doesn't care which computer does each job:

```
out("job", 6, C: Computers);    -- Job 6 to any computer
```

The advantage of the Linda model is its extreme flexibility. Note that a process may place a tuple in the tuple-space and terminate; only later will another process retrieve the tuple. Thus a Linda program is distributed in *time* as well as being distributed in *space* (among processes that may be on separate CPU's). Contrast this with Ada and occam which require processes to directly communicate with each other. The disadvantage of the Linda model is the overhead involved in maintaining the Tuple Space which requires potentially unbounded global memory. Even though the tuple-space is global, sophisticated algorithms have been developed for distributing it among many processors.

12.9 Exercises

1. Study the following attempt to solve the mutual-exclusion problem under the shared memory model where B1 and B2 are global Boolean variables with initial value False:

```
task body T1 is                                    Ada
begin
   loop
       B1 := True;
       loop
           exit when not B2;
           B1 := False;
           B1 := True;
       end loop;
       Critical_Section;
       B1 := False;
       Non_Critical_Section;
   end loop;
end T1;

task body T2 is
begin
   loop
       B2 := True;
       loop
           exit when not B1;
           B2 := False;
           B2 := True;
       end loop;
       Critical_Section;
       B2 := False;
       Non_Critical_Section;
   end loop;
end T2;
```

What is the intended meaning of the variables B1 and B2? Is it possible for both tasks to be in their critical sections at any time? Can the program deadlock? Is liveness achieved?

2. Check the semaphore solution to the mutual exclusion problem. Show that in *all* instruction interleavings, at most one task is in the critical section at any time. What about deadlock, liveness and fairness?

3. What happens in the solution to the mutual exclusion problem if the semaphore is given an initial value greater than 1?

4. Try to precisely define fairness. What is the connection between fairness and priority?

5. How would you implement a semaphore?

6. How does a Linda job dispatcher ensure that a specific job should go to a specific computer?

7. Write a Linda program for matrix multiplication. Each inner product is a separate "job"; an initial dispatching process fills the tuple space with "jobs"; worker processes remove "jobs" and return results; a final collecting process removes and outputs results.

8. Translate the Linda program for matrix multiplication into Ada. Solve the problem twice: once with separate tasks for the dispatcher and collector, and once with a single task that does both functions within a single **select**-statement.

PART IV

Programming
Large
Systems

13 Program Decomposition

Both beginning programmers and project managers frequently extrapolate from the ease with which one person can write a program, and assume that developing a software system is just as easy. All you have to do is to assemble a team and let them write the program. However, there is a wide gulf between writing (small) programs and creating (large) software systems, and many systems are delivered late, full of bugs and cost several times the original estimate.[1] The topic called *software engineering* deals with methods for organizing and controlling software development teams, and with notations and tools that support phases of the development process aside from programming. These include requirements specification, software design and software testing.

In this chapter and the next two, we will study programming language constructs that are designed to support the creation of large software systems. There is a clear trade-off: the less support the language offers for the development of large systems, the greater is the need for methods, conventions and notations that are external to the language itself. Since a programming language is of course required, it seems reasonable to integrate support for large systems within the language, and to expect the compiler to automate as much of the process as possible. We software engineers are always willing to automate someone else's job, but we often hesitate before adopting automation into programming languages.

The basic problem is: how should a large software system be decomposed into easily manageable components, that can be developed separately and then assembled into a system in which all the components cooperate with each other as planned? The discussion will begin with elementary "mechanical" methods for decomposing a program, and proceed to modern concepts, such as abstract data types and object-oriented programming, which guide

---

[1]The first frustrated project manager to write about these problems was Frederick P. Brooks, Jr., in his delightful and instructive book: *The Mythical Man-Month*, Addison-Wesley, 1972.

the system designer in creating semantically meaningful components.

Before commencing the discussion, a word to readers who are just beginning their study of programming. The concepts will be presented using small examples that fit into a textbook, and your natural reaction may be that these concepts are just unnecessary "bureaucracy". Be assured that generations of programmers have discovered the hard way that such bureaucracy is essential; the only question is whether it is carefully defined and implemented within a standard language, or invented and imposed by management for each new project.

13.1   Separate compilation

Originally, decomposition of programs was done solely to enable the programmer to compile components separately. Given the power of modern computers and the efficiency of compilers, this reason is less important than it used to be, but it is important to study separate compilation because the features that support it are often the same ones used for decomposition of a program into logical components. Even in very large systems which cannot be constructed without separate compilation, the decomposition into components is determined during program design without reference to compilation time. Since such components are usually relative small, the limiting factor in the time it takes to modify a program is usually link time rather than compile time.

Separate compilation in Fortran

When Fortran was developed, programs were fed into a computer using punched cards and there were no disks or program libraries as we know them today.[2] The unit of compilation in Fortran is identical with the unit of execution, namely the subprogram, called *subroutine*. Each subroutine is compiled, not only separately, but *independently*; no information is stored from one compilation to use in a subsequent one.

This means that absolutely no checking is done between the formal parameters and the actual parameters. You can supply a floating-point value for an integer parameter. Even worse, an array is passed as a pointer to the first component and the called subroutine has no way of knowing the size of the array or even the type of the component. It is even possible for a subroutine to attempt to access a non-existent actual parameter. In other

---

[2]When I wrote my first program, I was handed a deck of *binary* punched cards and told that it was the plotter driver!

words, matching formal and actual parameters is the task of the programmer; he/she must supply correct declarations of the parameter types and sizes both in the calling and called subroutines.

Since each subroutine is independently compiled, there is no way to directly share global data declarations. Instead, *common blocks* are defined:

```
subroutine S1
common /block1/ distance(100), speed(100), time(100)
real distance, speed, time
...
end
```

This declaration requests the allocation of 300 memory locations for floating-point values. All declarations for the same block are allocated to the same memory locations, so if another subroutine declares:

```
subroutine S2
common /block1/ speed(200), time(200), distance(200)
integer speed, time, distance
...
end
```

the two subroutines are using different names and different types to access the same memory! Mapping of common blocks is done by memory *location* and not by variable *name*. If a real variable is allocated twice the memory as an integer variable, speed(80) in the subroutine S2 is accessing the same memory as half of the variable distance(40) in S1. The effect is similar to the undisciplined use of union types in C or variant records in Pascal.

Independent compilation and common blocks are unlikely to cause problems for a single programmer writing a small program, but are extremely likely to cause problems in a ten-person team; meetings or inspections must be held to ensure that interfaces are correctly implemented. A partial solution is to use *include*-files especially for common blocks, but you still have to check that you are using the latest version of the include file, and to make sure that some clever programmer doesn't ignore the declarations in the file.

Separate compilation in C

C is unusual among programming languages in that the concept of a source code *file* appears in the language definition and is significant in terms of scope and visibility of identifiers. C encourages separate compilation to such an extent that by default every subprogram and every global variable can be accessed from anywhere in the program.

First some terminology: a *declaration* introduces a name into a program:

```
void proc(void);
```

A name may have many (identical) declarations, but exactly one of them will also be a *definition* which creates an entity of this name: allocates memory for variables or gives the implementation of a subprogram.

The following file contains a main program, as well as a global variable *definition* and a function *declaration*, both of which have external linkage by default:

```
/* File main.c */
int global;                 /* External by default */
int func(int);              /* External by default */

int main(void)
{
    global = 4;
    return func(global);
}
```

In a separate file, the definition (implementation) of the function is given; the variable global is declared again to enable the function to access it:

```
/* File func.c */
extern int global;              /* External, declaration only */

int func(int parm)
{
    return parm + global;
}
```

Note that another declaration of func is not needed, because the definition of the function in this file also serves as a declaration and by default it has external linkage. However, in order for func to access the global variable a declaration is needed, and the specifier extern must be used. If extern is not used, the declaration of global will be taken as a second definition of the variable. A linker error will occur since it is illegal to have two definitions of the same global variable in a program.

Compilation in C is independent in the sense that the result of one compilation is not stored for use by another. If a member of your team accidentally writes:

```
        /* File func.c */
extern float global;              /* External, declaration only */

int func(int parm)                /* External by default */
{
        return parm + global;
}
```

the program can still be compiled and linked, and it is only at run-time that an error occurs. On my computer, the integer value 4 assigned to global in main appears in the file func.c to be a very small floating-point number; when converted back to an integer, it becomes zero and the function returns 4 rather than 8.

As in Fortran a partial solution is to use include files so that the same declarations are accessed in all files. Both an extern declaration for a function or variable and a definition can appear within the same computation. Thus we put all the external declarations in one or more include files, while at most one ".c" file will contain the single definition of each function or variable:

```
        /* File main.h */
extern int global;                /* Declaration only */

        /* File func.h */
extern int func(int parm);        /* Declaration only */

        /* File main.c */
#include   "main.h"
#include   "func.h"
int global;                       /* Definition */
int main(void)
{
        return func(global) + 7;
}

        /* File func.c */
#include   "main.h"
#include   "func.h"
int func(int parm)                /* Definition */
{
        return parm + global;
}
```

static *specifier*

Anticipating the discussion in the next section, we now show how features of
the C decomposition can be used to emulate the module construction of other
languages. In a file containing dozens of global variables and subprogram
definitions, usually only a few of them need to be accessed from outside the
file. Each definition which is *not* used externally should be preceded by the
specifier static which indicates to the compiler that the declared variable or
subprogram is known only within the file:

```
static   int g1;                  /* Global only in this file */
         int g2;                  /* Global to all files */
static   int f1(int i) { ...};    /* Global only in this file */
int      f2(int i) { ...};        /* Global to all files */
```

This is known as *file scope* and is used where other languages would have
module scope. It would be better of course if the default specifier were
static rather than extern; however, it is not difficult to get into the habit of
prefixing every global declaration with static.

A source of confusion in C is the fact that static has another meaning,
namely that it specifies that the lifetime of a variable is the entire execution
of the program. As we discussed in Section 7.4, local variables within a
procedure have a lifetime limited to a single invocation of the procedure.
Global variables, however, have *static* lifetime, that is they are allocated when
the program begins and are not deallocated until the program terminates.
Static lifetime is the normal behavior we expect from global variables; in fact,
global variables declared with extern also have static lifetime!

The static specifier can also be used on local variables to request static
lifetime:

```
void proc(void)
{
    static bool first_time = true;
    if (first_time) {
        /* Statements executed the first time that proc is called */
        first_time = false;
    }
    ...
}
```

To summarize: all global variables and subprograms in a file should be
declared static, unless it is explicitly required that they be accessible outside
the file. In this case, they should be defined in one file without any specifier,
and exported by declaring them in an include file with the extern specifier.

13.2 Why are modules needed?

In the previous section we approached the decomposition of programs from a purely mechanical standpoint, namely the desire to separately edit and compile parts of the program in separate files. Starting in this section, we discuss decomposition of programs into components that are created to express the design of the program, and only incidentally to allow separate compilation. But first let us ask why is such decomposition necessary?

You may have been taught that the human brain is only capable of dealing with a small amount of material at any one time. In terms of programming, this is usually expressed by requiring that a single subprogram be no longer than one "page".[3] The subprogram is considered to be a conceptual unit: a sequence of statements performing a certain function. If the subprogram is small enough, say 25 to 100 lines, we will be able to completely and easily understand the relationships among the statements that compose the subprogram.

But to understand an entire program, we must understand the relationships among the subprograms that compose it. By analogy, it ought to be possible to understand programs composed of 25 to 100 subprograms, which totals 625 to 10,000 lines. This size program is relatively small compared to industrial and commercial software systems that contain 100,000, if not one million, lines. Experience shows that 10,000 lines is probably an upper limit on the size of a monolithic program, and that a new structuring mechanism is needed in order to build and maintain larger software systems.

The standard term for the mechanism used to structure large programs is *module*, though the two languages that we are concentrating on use other terms: *packages* in Ada and *classes* in C++. Standard Pascal does not define any method for separate compilation or for decomposing programs. For example, the first Pascal compiler was a *single* program containing over 8,000 lines of Pascal code. Rather than modify Pascal, Wirth developed a new (though similar) language called Modula which takes its name from the central concept of modules. Unfortunately, many vendors extended Pascal with incompatible module constructs, so Pascal is not suitable for writing portable software. Because modules are so important to software development, we choose to focus the discussion on Ada which has an elegant module construct called *packages*.

---

[3]This of course dates from the days when programs could be read only if printed out on paper, and a single page could hold about 50 lines. Today we would restrict a subprogram to about half that size so that it could be completely displayed on the screen (unless you have a workstation with a large screen!).

13.3 Packages in Ada

The basic concept underlying modules in general and Ada packages in particular is that computational resources like data and subprograms should be *encapsulated*[4] into a unit. Access to components of the unit is permitted only according to an explicit interface specification. Figure 13.1 shows a graphical notation (called *Booch-Buhr diagrams*) used in Ada designs. The large

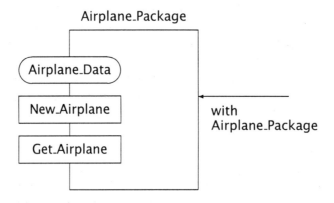

Figure 13.1 Diagram of a package

rectangle denotes the package Airplane_Package containing hidden computational resources, while the small rectangles are meant to look like windows that allow the user of the package access to the hidden resources. The oval rectangle denotes that a type is exported; the other two are subprograms. From each unit that uses the resources of the package, an arrow is drawn which points to the package.

Declaring a package

A package is composed of two parts: a *specification* and a *body*. The body encapsulates the computational resources, while the specification defines the interface to these resources. The package in the following example is intended to represent a component of an air-traffic control system[5] that stores a description of all the airplanes in the airspace being controlled. The package specification declares a type and two interface subprograms:

---

[4]As in the word "capsule".

[5]TRACON, from Wesson International, is a simulation of such a system on a PC and will give you an idea of the type of program we are discussing.

```
package Airplane_Package is
    type Airplane_Data is
        record
            ID: String(1..80);
            Speed: Integer range 0..1000;
            Altitude: Integer 0..100;
        end record;
    procedure New_Airplane(Data: in Airplane_Data; I: out Integer);
    procedure Get_Airplane(I: in Integer; Data: out Airplane_Data);
end Airplane_Package;
```

The package specification contains only procedure declarations—terminated by a semicolon, not procedure bodies—which are denoted by the reserved word is and a block. The declaration serves only as a specification of a computational resource that the package provides.

In the package body, all resources that were promised must be supplied. In particular, for every subprogram declaration, a subprogram body must exist with exactly the same declaration:

```
package body Airplane_Package is
    Airplanes: array(1..1000) of Airplane_Data;
    Current_Airplanes: Integer range 0..Airplanes'Last;

    function Find_Empty_Entry return Integer is
    begin
        ...
    end Find_Empty_Entry;

    procedure New_Airplane(Data: in Airplane_Data; I: out Integer) is
        Index: Integer := Find_Empty_Entry;
    begin
        Airplanes(Index) := Data;
        I := Index;
    end New_Airplane;

    procedure Get_Airplane(I: in Integer; Data: out Airplane_Data) is
    begin
        Data := Airplanes(I);
    end Get_Airplane;
end Airplane_Package;
```

What has this accomplished? The data structure used to hold the airplanes, here a fixed-size array, is encapsulated within the package body. The rule in Ada is that a change in a package body only, does not require modification either of the package specification or of any other program component that uses the package. Furthermore, it is not even necessary to recompile the specification or any component that uses the package. For example, if you subsequently need to replace the array by a linked list, no other component of the system need be modified *provided* that the interface, as listed in the package specification, is not modified:

```
package body Airplane_Package is
    type Node;
    type Ptr is access Node;
    type Node is
        record
            Info:  Airplane_Data;
            Next:  Ptr;
        end record;

    Head: Ptr;                      -- Head of linked list

    procedure New_Airplane(Data:  in Airplane_Data; I: out Integer) is
    begin
        ...                         -- New implementation
    end New_Airplane;

    procedure Get_Airplane(I: in Integer; Data:  out Airplane_Data) is
    begin
        ...                         -- New implementation
    end Get_Airplane;
end Airplane_Package;
```

Encapsulation is not just for convenience but also for reliability. The user of the package is not allowed to directly access data or internal subprograms (like Find_Empty_Entry) of the package body. Thus no other programmer on the team can accidentally (or maliciously) modify the data structure in a manner that was not intended. A bug in the implementation of a package is necessarily within the code of the package body, and not the result of some code written by a member of the team not responsible for the package.

Both the package specification and the package body are distinct units and can be separately compiled. However, they are considered to be a single scope in terms of declarations, so for example, the type Airplane_Data is known within the body. This means of course that the specification must be compiled before the body. Unlike C, there is no concept of "file", and declarations in Ada only exist within a unit such as a subprogram or package. Several compilation units can be in the same file, though it is usually more convenient to write each one in a separate file.

The convention for writing C programs suggested in the previous section attempts to imitate the encapsulation supplied by Ada packages. The include files containing the external declarations correspond to the package specifications, and by writing static on all global variables and subprograms in a file the effect of a package body is achieved. Of course this is just "bureaucracy" and can easily be circumvented, but it is a good way of structuring C programs.

Using a package

An Ada program (or another package) can access the computational resources of a package by writing a *context clause* before the first line of the program:

```
with Airplane_Package;
procedure Air_Traffic_Control is
    A: Airplane_Package.Airplane_Data;
    Index: Integer;
begin
    while ... loop
        A := ...;                    -- Create record
        Airplane_Package.New_Airplane(A, Index);
                             -- Store in data structure
    end loop;
end Air_Traffic_Control;
```

The with-clause tells the compiler that this program is to be compiled in an environment that includes all the declarations of Airplane_Package. The syntax for naming components of a package is like the syntax for selecting record components. Since each package must have a distinct name, components of a package can have identical names and no conflict will arise. This means that the management of the *name space*, the set of names, in a software project is simplified, and need only be controlled at the level of package names. Compare this with C where an identifier that is exported from a file is visible to all other files, so it is not sufficient just to ensure that file names are distinct.

The with-clause adds the expanded names to the name space of a compilation; it is also possible to include a use-clause[6] to "open" the name space

---

[6]The use-clause in Ada is similar to the with-statement in Pascal which adds the field names of a record to the name space. Note also that Turbo Pascal (a trademark of Borland International,

and allow direct naming of components appearing in a specification:

```
with Airplane_Package;
use Airplane_Package;
procedure Air_Traffic_Control is
    A: Airplane_Data;          -- Directly visible
    Index: Integer; begin
    New_Airplane(A, Index);    -- Directly visible
end Air_Traffic_Control;
```

One difficulty with use-clauses is that you may encounter ambiguity if use-clauses for two packages expose the same name, or if a local declaration exists with the same name as that in a package. The language rules specify what the compiler's response must be in cases of ambiguity.

More importantly, however, a unit that with's and then use's a lot of packages can become practically impossible to read. A name like Put_Element could come from almost any package, while the location of the definition of Airplane_Package.Put_Element is obvious. The situation is similar to that of a C program with many include files: you simply have no easy way of locating declarations, and the only solution is an external software tool or bureaucratic naming conventions.

Ada programmers should take advantage of the self-documenting aspect of with'ed units, and employ use-clauses only in small segments of a program where the intent is clear and the full notation would be extremely tedious. Fortunately, it is possible to put a use-clause within a local procedure:

```
procedure Check_for_Collision is
    use Airplane_Package;
    A1: Airplane_Data;
begin
    Get_Airplane(1, A1);
end Check_for_Collision;
```

In most programming languages the *importing* unit automatically obtains all the public resources of the imported unit. Some languages like Modula allow the importing unit to specify exactly which resources it needs. This method can avoid the name space overload caused by the inclusive nature of use-clauses in Ada.

Inc.) contains uses-clauses which access declarations from other units similarly to the Ada with-clause. Don't get confused!

Compilation order

with-clauses impose a natural order on compilation: a package specification must be compiled *before* its body, and *before* any unit that with's it. However, the ordering is partial, that is, there is no required compilation order between the package body and the units that use the package. You can fix a bug either in the package body or in the using unit without recompiling the other, but modifying a package specification requires recompilation both of the body and of all using units. In a very large project, modifications of package specifications should be avoided because they can trigger an avalanche of recompilations: P1 is used by P2 which is used by P3, and so on.

The fact that the compilation of one unit requires the results of the compilation of another means that an Ada compiler must contain a *library* to store compilations. The library may simply be a directory containing internally generated files, or it may be a sophisticated database. Regardless of the method used, a library manager is a central component of an Ada implementation, not just an optional software tool. The Ada library manager enforces the rule that changing a package specification requires the recompilation of the body and the using units. Thus an Ada compiler already includes a make tool that in other programming environments is an optional utility rather than part of the language support.

13.4 Abstract data types in Ada

Airplane_Package is an *abstract data object*. It is *abstract* because the user of the package does not know if the database of airplanes is implemented as an array, a list or a tree. The only access to the database is through the interface procedures in the package specification, which enable the user to abstractly create and retrieve a value of type Airplane_Data without knowledge of how it is stored.

The package is a *data object* because it actually contains data: the array and any other variables declared in the package body. It is correct to look upon Airplane_Package as a glorified variable: memory must be allocated for it and there are certain operations which can modify its value. It is not a first-class object because it does not have all the privileges of an ordinary variable: you cannot assign to a package or pass a package as a parameter.

Suppose now that we need *two* such databases; perhaps one for the simulated air-traffic control console, and one for a simulation scenario manager that creates and initializes new airplanes. It would be possible to write two packages, each with slightly different names, or to write a generic package and instantiate it twice, but these are very limited solutions. What we would really like to do is to declare as many such objects as we need, just like we declare integers. In other words, we want to be able to construct an *abstract data type (ADT)* which is just like an abstract data object, except that it does not contain any "variables". Instead, like other types an ADT will specify a set of values and a set of operations on these values, and we leave it to other program components to actually declare variables of the type.

An ADT in Ada is a package which contains only constant, type and subprogram declarations. The package specification includes a type declaration so that other units can declare one or more Airplanes:

```
package Airplane_Package is
    type Airplane_Data is ... end record;
    type Airplanes is
        record
            Database: array(1..1000) of Airplane_Data;
            Current_Airplanes: Integer 0..Airplanes'Last;
        end record;
    procedure New_Airplane(
        A: in out Airplanes; Data: in Airplane_Data; I: out Integer);
    procedure Get_Airplane(
        A: in out Airplanes; I: in Integer; Data: out Airplane_Data);
end Airplane_Package;
```

The package body is as before except that there are no global variables in the body:

```
package body Airplane_Package is
    function Find_Empty_Entry ... ;
    procedure New_Airplane ...;
    procedure Get_Airplane ...;
end Airplane_Package;
```

The program that uses the package can now declare one or more variables of the type supplied by the package. In fact the type is an ordinary type and can be used in further type definitions and as the type of a parameter:

```
with Airplane_Package;
procedure Air_Traffic_Control is
    Airplane: Airplane_Package.Airplanes;
            -- Variable of the ADT
    type Ptr is access Airplane_Package.Airplanes;
            -- Type with component of the ADT
```

```
    procedure Display(Parm: in Airplane_Package.Airplanes);
            -- Parameter of the ADT
    A: Airplane_Package.Airplane_Data;
    Index: Integer;
begin
    A := ... ;
    Airplane_Package.New_Airplane(Airplane, A, Index);
    Display(Airplane);
end Air_Traffic_Control;
```

There is a price to be paid for using ADT's instead of abstract data objects: since there is no longer *one* implicit object in the package body, every interface procedure must contain an extra parameter that explicitly informs the subprogram which object to process.

Now you are supposed to complain: what about "abstract"? Since the type **Airplanes** is now declared in the package specification, we have lost all the abstraction; it is no longer possible to change the data structure without potentially invalidating every other unit that uses the package. Furthermore, some team member can secretly ignore the interface procedures and write a "better" interface. We have to find a solution where the name of the type is in the specification so that it can be used, but the details of the implementation are encapsulated—something like the following:

```
package Airplane_Package is
    type Airplane_Data is ... end record;
    type Airplanes;               -- Incomplete type declaration
    ...
end Airplane_Package;

package body Airplane_Package is
    type Airplanes is            -- Complete type declaration
        record
            Database: array(1..1000) of Airplane_Data;
            Current_Airplanes: Integer 0..Airplanes'Last;
        end record;

    ...
end Airplane_Package;
```

Take a few minutes to analyze this proposal yourself before continuing.

As far as the package is concerned, there is no problem with these declarations, because the specification and the body form a single declarative region. The problems begin when we try to use the package:

```
with Airplane_Package;
procedure Air_Traffic_Control is
    Airplane_1: Airplane_Package.Airplanes;
    Airplane_2: Airplane_Package.Airplanes;

    ...
end Air_Traffic_Control;
```

Ada is designed so that compilation of a package specification is sufficient to enable compilation of any unit using the package. If fact, the package body need not even exist when the using unit is compiled. But to compile the above program, the compiler must know how much memory to allocate for Airplane_1 and Airplane_2; similarly, if this variable is used in an expression or passed as a parameter, the compiler must know the size of the variable. Thus if the representation of an ADT is encapsulated in the package body, it will be impossible to compile the program.

Private types

Since we are dealing with practical programming languages which have to be compiled, there is no choice but to return the complete type specification to the package specification. To achieve abstraction, a combination of self-delusion and a language rule is used:

```
package Airplane_Package is
    type Airplane_Data is ... end record;
    type Airplanes is private;
                                    -- Details to be supplied later
    procedure New_Airplane(Data: in Airplane_Data; I: out Integer);
    procedure Get_Airplane(I: in Integer; Data: out Airplane_Data);
private
    type Airplanes is              -- Complete type declaration
        record
            Database: array(1..1000) of Airplane_Data;
            Current_Airplanes: Integer 0..Airplanes'Last;
        end record;
end Airplane_Package;
```

The type itself is initially declared as a *private type*, while the complete type definition is written in a special section of the package specification that is introduced by the keyword private. The data type is abstract because the compiler enforces a rule that units with'ing the package are not allowed to access information written in the private part. They are only permitted to access the private data type through the interface subprograms in the public part of the specification; these subprograms are implemented in the body which can access the private part. Since the code of the using units does not depend upon the private part, it is possible to modify declarations in the private part without invalidating the using units; of course, recompilation will be necessary because a change in the private part could require a different amount of memory to be allocated.

Since you cannot make explicit use of the information in the private part, you should "pretend" that you cannot even see it. For example, you should not make a special effort to write algorithms that are extremely efficient if a private type is implemented as an array but not as a list, because the project team leader may eventually modify the implementation.

Limited types

An object (variable or constant) of a private type can be declared, and the operations of assignment and equality checking can be performed on objects of private type, since these operations are done bitwise without knowledge of the internal structure. There is, however, a conceptual problem with allowing assignment and equality. Suppose that an implementation is changed from an array to a pointer:

```
package Airplane_Package is
    type Airplanes is private;
    ...
private
    type Airplanes_Info is
        record
            Database: array(1..1000) of Airplane_Data;
            Current_Airplanes: Integer 0..Airplanes'Last;
        end record;
    type Airplanes is access Airplanes_Info;
end Airplane_Package;
```

We promised that modifying the private part does not require a modification of the using units, but this is not true here because assignment is that of the pointers and not the designated objects:

```
with Airplane_Package;
procedure Air_Traffic_Control is
    Airplane_1: Airplane_Package.Airplanes;
    Airplane_2: Airplane_Package.Airplanes;
```

```
begin
    Airplane_1 := Airplane_2;    -- Pointer assignment
end Air_Traffic_Control;
```

If assignment and equality are not meaningful (for example comparing two arrays that implement databases), Ada allows you to further declare a private type as limited. Objects of limited types cannot be assigned or compared, but you can explicitly write your own versions of these operations. This will solve the problem just described; in the transformation between the two implementations, a modification in the package body of the explicit code for assignment and equality can be done to ensure that these operations are still meaningful. Non-limited private types should be restricted to "small" objects that are not likely to undergo modifications other than adding or changing a field in a record.

Note that if a private type is implemented by a pointer, it doesn't really matter what the designated type is under the assumption that all pointers are represented the same way. Ada does in fact make this assumption and thus the designated type can be defined in the package body. Now, changing the data structure does not even require recompilation of the with'ing units, at the cost of indirect access to each object of the type:

```
package Airplane_Package is
    type Airplanes is private;

    ...
private
    type Airplanes_Info;            -- Incomplete type declaration
    type Airplanes is access Airplanes_Info;
end Airplane_Package;

package body Airplane_Package is
    type Airplanes_Info is          -- Completion in the body
        record
            Database: array(1..1000) of Airplane_Data;
            Current_Airplanes: Integer 0..Airplanes'Last;
        end record;
end Airplane_Package;
```

ADT's are a powerful method of structuring programs because of the clear separation between specification and implementation:

- Using ADT's, it becomes possible to make major modifications of individual program components reliably, without causing bugs in unrelated parts of the program.

- ADT's can be used as a management tool: the project architect designs the interfaces and each team member is given one or more ADT's to implement.

- It is possible to perform testing and partial integration by supplying degenerate implementations of missing package bodies.

In Chapter 14 we will expand on the role of ADT's as the basis of object-oriented programming.

13.5 How to write modules in C++

C++ is an extension of C and thus the concept of file as a unit for structuring programs still exists. The most important extension relative to C is the introduction of *classes* which implement abstract data types directly, unlike Ada which uses a combination of the two concepts: package and private data type. In the next chapter we will discuss object-oriented programming which is based on classes; in this section we will explain the basic concepts of classes and show how they can be used to define modules.

A class is like a package specification that declares one or more private types:

```
class Airplanes {
public:
    struct Airplane_Data {
        char id[80];
        int speed;
        int altitude;
    };
    void new_airplane(const Airplane_Data & a, int & i);
    void get_airplane(int i, Airplane_Data & a) const;

private:
    Airplane_Data database[1000];
    int current_airplanes;
    int find_empty_entry();
};
```

Note that the name of the class, that is the name of the type, also serves as the name of the unit of encapsulation; there is no separate module name. A class has a public part and a private part. By default, components of a class are private so the public specifier is needed before the public part. In fact, by using public and private specifiers, the public and private parts can be interspersed, unlike Ada which requires that there be exactly one list of declarations for each:

```
class C {
public:
    ...
private:
    ...
public:
    ...
private:
    ...
};
```

The declarations in the public part are accessible by any unit using this class, while the declarations in the private part are only accessible within the class. As a further means of control, the const specifier on get_airplane means that the subprogram will not modify any of the data within an object of the class. Such subprograms are called *inspectors.*

Since a class is a type, objects (constants and variables) of the class, called *instances*, can be declared:

```
Airplanes Airplane;                  // Instance of class Airplanes
```

```
int index;
Airplanes::Airplane_Data a;
Airplane.new_airplane(a, index);   // Call a subprogram on an instance
```

Similarly, a parameter type can be a class. Each instance will be allocated memory for all variables declared in the class, just as a variable of record type is allocated memory for all fields.

The syntax of the subprogram call is different from the Ada syntax because of a difference in the basic concept. The Ada call:

```
Airplane_Package.New_Airplane(Airplane, A, Index);
```

looks upon the package as supplying a resource, the procedure New_Airplane, which must be supplied with a specific object Airplane. C++ considers the object Airplane to be an instance of the class Airplanes, and if you send the object the *message* new_airplane, the corresponding procedure will be executed for this object.

Note that even subprograms like find_empty_entry which are only needed internally to implement the class, are declared in the class definition. C++

has nothing similar to a package body, which is a unit that encapsulates the implementation of the interface and other subprograms. Of course, the internal subprogram is not available for access by other units because it is declared within the private part. The problem in C++ is that if it is necessary to modify the declaration of find_empty_entry or to add another private subprogram, it will be necessary to recompile all units of the program which use this class; in Ada, a modification to the package body does not affect the rest of the program. To achieve true separation of interface and implementation of C++, you must declare the interface as an abstract class and then derive a concrete class which contains the implementation (see Section 15.1).

Where are the subprograms of a class implemented? The answer is that they can be implemented anywhere, in particular, in a separate file which accesses the class definition through an include file. A *scope resolution operator* "::" identifies each subprogram as belonging to a specific class:

```
// Some file
#include "Airplanes.h"          // Contains class declaration

void Airplanes::new_airplane(const Airplane_Data & a, int & i)
{
    . . .
}
void Airplanes::get_airplane(int i, Airplane_Data & a) const
{
    . . .
}
int Airplanes::find_empty_entry()
{
    . . .
}
```

Note that the internal subprogram find_empty_entry must be declared within the (private part) of the class so that it can access private data.

Namespaces

One of the last additions to the definition of C++ was the *namespace* construct which enables the programmer to limit the scope of otherwise global entities in a manner similar to that of an Ada package. A clause similar to the Ada use-clause opens the namespace:

```
namespace N1{
    void proc();                  // Procedure in namespace
};
namespace N2{
    void proc();                  // Different procedure
};

N1::proc();                       // Scope resolution operator to access

using namespace N1;
proc();                           // OK
using namespace N2;
proc();                           // Now ambiguous
```

Unfortunately, the C++ language does not define a library mechanism: class declarations must still be shared through include files. A development team must establish procedures for updating include files, preferably using software tools to warn the team members if two compilations are not using the same version of an include file.

13.6 Exercises

1. Write a main program in C that calls an external function f with an int parameter; in another file, write a function f that has a float parameter which it prints. Compile, link and run the program. What does it print? Try to compile, link and run the *same* program in C++.

2. Write a program to implement an abstract data type for a queue, and a main program that declares and uses several queues. The queue should be implemented as an array that is declared in the private part of an Ada package or C++ class. Then change the implementation to a linked list; the main program should be run unaltered.

3. What happens if you try to assign one queue to another? Solve the problem by using a limited private type in Ada, or a *copy-constructor* in C++.

4. In C and C++, a subprogram declaration need not have parameter names:

```
int func(int, float, char*);                                    C
```

Why is this so? Should you use parameter names anyway? Why does Ada require parameter names in a package specification?

5. Ada has a construct for separate compilation that is independent of the package construct:

```
procedure Main is                                    Ada
    Global: Integer;
    procedure R is separate;    -- Separately compiled procedure
end Main;

separate(Main)                   --Another file
procedure R is
begin
    Global := 4;                 -- Ordinary scope rules
end R;
```

The fact that a local package or procedure body is separately compiled does not change its scope and visibility. How can this be implemented? Does a change in a separate unit require recompilation of the parent unit? Why? Conversely, how does a change in the parent unit affect the separate unit?

6. Since a separate unit is a compilation unit, it can have its own context clause:

```
with Text_IO;                                        Ada
separate(Main)
procedure R is

    . . .
end R;
```

Why would this be done?

7. The following Ada program does not compile; why?

```
package P is                                         Ada
    type T is (A, B, C, D);
end P;

with P;
procedure Main is
    X: P.T;
begin
    if X = T.A then ... end if;
end Main;
```

There are four ways to solve the problem; what are the advantages and disadvantages of each: (a) use-clause, (b) prefix notation, (c) renames, (d) use type-clause in Ada 95?

14   Object-Oriented Programming

14.1   Object-oriented design

The previous chapter discussed language support for structuring programs, but it did not attempt to answer the question: how should programs be decomposed into modules? Normally, this subject would be studied in a course on software engineering, but one method of decomposition called *object-oriented programming* (OOP) is so important that modern programming languages directly support this method. The next two chapters will be devoted to the topic of language support for OOP.

When designing a program, the natural approach is to examine the requirements in terms of functions or operations, that is to ask: what should the program *do*? For example, software to support the tasks of an airline reservations clerk would have its requirements stated as follows:

1. Accept the customer's destination and departure date from the clerk.

2. Display the available flights to the clerk.

3. Accept the reservation request for a specific flight from the clerk.

4. Confirm the reservation and print the ticket.

This translates naturally into the design shown in Figure 14.1 with a module for each function and a "main" module to call the others.

Unfortunately, this design is not *robust*; even minor modifications in the requirements can require extensive modifications of the software. For example, suppose that the airline improves working conditions by replacing obsolete display terminals. The new terminals are likely to require modifications to all four modules; similarly, a new code-sharing arrangement with another airline will require extensive modifications.

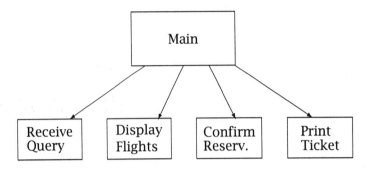

Figure 14.1 Functional decomposition

But we all know that software modification is extremely error-prone; a design which is not robust will thus cause the delivered software system to be unreliable and unstable. You might object that people should refrain from modifying software, but the whole justification for software is that it is "soft" and thus "inexpensive" to change; otherwise, all applications would be efficiently wired-in like the program of a pocket calculator.

Software can be made much more robust and reliable by changing the focus of our design criteria. The correct question to ask is: *on what* is the software working? The emphasis is changed from a focus on functionality to a focus on external devices, internal data structures, and real-world models, collectively called *objects*. A module should be constructed for every "object", and should contain all data and operations needed to implement the object. In the example we can identify several objects as shown in Figure 14.2.

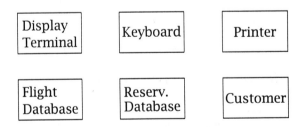

Figure 14.2 Object-oriented design

External devices such as the display terminal and the printer are identified as objects, as are the databases of flight information and reservations. In addition, we have designed an object **Customer**, whose purpose is to model an imaginary form on which the clerk enters data until the flight is confirmed and the ticket issued. This design is robust to modifications:

- Modifications to use a different terminal can be limited to the Terminal object. The programming of this object maps the customer data into actual display and keyboard commands, so the Customer object need not be modified, just the mapping onto the new hardware.

- Code-sharing may certainly require a total reorganization of the database, but as far as the rest of the program is concerned, one two-letter airline code is the same as another.

Object-oriented design is not limited to modelling real-world objects; it can also be used to create reusable software components. This is directly linked with one of the programming language concepts we have emphasized: abstraction. Modules implementing data structures can be designed and programmed as objects which are instances of an abstract data type together with the operations to manipulate the data. Abstraction is achieved by hiding the representation of the data type within the object.

In fact, the main difference between object-oriented design and "ordinary" programming is that in ordinary programming we are limited to predefined abstractions, while in object-oriented design we can define our own abstractions. For example, floating-point numbers (Chapter 9) are nothing more than a useful abstraction of a difficult manipulation of data in the computer. It would be helpful if all programming languages contained predefined abstractions for every object we would ever need (complex numbers, rational numbers, vectors, matrices, etc., etc.), but there is no end to the useful abstractions. Eventually a programming language has to stop and leave the work to the programmer.

How can a programmer create new abstractions? One way is to use coding conventions and documentation ("the first element of the array is the real part and the second is the imaginary part"). Alternatively, the language can supply a construct like Ada private types which enable the programmer to explicitly define new abstractions; these abstractions will be compiled and checked just like predefined abstractions. OOP can (and should) be done in ordinary languages, but like other ideas in programming, it works best when done in languages that directly support the concept. The basic construct used in languages that support OOP is the abstract data type that was discussed in the previous chapter, but it is important to realize that object-oriented design is more general and extends to abstracting external devices, models of the real world, and so on.

Object-oriented design is extremely difficult. The reason is that it requires a great deal of experience and judgement to decide if something deserves to become an object or not. First-time users of object-oriented design tend to become over-enthusiastic and make everything an object; this leads to programs so dense and tedious that all the advantages of the method are lost. The best rule-of-thumb to use is based on the concept of *information hiding*:

> Every object should hide one major design decision.

It helps to ask yourself: "is the decision likely to change over the lifetime of the program?".

The specific display terminals and printers chosen for a reservation system are clearly subject to upgrading. Similarly, decisions on database organization are likely to change, if only to improve performance as the system grows. On the other hand, it could be argued that the customer data form is unlikely to change, and need not be a separate object. Even if you don't agree with our design decision to create a Customer object, you should agree that object-oriented design is a good framework in which to discuss design issues and to argue the merits of one design over another.

The following sections will discuss language support for OOP using two languages: C++ and Ada 95. First we look at C++ which was designed by adding a single integrated construct for OOP on top of C which does not even have support for modules. Then we will see how full object-oriented programming is defined in Ada 95 by adding a few small constructs to Ada 83 which already had many features that partially supported OOP.

14.2   Object-oriented programming in C++

A programming language is said to support OOP if it includes constructs for:

- Encapsulation and data abstraction

- Inheritance

- Dynamic polymorphism

Let us recall the discussion of encapsulation and data abstraction from the previous chapter.

Modules such as Ada packages encapsulate computational resources, exposing only an interface specification. Data abstraction can be achieved by specifying the data representation in the private part which cannot be accessed from other units. The unit of encapsulation and abstraction in C++ is the *class* which contains data type and subprogram declarations. Actual objects, called *instances*, are created from the class. An example of a class in C++ is:

```
class Airplane_Data {
public:
    char *get_id(char *s) const  {return id;}
    void set_id(char *s)         {strcpy(id, s);}
    int get_speed() const        {return speed;}
    void set_speed(int i)        {speed = i;}
    int get_altitude() const     {return altitude;}
    void set_altitude(int i)     {altitude = i;}
private:
    char id[80];
    int speed;
    int altitude;
};
```

This example extends the example of the previous chapter by creating a separate class for the data on each airplane. The class can now be *used* by another class, for example by one that defines a data structure for storing many airplanes:

```
class Airplanes {
public:
    void New_Airplane(Airplane_Data, int &);
    void Get_Airplane(int, Airplane_Data &) const;
private:
    Airplane_Data database[100];
    int current_airplanes;
    int find_empty_entry();
};
```

Each class is designed to encapsulate a set of data declarations. The data declarations in the private part can be modified without modifying programs that use the class (called *clients* of the class), though you will need to recompile. A class will have a set of interface functions which will retrieve and update data values that are internal to the class.

You may question why Airplane_Data should be made a separate class, rather than just being declared as an ordinary public record. This is a debatable design decision: data should be hidden in a class if you believe that the internal representation is likely to change. For example, you may know that one customer prefers to measure altitude in English units (feet) while another prefers metric units (meters). By defining a separate class for Airplane_Data, you can use the same software for both customers and only change the implementation of the access functions.

There is a price to pay for this flexibility; *every* access to a data value requires a subprogram call:

```
Aircraft_Data a;              // Instance of the class
int alt;

alt = a.get_altitude();       // Get value hidden in instance
alt = (alt * 2) + 1000;
a.set_altitude(alt);          // Return value to instance
```

instead of a simple assignment statement if a were a public record:

```
a.alt = (a.alt * 2) + 1000;
```

Programming can be very tedious and the resulting code hard to read and understand, because the access functions obscure the intended processing. Thus classes should be defined only when there is a clear advantage to be obtained from hiding implementation details of an abstract data type.

However, there need not be any significant run-time overhead for encapsulation. As shown in the example, the body of the interface function can be written within the class declaration; in this case the function is an *inline* function,[1] which means that the mechanism of a subprogram call and return (see Chapter 7) is not used. Instead, the code for the subprogram body is inserted directly within the sequence of code at the point of call. Since inlining trades space for time, it should be restricted to very small subprograms (no more than two or three instructions). Another factor to consider before inlining a subprogram is that it introduces additional compilation conditions. If you modify an inlined subprogram, all clients must be recompiled.

14.3 Inheritance

In Section 4.6 we showed how in Ada one type can be derived from another so that the derived type has a copy of the values and a copy of the operations that were defined for the parent type. Given the parent type:

---

[1]In C++ a function can be inline even if the body is written separately and not in the class declaration.

```ada
package Airplane_Package is                                        Ada
    type Airplane_Data is
        record
            ID: String(1..80);
            Speed: Integer range 0..1000;
            Altitude: Integer range 0..100;
        end record;
    procedure New_Airplane(Data: in Airplane_Data; I: out Integer);
    procedure Get_Airplane(I: in Integer; Data: out Airplane_Data);
end Airplane_Package;
```

a derived type can be declared in another package:

```ada
type New_Airplane_Data is                                          Ada
    new Airplane_Package.Airplane_Data;
```

You can declare new subprograms that operate on the derived type and you can replace a subprogram of the parent type with a new one:

```ada
procedure Display_Airplane(Data: in New_Airplane_Data);            Ada
            -- Additional subprogram
procedure Get_Airplane(Data: in New_Airplane_Data; I: out Integer);
            -- Replaced subprogram
            -- Subprogram New_Airplane copied from Airplane_Data
```

Derived types form a family of types and a value of any type in the family can be converted to that of another type in the family:

```ada
A1: Airplane_Data;                                                 Ada
A2: New_Airplane_Data := New_Airplane_Data(A1);
A3: Airplane_Data := Airplane_Data(A2);
```

Furthermore, you can even derive from a private type, though of course all subprograms for the derived type must be defined in terms of public subprograms of the parent type.

The problem with derived types in Ada is that only the *operations* can be extended, not the data components that form the type. For example, suppose that the air-traffic control system must be modified so that for supersonic aircraft the Mach number[2] is stored in addition to the existing data. One possibility is simply to modify the existing record to include the extra field. This solution is acceptable if the modification is made during the initial development of the program. However, if the system has already

---

[2]The speed in terms of the speed of sound.

been tested and installed, it would be better to find a solution that does not require all the existing source code to be recompiled and checked.

The solution is to use *inheritance*, which is a way of extending an existing type, not just by adding and modifying operations, but also by adding data to the type. In C++ this is done by deriving one class from another:

```
class SST_Data: public Airplane_Data {          C++
private:
    float mach;
public:
    float get_mach() const {return mach;};
    void set_mach(float m) {mach = m;};
};
```

The derived class SST_Data is derived from an existing class Airplane_Data. This means that every data element and subprogram that are defined for the *base class*[3] are also available in the derived class. In addition, values of the derived class SST_Data will each have an additional data component mach, and there are two new subprograms that can be applied to values of the derived type.

The derived class is an ordinary class in the sense that instances can be declared and subprograms invoked:

```
SST_Data s;                                      C++

s.set_speed(1400);          // Inherited subprogram
s.set_mach(2.4);            // New subprogram
```

The subprogram called for set_mach is the one which is declared within class SST_Data, while the subprogram called for set_speed is the one inherited from the base. Note that the derived class can be compiled and linked without modifying and recompiling the base class; thus existing code need not be affected by the extension.

14.4 Dynamic polymorphism in C++

When one class is derived from another class, you can *override* inherited subprograms in the derived class by redefining the subprogram:

---

[3]Parent type in Ada is roughly the same as base class in C++.

```
class SST_Data: public Airplane_Data {
public:
    int get_speed() const;      // Override
    void set_speed(int);        // Override
};
```

Given a call:

```
obj.set_speed(100);
```

the decision as to which of the subprograms to call—the subprogram inherited from Airplane_Data or the new one in SST_Data—is made at compile-time based on the class of the object obj. This is called *static binding* or *early binding*, since the decision is made before the program is run, and each call is always to the same subprogram.

However, the whole point of inheritance is to create a group of classes with similar properties, and it is reasonable to expect that it should be possible to assign a value belonging to any of these classes to a variable. What should happen when a subprogram is called for such a variable? The decision as to which subprogram to call must be made at run-time because the value held in the variable is not known until then; in fact, the variable may hold values of different classes at different times during the program. The terms used to denote the ability to select subprograms at run-time are *dynamic polymorphism, dynamic binding, late binding*, and *run-time dispatching*.

In C++, *virtual functions* are used to denote those subprograms for which dynamic binding is performed:

```
class Airplane_Data {
private:
    ...
public:
    virtual int get_speed() const;
    virtual void set_speed(int);
    ...
};
```

A subprogram in the derived class with the same name and parameter signature as that of a virtual subprogram in the parent class is also considered virtual. You are not required to repeat the virtual specifier, but it is good practice to do so for clarity:

```
class SST_Data : public Airplane_Data {
private:
    float mach;
public:
    float get_mach() const;          // New subprogram
    void set_mach(float m);          // New subprogram
    virtual int get_speed() const;   // Override virtual subprogram
    virtual void set_speed(int);     // Override virtual subprogram
    ...
};
```

Consider now the procedure update which takes a reference parameter to the base class:

```
void update(Airplane_Data & d, int spd, int alt)
{
    d.set_speed(spd);                // What type does d point to ??
    d.set_altitude(alt);             // What type does d point to ??
}


Airplane_Data a;
SST_Data s;

void proc()
{
    update(a, 500, 5000);            // Call with Airplane_Data
    update(s, 800, 6000);            // Call with SST_Data
}
```

The idea of derived classes is that a derived value *is* a base value (perhaps with additional fields), so update can also be called with the value s of the derived class SST_Data. Within update, the compiler has no way of knowing what d points to: a value of Airplane_Data or a value of SST_Data. So it has no way of compiling an unambiguous call to set_speed which is defined differently for the two types. Therefore, the compiler must create code to *dispatch* the call to the correct subprogram at run-time, depending on the class of the value pointed to by d. The first call in proc passes a value of type Airplane_Data to d, so the call to set_speed will be dispatched to the subprogram defined in the class Airplane_Data while the second call will be dispatched to the subprogram defined in SST_Data.

Let us stress the advantages of dynamic polymorphism: you can write large portions of a program in a completely general fashion using calls to virtual subprograms. The specialization of the processing to a specific class in a family of derived classes is made only at run-time, by dispatching on the virtual subprograms. Furthermore, if you ever need to add derived classes to the family, none of the existing code need be modified or recompiled, because any change in the existing computation is solely limited to the new implementations of the virtual subprograms. For example, if we derive another class:

```
class Space_Plane_Data : public SST_Data {
    virtual void set_speed(int);      // Override virtual subprogram
private:
    int reentry_speed;
};

Space_Plane_Data sp;
update(sp, 2000, 30000);
```

the file containing the definition of update need not be recompiled, even though (i) a new subprogram has overridden set_speed, and (ii) the value of the formal parameter d of update contains an additional field reentry_speed.

When is dynamic polymorphism used?

Let us declare a base class with a virtual subprogram and an ordinary non-virtual subprogram, and let us derive a class that adds an additional field and supplies new declarations for both subprograms:

```
class Base_Class {
private:
    int Base_Field;
public:
    virtual void virtual_proc();
    void ordinary_proc();
};
class Derived_Class : public Base_Class {
private:
    int Derived_Field;
public:
    virtual void virtual_proc();
    void ordinary_proc();
};
```

Next let us declare instances of the classes as variables. Assignment of a value of the derived class to a variable of the base class is permitted:[4]

```
Base_Class        Base_Object;
Derived_Class     Derived_Object;
if (...) Base_Object = Derived_Object;
```

because the derived object *is* a base object (plus extra information), and the extra information can be ignored in the assignment (Figure 14.3).

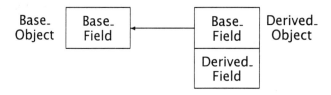

Figure 14.3 Direct assignment of a derived object

Furthermore, a call to a subprogram (whether virtual or not) is unambiguous and the compiler can use static binding:

```
Base_Object.virtual_proc();
Base_Object.ordinary_proc();
Derived_Object.virtual_proc();
Derived_Object.ordinary_proc();
```

Suppose, however, that indirect allocation is used and a pointer to a derived class is assigned to a pointer to the base class:

```
Base_Class*       Base_Ptr = new Base_Class;
Derived_Class*    Derived_Ptr = new Derived_Class;
if (...) Base_Ptr = Derived_Ptr;
```

In this case the semantics are different since the base pointer points to the *complete* derived object and no truncation is done (Figure 14.4). There is no implementation problem because we assume that all pointers are represented identically regardless of the designated type.

What is important to note is that following the pointer assignment, the *compiler* no longer has any information as to the type of the designated object. Thus it has no way of binding a call:

```
Base_Ptr->virtual_proc();
```

---

[4]See section 15.3 on assignment of objects from base to derived classes.

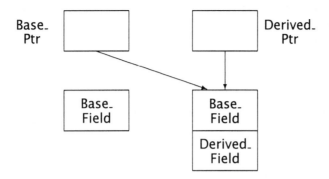

Figure 14.4 Indirect assignment of a derived object

to the correct subprogram and dynamic dispatching must be done. A similar situation occurs when a reference parameter is used as was shown above.

This situation is potentially confusing since programmers usually don't distinguish between a variable and a designated object. After the following statements:

```
int i1 = 1;
int i2 = 2;
int *p1 = &i1;          // p1 points to i1
int *p2 = &i2;          // p2 points to i2
p1 = p2;                // p1 also points to i2
i1 = i2;                // i1 has the same value as i2
```

you expect that i1==i2 and that *p1==*p2; this is certainly true as long as the types are exactly the same, but it is not true for assignment from a derived to a base class because of the truncation. When using inheritance you have to remember that the designated object may not be of the same type as the designed type in the pointer declaration.

There is a pitfall in the semantics of dynamic polymorphism in C++: if you look carefully, you will note that the discussion was about dispatching to an overridden *virtual* subprogram. But there may also be ordinary subprograms in the class which are overridden:

```
Base_Ptr = Derived_Ptr;
Base_Ptr->virtual_proc();     // Dispatches on designated type
Base_Ptr->ordinary_proc();    // Statically bound to base type !!
```

There is a semantic difference between the two calls: the call to the virtual subprogram is dispatched at run-time according to the *type of the designated object*, in this case Derived_Class; the call to the ordinary subprogram is bound at compile-time according to the *type of the pointer*, in this case Base_Class. This difference is dangerous because a modification that changes a non-virtual subprogram to a virtual subprogram, or conversely, can cause bugs in the entire family of classes derived from the base class.

> Dynamic dispatching in C++ is done on calls to virtual subprograms made through a pointer or reference.

Implementation

Earlier we noted that if a subprogram is not found in a derived class, a search is made in ancestor classes until a definition of the subprogram is found. In the case of static binding, the search can be made at compile-time: the compiler looks at the base class of the derived class, then at its base class, and so on, until an appropriate subprogram binding is found. Then an ordinary procedure call can be compiled to that subprogram.

If virtual subprograms are used, the situation is more complicated because the actual subprogram to call is not known until run-time. Note that if a virtual subprogram is called with an object of a specific type, as opposed to a reference or pointer, static binding can still be used. Otherwise, deciding which subprogram to call is based on (1) the name of the subprogram, and (2) the class of the object. But (1) is known at compile-time, so all we need to do is to simulate a **case**-statement on the class.

The usual implementation is slightly different; for each class with virtual subprograms, a dispatch table is maintained (Figure 14.5). Each value of a class must "drag" with it an *index* into the dispatch table for the derivation family in which it is defined. The dispatch table entries are pointers to jump tables; in each jump table there is an entry for each virtual subprogram. Note that two jump table entries can point to the same procedure; this will happen when a class does not override a virtual subprogram. In the Figure, cls3 is derived from cls2 which in turn is derived from the base class cls1. cls2 has overridden p2 but not p1, while cls3 has overridden both subprograms.

When a dispatching subprogram call ptr->p1() is encountered, code such as the following is executed, where we assume that the implicit index is the first field of the designated object:

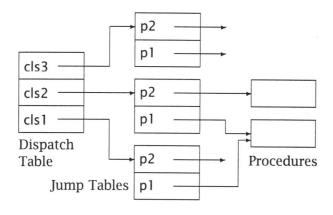

Figure 14.5 Implementation of dynamic polymorphism

```
load      R0,ptr          Get address of object
load      R1,(R0)         Get index of designated object
load      R2,&dispatch    Get address of dispatch table
add       R2,R1           Compute address of jump table
load      R3,(R2)         Get address of jump table
load      R4,p1(R3)       Get address of procedure
call      (R4)            Call procedure, address is in R4
```

Even without further optimization, run-time overhead is relatively small, and more importantly *fixed*, so in most applications there is no need to refrain from using dynamic polymorphism. Even so the overhead does exist and run-time dispatching should be used after careful analysis. Avoid either extreme: excessive use of dynamic polymorphism just because it is a "good idea", or refraining from its use because it is "inefficient".

Note that the fixed overhead is obtained because the dynamic polymorphism is limited to the fixed set of classes derived from a base class (so a fixed-size dispatch table can be used), and to the fixed set of virtual functions that can be overridden (so the size of each jump table is also fixed). It was a significant achievement of C++ to show that dynamic polymorphism can be implemented without an unbounded run-time search.

14.5 Object-oriented programming in Ada 95

Ada 83 fully supports encapsulation with the package construct and partially supports inheritance through derived types. Derived types do not support full inheritance because when you derive a new type you can only add new operations but not new data components. In addition, the only polymorphism is the static polymorphism of variant records. In Ada 95, full inheritance is supported by enabling the programmer to *extend* a record when deriving a type. To denote that a parent record type is eligible for inheritance, it must be declared as a *tagged* record type:

```
package Airplane_Package is
    type Airplane_Data is tagged
        record
            ID: String(1..80);
            Speed: Integer range 0..1000;
            Altitude: Integer 0..100;
        end record;
end Airplane_Package;
```

The tag is similar to the Pascal tag and the Ada discriminant in variant records in that it is used to distinguish between the different types that are derived from each other. Unlike those constructs, a tag of a tagged record is implicit and the programmer does not need to explicitly access it.[5] Looking ahead, this implicit tag will be used to dispatch subprogram calls for dynamic polymorphism.

To create an abstract data type, the type should be declared as private and the full type declaration given in the private part:

```
package Airplane_Package is
    type Airplane_Data is tagged private;
    procedure Set_ID(A: in out Airplane_Data; S: in String);
    function Get_ID(A: Airplane_Data) return String;
    procedure Set_Speed(A: in out Airplane_Data; I: in Integer);
    function Get_Speed(A: Airplane_Data) return Integer;
    procedure Set_Altitude(A: in out Airplane_Data; I: in Integer);
    function Get_Altitude(A: Airplane_Data) return Integer;
private
    type Airplane_Data is tagged
        record
            ID: String(1..80);
            Speed: Integer range 0..1000;
            Altitude: Integer 0..100;
        end record;
end Airplane_Package;
```

---

[5]If necessary, the tag can be read by using an attribute on an object of a tagged type.

The subprograms defined *within* a package specification containing the declaration of a tagged type (along with predefined operations on the type) are called *primitive subprograms*, and are the subprograms that are inherited upon derivation. Inheritance is done by *extending* a tagged type:

```
with Airplane_Package; use Airplane_Package;
package SST_Package is
    type SST_Data is new Airplane_Data with
        record
            Mach: Float;
        end record;
    procedure Set_Speed(A: in out SST_Data; I: in Integer);
    function Get_Speed(A: SST_Data) return Integer;
end SST_Package;
```

The values of this derived type are a copy of those of the parent type Airplane_Data together with the additional record field Mach. The operations defined for the type are a copy of the primitive subprograms; these operations may be overridden. Of course other unrelated subprograms may be declared for the derived type.

Ada does not have a special syntax for calling primitive subprograms:

```
A: Airplane_Data;
Set_Speed(A, 100);
```

The object A is syntactically an ordinary parameter and from its type the compiler can deduce which subprogram to call. The parameter is called a *controlling parameter* because it controls which subprogram is chosen. The controlling parameter need not be the first parameter and there may be more than one (provided that they are all of the same type). Contrast this with C++ which uses a special syntax to call a subprogram declared in a class:

```
Airplane_Data a;                                    C++
a.set_speed(100);
```

The object a is the *distinguished receiver* of the message set_speed. The distinguished receiver is an implicit parameter, in this case denoting that the speed will be set for object a.

Dynamic polymorphism

Before discussing dynamic polymorphism in Ada 95, we have to deal with a difference in terminology between Ada and other object-oriented languages.

C++ uses the term class to represent a data type which is used to create instances of the type. Ada 95 continues to use the terms types and objects, even for tagged types and objects which are known in other languages as classes and instances. The word *class* is used to denote the set of all types that are derived from a common ancestor, what we have called a family of classes in C++. The following discussion is best done in the correct Ada 95 terminology; be careful not to confuse the new use of the word class with its use in C++.

With every tagged type T is associated a type called a *class-wide type*, denoted T'Class. All types derived from a type T are *covered* by T'Class. A class-wide type is unconstrained, and an unconstrained object of the type cannot be declared, any more than we can declare an object of an unconstrained array:

```
type Vector is array(Integer range <>) of Float;
V1: Vector;                          -- Illegal, no constraint

type Airplane_Data is tagged record ... end record;
A1: Airplane_Data'Class;             -- Illegal, no constraint
```

However, an object of class-wide type can be declared if it is given an initial value:

```
V2: Vector := (1..20=>0.0);          -- OK, constrained

X2: Airplane_Data;                   -- OK, specific type
X3: SST_Data;                        -- OK, specific type
A2: Airplane_Data'Class := X2;       -- OK, constrained
A3: Airplane_Data'Class := X3;       -- OK, constrained
```

Like an array, once a class-wide object is constrained, its constraint cannot be changed. Class-wide types can be used in the declaration of local variables in a subprogram that takes a parameter of class-wide type, again just like unconstrained arrays:

```
procedure P(S: String; C: in Airplane_Data'Class) is
    Local_String: String := S;
    Local_Airplane: Airplane_Data'Class := C;
begin
    ...
end P;
```

Dynamic polymorphism occurs when an *actual* parameter is of a class-wide type, while the *formal* parameter is of a specific type belonging to the class:

```
with Airplane_Package; use Airplane_Package;
with SST_Package; use SST_Package;
procedure Main is
    procedure Proc(C: in out Airplane_Data'Class; I: in Integer) is
    begin
        Set_Speed(C, I);        -- What type is C ??
    end Proc;

    A: Airplane_Data;
    S: SST_Data;
begin        -- Main
    Proc(A, 500);              -- Call with Airplane_Data
    Proc(S, 1000);             -- Call with SST_Data
end Main;
```

The *actual* parameter C in the call to Set_Speed is of the class-wide type, but there are two versions of Set_Speed whose *formal* parameter is either of the parent type or of the derived type. At run-time the type of C will change from one call to another, so dynamic dispatching is needed to disambiguate the call.

Figure 14.6 will help you understand the role of the formal and actual parameters in dispatching. The call to Set_Speed at the top of the figure

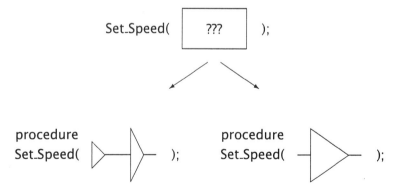

Figure 14.6 Dynamic dispatching in Ada 95

has an *actual* parameter which is of class-wide type. This means that only when the subprogram is called, do we know whether the type of the actual parameter is Airplane_Data or SST_Data. However, the procedure declarations shown at the bottom of the figure each have a formal parameter of a specific type. As shown by the arrows, the call must be dispatched according to the type of the actual parameter.

Note that dispatching is only done if needed; if the compiler can resolve the call statically, it will do so. The following calls need no dispatching because the call is with an *actual* parameter of a specific type and not a class-wide type:

```
Set_Speed(A, 500);
Set_Speed(S, 1000);
```

Similarly, if the *formal* parameter is of class-wide type then no dispatching is needed. The calls to Proc are calls to a single unambiguous procedure; the formal parameter is of a class-wide type which matches an actual parameter of any type that is covered by the class. Referring to Figure 14.7, if the declaration of Set_Speed were:

```
procedure Set_Speed(A: in out Airplane'Class: I: in Integer);
```

then any actual parameter of the class will "fit into" the class-wide formal parameter. No dispatching is needed, because every call is to the same subprogram.

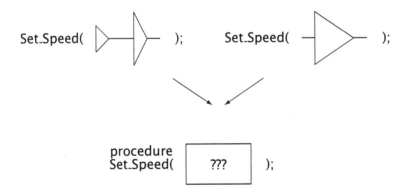

Figure 14.7 Class-wide formal parameter

The designated type of an access type can be a class-wide type. A pointer of this type can designate any object whose type is covered by the class-wide type and dispatching can be done by simply dereferencing the pointer:[6]

---

[6] Ada 95 also defines an anonymous access type that can dispatch without dereferencing.

```
type Class_Ptr is access Airplane_Data'Class;
Ptr: Class_Ptr := new Airplane_Data;

if (...) then Ptr := new SST_Data; end if;

Set_Speed(Ptr.all);            -- What type does Ptr point to ??
```

> Dynamic polymorphism in Ada 95 occurs when the actual parameter is of a class-wide type and the formal parameter is of a specific type.

While the run-time implementation of dispatching is similar in Ada 95 and C++, the *conditions* for dispatching are quite different:

- In C++, a subprogram must be declared virtual for dispatching to be done. All indirect calls to the virtual subprogram are dispatching.[7]

- In Ada 95, any inherited subprogram can be overridden and implicitly becomes dispatching. The dispatching is only done as needed if required by a specific call.

The main advantage of the Ada approach is that it is not necessary to specify in advance whether dynamic polymorphism is to be used. This means that the semantic difference between the call to a virtual and to a non-virtual subprogram does not exist. Suppose that Airplane_Data has been defined as tagged but that no derivations have been done. In that case an entire system can be built in which all calls are statically resolved. Later, if derived types are declared, they can use dispatching without the need to modify or recompile the existing code.

14.6 Exercises

1. A software development method called *top-down* programming advocates writing the program in terms of high-level abstract operations and then progressively refining the operations until programming language statements are reached. Compare this method with object-oriented programming.

---

[7]The compiler may optimize away dynamic dispatching. For example, if the actual parameter is a variable rather than a reference or a pointer, the call can be statically resolved as in Ada 95.

2. Would you make Aircraft-Data an abstract data type or would you expose the fields of the class?

3. Check that you can inherit from a C++ class or Ada 95 package with a tagged type without recompiling existing code.

4. Write a heterogeneous queue in Ada 95: declare a tagged type Item, specify the queue in terms of Item and then derive from Item for each of Boolean, Integer and Character.

5. Write a heterogeneous queue in C++.

6. Check that in C++ dispatching occurs for a reference parameter but not for an ordinary parameter.

7. In Ada 95, a tagged type can be extended privately:

```
with Airplane-Package; use Airplane-Package;
package SST-Package is
    type SST-Data is new Airplane-Data with private;
    procedure Set-Speed(A: in out SST-Data; I: in Integer);
    function Get-Speed(A: SST-Data) return Integer;
private
    . . .
end SST-Package;
```

What are the advantages and disadvantages of private extension?

8. Study the machine instructions generated by your Ada 95 or C++ compiler for dynamic polymorphism.

15 More on Object-Oriented Programming

In this chapter we will survey additional constructs that exist in object-oriented languages. These are not simply clever features added on to the languages, but technical constructs that must be mastered if you wish to become competent in object-oriented programming techniques. The survey is not comprehensive; for details you will need to consult textbooks on the languages.

The chapter is divided into six sections:

1. Structuring classes:

   - Abstract classes are used to create an abstract interface that may be implemented by one or more inheriting classes.
   - Generics (Ada) and templates (C++) can be combined with inheritance to parameterize classes with other classes.
   - Multiple inheritance: A class can be derived from two or more parent classes and inherit data and operations from each one.

2. Access to private components: Are components in the private part of a package or class always private, or is it possible to export them to derived classes or to clients?

3. Class data: This section discusses the creation and use of data components in a class.

4. Eiffel: The Eiffel language was designed to support OOP as the only method of structuring programs; it is instructive to compare the constructs of Eiffel with those of Ada 95 and C++, where support for OOP was added to an existing language.

5. Design considerations: (a) What are the trade-offs between using and inheriting from a class? (b) What can inheritance be used for? (c) What is the relationship between overloading and overriding?

6. We conclude with a summary of methods for dynamic polymorphism.

15.1 Structuring classes

Abstract classes

When a class is derived from a base class, the assumption is that the base class contains most of the required data and operations, while the derived class just adds additional data, and adds or modifies some operations. In many designs it is better to think of a base class as a framework defining common operations for an entire family of derived classes. For example, a family of classes for I/O or graphics may define common operations such as get and display which will be defined for each derived class. Both Ada 95 and C++ support such abstract classes.

We will demonstrate abstract classes by giving multiple implementations of the same abstraction: the abstract class will define a Set data structure[1] and the derived classes will implement the set in two different ways. In Ada 95, the word abstract denotes an abstract type and abstract subprograms associated with the type:

```
package Set_Package is                                              Ada
    type Set is abstract tagged null record;
    function Union(S1, S2: Set) return Set is abstract;
    function Intersection(S1, S2: Set) return Set is abstract;
end Set_Package;
```

You cannot declare an object of an abstract type, nor can you call an abstract subprogram. The type serves only as a framework for deriving concrete types, and the subprograms must be overridden with concrete subprograms.

First, we derive a type which implements a set using an array of Booleans:

```
with Set_Package;                                                  Ada
package Bit_Set_Package is
    type Set is new Set_Package.Set with private;
    function Union(S1, S2: Set) return Set;
    function Intersection(S1, S2: Set) return Set;
private
```

---

[1]This is only a small fragment of a useful class for sets.

```
        type Bit_Array is array(1..100) of Boolean;
        type Set is new Set_Package.Set with
            record
                Data: Bit_Array;
            end record;
    end Bit_Set_Package;
```

Of course a package body is needed to implement the operations.

The derived type is a concrete type with concrete data components and operations, and it can be used like any other type:

```
    with Bit_Set_Package; use Bit_Set_Package;                        Ada
    procedure Main is
        S1, S2, S3: Set;
    begin
        S1 := Union(S2, S3);
    end Main;
```

Suppose now that in another part of the program, you need a different implementation of sets, one that uses linked lists instead of arrays. You can derive an additional concrete type from the abstract type and use it in place of, or in addition to, the previous implementation:

```
    with Set_Package;                                                 Ada
    package Linked_Set_Package is
        type Set is new Set_Package.Set with private;
        function Union(S1, S2: Set) return Set;
        function Intersection(S1, S2: Set) return Set;
    private
        type Node;
        type Pointer is access Node;
        type Set is new Set_Package.Set with
            record
                Head: Pointer;
            end record;
    end Linked_Set_Package;
```

The new implementation can be used by another unit; in fact, you can change the implementation used in existing units simply by replacing the context clause:

```ada
with Linked_Set_Package; use Linked_Set_Package;
procedure Main is
    S1, S2, S3: Set;
begin
    S1 := Union(S2, S3);
end Main;
```
Ada

In C++, an abstract class is created by declaring a *pure* virtual function, denoted by an "initial value" 0 for the function.[2] An abstract class for sets in C++ is:

```cpp
class Set {
public:
    virtual void Union(Set&, Set&) = 0;
    virtual void Intersection(Set&, Set&) = 0;
};
```
C++

It is impossible to define instances of abstract classes; they can only be used as base classes in a derivation:

```cpp
class Bit_Set : public Set {
public:
    virtual void Union(Set&, Set&);
    virtual void Intersection(Set&, Set&);
private:
    int data[100];
};

class Linked_Set : public Set {
public:
    virtual void Union(Set&, Set&);
    virtual void Intersection(Set&, Set&);
private:
    int data;
    Set *next;
};
```
C++

The concrete derived classes can be used like any other class:

---

[2]The syntax was chosen to be similar to the syntax for a null pointer, using "0" rather than a new keyword.

```cpp
void proc()                                              C++
{
    Bit_Set b1, b2, b3;
    Linked_Set l1, l2, l3;

    b1.Union(b2, b3);
    l1.Union(l2, l3);
}
```

Note the difference in syntax between the two languages that comes from the different ways that they approach OOP. In Ada 95 an ordinary function is defined which takes two sets and returns a third. In C++, one of the sets is the distinguished receiver. The intended interpretation of:

```
b1.Union(b2, b3);
```

is that the instance b1, the distinguished receiver of the operation Union, will receive the result of the operation on the two parameters b2 and b3, and use it to replace the current value of its internal data.

For a set class, you may prefer to overload predefined operators like "+" and "*" instead of using names like Union and Intersection. This is possible in both C++ and Ada 95.

All the implementations of the abstract class are in the class-wide type Set'Class. Values of the abstract class-wide type will be dispatched to the correct concrete specific type, that is to the correct implementation. Thus abstract types and operations enable the programmer to write implementation-independent software.

Generics

In Section 10.3 we discussed generic subprograms in Ada, which enable the programmer to create a template for a subprogram and then to instantiate the subprogram for various types. Generics are more commonly applied to Ada packages; for example, a package that maintains a list would be generic on the type of the list element. In addition, it could be generic on a function to compare list elements so that the list can be sorted:

```ada
generic                                                  Ada
    type Item is private;
    with function "<"(X, Y: in Item) return Boolean;
package List_Package is
    type List is private;
```

```
      procedure Put(I: in Item; L: in out List);
      procedure Get(I: out Item; L: in out List);
   private
      type List is array(1..100) of Item;
   end List_Package;
```

This package can now be instantiated for any element type:[3]

```
   package Integer_List is new List_Package(Integer, Integer."<");      Ada
```

The instantiation creates a new type and you can declare and use objects of that type:

```
   Int_List_1, Int_List_2: Integer_List.List;                          Ada
```

```
   Integer_List.Put(42, Int_List_1);
   Integer_List.Put(59, Int_List_2);
```

Ada has a rich set of generic formal parameter notations which are used in the contract model to restrict the actual parameters to a certain class of types, such as discrete types or floating-point types. In Ada 95, this was generalized to allow generic formal parameters to specify programmer-defined classes of types:

```
   with Set_Package;                                                   Ada
   generic
      type Set_Class is new Set_Package.Set;
   package Set_IO is

      ...

   end Set_IO;
```

This specification means that the generic package can be instantiated with any type derived from the tagged type Set, such as Bit_Set and Linked_Set. All operations from Set such as Union can be used within the generic package, because we know by the contract model that any instantiation will be with a type derived from Set, and hence they will inherit or override these operations.

Templates

In C++, class templates can be defined:

---

[3]A generic subprogram formal parameter declared as follows:

```
      with function "<"(X, Y: in Item) return Boolean is <>;
```

specifies that if a subprogram with the appropriate signature is visible when instantiation is done, it can be used by default if an actual parameter is not given. This avoids the need to write such things as Integer."<".

```
template <class Item>                                          C++
    class List {
        void put(const Item &);
    };
```

Once the class template is defined, you can define objects of this class by supplying the template parameter:

```
List<int> Int_List1;                                          C++
        // Int_List is a List instantiated with int
```

Like Ada, C++ enables the programmer to supply particular subprograms for use in an instantiation by a specific class (a process called *specialization*), or to use default subprograms that exist for the class.

There is an important difference between Ada generics and C++ templates. In Ada, an instantiation of a generic package that defines a type will give you a specific *package* containing a specific type. It takes another step to obtain an object. In C++, the instantiation gives an object directly and there is no specific class defined. To define another object, you just instantiate the template again:

```
List<int> Int_List2;              // Another object            C++
```

The compiler and linker are responsible for keeping track of all instantiations by the same type, to ensure that the code for the operations of the class template is not replicated for each object.

A further difference between the languages is that C++ does not use the contract model, so there is the possibility that an instantiation will cause a compilation error in the template itself (see Section 10.3).

Multiple inheritance

The discussion of derived classes has always been in terms of deriving from a single base, so that a family of classes forms a tree. During the object-oriented design, it is likely that a class will have characteristics of two or more existing classes, and it seems reasonable to derive the class from several base classes. This is called *multiple inheritance*. Figure 15.1 shows that an Airplane can be multiply derived from Winged_Vehicle and Motorized_Vehicle, while the Winged_Vehicle is also a (single) base of Glider. Given the two classes:

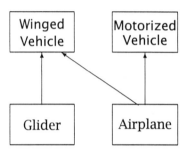

Figure 15.1 Multiple inheritance

```
class Winged_Vehicle {                                          C++
public:
    void display(int);
protected:
    int Wing_Length;
    int Weight;
};
```

```
class Motorized_Vehicle {
public:
    void display(int);
protected:
    int Power;
    int Weight;
};
```

a class can be derived by multiple inheritance:

```
class Airplane :                                                C++
    public Winged_Vehicle, public Motorized_Vehicle {
public:
    void display_all();
};
```

The problem that must be solved in order to use multiple inheritance is what to do with data and operations, such as Weight and display, that are inherited from more than one base class. In C++, ambiguities caused by multiply-defined components must be explicitly resolved using the scope resolution operator:

```cpp
void Airplane::display_all()
{
    Winged_Vehicle::display(Wing_Length);
    Winged_Vehicle::display(Winged_Vehicle::Weight);
    Motorized_Vehicle::display(Power);
    Motorized_Vehicle::display(Motorized_Vehicle::Weight);
};
```

C++

This is unfortunate since the whole point of inheritance is to allow direct
access to unmodified data and operations of the base. The implementation
of multiple inheritance is much more difficult than the implementation of
single inheritance that we described in Section 14.4. See Sections 10.1c
through 10.10c of the Annotated Reference Manual for details.

The importance of multiple inheritance in OOP is the subject of much
debate. Some programming languages such as Eiffel encourage the use
of multiple inheritance, while others like Ada 95 and Smalltalk have no
facilities for multiple inheritance. These languages claim that the problems
that multiple inheritance can solve have elegant solutions using other features
of the language. For example, we noted above that generic parameters of
tagged types in Ada 95 can be used to create new abstractions by combining
existing abstractions. Clearly, the availability of multiple inheritance has
a deep influence on the design and programming of a system according
to object-oriented principles. Thus it is difficult to talk about language-
independent object-oriented design; even at the very earliest stages of the
design you should have a specific programming language in mind.

15.2 Access to private components

Friends in C++

Within a C++ class declaration, you can include the declaration of *friend*
subprograms or classes, which are subprograms or classes that have full
access to private data and operations of the class:

```cpp
class Airplane_Data {
private:
    int speed;

    friend void proc(const Airplane_Data &, int &);
    friend class CL;
};
```

The subprogram proc and the subprograms of the class CL can access private components of Airplane_Data:

```
void proc(const Airplane_Data & a, int & i)
{
    i = a.speed;                  // OK, we're friends
}
```

The subprogram proc can then pass on the internal components of the class using reference parameters or pointers as shown. Thus the "friend" has exposed to public view all the secrets of the abstraction.

The motivation behind granting access to otherwise private elements is taken from operating systems which have been designed to explicitly grant specific privileges, called *capabilities*. This concept is less applicable to programming languages because one of the aims of OOP is to create closed, reusable components. From a design point of view, friends are problematic because we are asking the *component* to have knowledge of who is using it, which is certainly not compatible with reusable components that you buy or borrow from another project. Another serious problem with the friend construct is that it may be used too often to "patch" problems in a program instead of rethinking an abstraction. Excessive use of friend will clearly break the abstractions that were so carefully designed.

A valid use of friends is in cases when an abstraction is composed of two distinct elements. In this case, two classes may be declared which are friends of each other. For example, suppose that the class Keyboard needs direct access to the class Display in order to echo a character; conversely, the class Display needs to be able to put a character obtained from a touch-screen interface into the internal buffer of class Keyboard:

```
class Display {
private:
    void echo(char c);
    friend class Keyboard;      // Let Keyboard call echo
};

class Keyboard {
private:
    void put_key(char c);
    friend class Display;       // Let Display call put_key
};
```

The use of friend avoids either of two unsatisfactory solutions: unnecessarily making the subprograms public, or merging the two classes into a single large class just because they have one single operation in common.

Another use of friend is to solve a syntactic problem associated with the fact that a subprogram in a C++ class has a distinguished receiver such as obj1 in the call obj1.proc(obj2). This makes for an asymmetry in subprograms that would otherwise be symmetrical in their parameters. The standard example is overloading of arithmetic operators. Suppose that we wish to overload "+" on complex numbers, while allowing the operation to implicitly convert a floating-point parameter to a complex value:

```
complex operator+(float);
complex operator+(complex);
```

Consider the expression x+y where either x or y can be float and the other complex. The first declaration is correct for complex x and float y because x+y is equivalent to x.operator+(y), which will dispatch on the distinguished receiver of type complex. However, the second declaration for x+y with x of type float will attempt to dispatch on the type float, but the operator was declared in the class complex.

The solution is to declare all these operators as friends of a class, rather than as operations of the class:

```
friend complex operator+(complex, complex);
friend complex operator+(complex, float);
friend complex operator+(float, complex);
```

While this construct is popular in C++, there is actually a better solution which does not require friend.[4] The operator "+=" can be defined as a member function (see ARM, p. 249) and then "+" can be defined as an ordinary function outside the class:

```
complex operator+(float left, complex right)
{
    complex result = complex(left);
    result += right;          // result is distinguished receiver
    return result;
}
```

Access specifiers in C++

When one class is derived from another, we have to ask if the derived class can access the components of the base class. In the following example, database is declared to be private so it is not accessible in a derived class:

---

[4] I would like to thank Kevlin A.P. Henney for showing me how to do this.

```
lass Airplanes {
private:
    Airplane_Data database[100];
};
class Jets : public Airplanes {
    void process_jet(int);
};
void Jets::process_jet(int i)
{
    Airplane_Data d = database[i];        // Error, not accessible !
};
```

If an instance of class Jets is declared, it will contain memory for database but that component is not accessible to any subprogram in the derived class.

There are three access specifiers in C++:

- A public component is accessible to any user of the class.

- A protected component is accessible within the class, and within a class derived from it.

- A private component is accessible only within the class.

In the example, if database is just protected and not private, it can be accessed from the derived class Jets:

```
class Airplanes {
protected:
    Airplane_Data database[100];
};
class Jets : public Airplanes {
    void process_jet(int);
};
void Jets::process_jet(int i)
{
    Airplane_Data d = database[i];        // OK, in derived class
};
```

though this may not be a good idea because it exposes an abstraction. It would probably be better even for the derived class to manipulate the inherited components using public or protected *subprograms*. Then if the internal representation changes, only a few subprograms need be modified.

C++ allows the accessibility of a class component to be modified during derivation. Normally you would use public derivation (as we have done in all the examples) which retains the base class accessibility. However, you can also derive private'ly in which case both public and protected components become private:

```
class Airplanes {
protected:
    Airplane_Data database[100];
};
class Jets : private Airplanes {          // private derivation
    void process_jet(int);
};
void Jets::process_jet(int i)
{
    Airplane_Data d = database[i];        // Error, not accessible
};
```

Child packages in Ada

In Ada, only a package body has access to private declarations. This makes it impossible to directly share private declarations between packages, in the same way that sharing is possible with protected declarations in C++. Ada 95 provides for sharing private declarations through an additional structuring facility called *child packages*. We will limit the discussion here to the use of child packages for this purpose, even though they are extremely useful in any situation in which you wish to extend an existing package without modifying or recompiling it.

Given the private type Airplane_Data defined in a package:

```
package Airplane_Package is
    type Airplane_Data is tagged private;
private
    type Airplane_Data is tagged
        record
            ID: String(1..80);
            Speed: Integer range 0..1000;
            Altitude: Integer 0..100;
        end record;
end Airplane_Package;
```

the type can be extended in a child package:

```
package Airplane_Package.SST_Package is
    type SST_Data is tagged private;
    procedure Set_Speed(A: in out SST_Data; I: in Integer);
private
    type SST_Data is new Airplane_Data with
        record
            Mach: Float;
        end record;
end Airplane_Package.SST_Package;
```

Given a package P1 and its child P1.P2, P2 belongs to the scope of the parent P1 as if it were declared immediately after the specification of the parent. Within the private part and the body of the child package, the private declarations of the parent are visible:

```
package body Airplane_Package.SST_Package is
    procedure Set_Speed(A: in out SST_Data; I: in Integer) is
    begin
        A.Speed := I;              -- OK, private field in parent
    end Set_Speed;
end Airplane_Package.SST_Package;
```

Of course the public part of the child package cannot access the private part of the parent, otherwise the child could expose the secrets of the parent package.[5]

15.3 Class data

Constructors and destructors

A *constructor* is a subprogram that is called when an object of a class is created; similarly, a *destructor* is called when the object is destroyed. Actually, every object (variable) that is defined in any language requires that processing be done when the variable is created and destroyed, if only to allocate and deallocate memory. In object-oriented languages, the programmer is allowed to specify such processing.

Constructors and destructors can be defined in C++ for any class; in fact if you do not define your own, defaults will be supplied by the compiler. The syntax of a constructor is a subprogram with the name of the class, and the syntax of the destructor is the name with a prefixed symbol "~":

---

[5]A child package can be declared private in which case its visible part *can* access the private part, but then the child package cannot be used outside of the parent and its descendants.

```cpp
class Airplanes {                                            C++
private:
    Airplane_Data database[100];
    int current_airplanes;
public:
    Airplanes(int i = 0) : current_airplanes(i) { };
    ~Airplanes();
};
```

Upon creation of an Airplanes database, the count of airplanes receives the value of the parameter i, which has a default value of zero:

```cpp
Airplanes a1(15);           // current_airplanes = 15
Airplanes a2;               // current_airplanes = 0
```

When the database is destroyed the code of the destructor (not shown) will be executed.

It is possible to define several constructors which are overloaded on the parameter signatures:

```cpp
class Airplanes {                                            C++
public:
    Airplanes(int i = 0) : current_airplanes(i) { };
    Airplanes(int i, int j) : current_airplanes(i+j) { };
    ~Airplanes();
};


Airplanes a3(5,6);          // current_airplanes = 11
```

C++ also has a *copy constructor* which allows programmer-defined processing when an object is initialized with the value of an existing object, or more generally when one object is assigned to another. The full definition of constructors and destructors in C++ is quite complicated; for details see Chapter 12 of the Annotated Reference Manual.

In Ada 95, explicit constructors and destructors usually are not declared. For simple initialization of variables, it suffices to use default values for record fields:

```ada
type Airplanes is tagged                                    Ada
    record
        Current_Airplanes: Integer := 0;
    end record;
```

or discriminants (Section 10.4):

```
type Airplanes(Initial: Integer) is tagged
    record
        Current_Airplanes: Integer := Initial;
    end record;
```

Explicit programmer-defined processing is possible by deriving the type from an abstract type called Controlled. This type supplies abstract subprograms for Initialization, Finalization and Adjust (for assignment) that you can override with the specific processing you require. For details, see the package Ada.Finalization described in Section 7.6 of the Ada 95 Language Reference Manual.

Class-wide objects

Memory is allocated for each instance of a class:

```
class C {                                               C++
    char s[100];
};
```

```
C c1, c2;                        // 100 characters for each of c1 and c2
```

Occasionally, it is useful to have a variable that is common to all instances of the class. For example, to assign a serial number to each instance, we would keep a variable last to record the last number assigned. In Ada this is obviously done by including an ordinary variable declaration in the package body:

```
package body P is                                       Ada
    Last: Integer := 0;
end P;
```

while in C++, a special syntax is needed:

```
class C {                                               C++
    static int last;              // Declaration
    char s[100];
};
```

```
int C::last = 0;                 // Definition, accessible outside file
```

The specifier static in this case means that one class-wide object will be allocated. You have to explicitly define the static component outside the class definition. Note that a static class component has external linkage and can be accessed from other files, unlike a static declaration in file scope.

Up- and down-conversion

In Section 14.4 we described how a value of a derived class can be implicitly converted in C++ to a value of its base class. This is called *up-conversion*, because the conversion is upwards from a descendant to any of its ancestors. It is also called *narrowing*, because the derived type is "wide" (since it has extra fields), while the base type is "narrow", having only the fields that are common to all types in its derivation family. Recall that up-conversion occurs only when a value of a derived type is directly assigned to a variable of the base type, not when a pointer is assigned from one variable to another.

Down-conversion from a value of a base type to a value of a derived type ii not allowed because we don't know what values to put in the "extra" fields. Consider, however, the case of a pointer to a base type:

```
Base_Class*      Base_Ptr = new Base_Class;                     C++
Derived_Class*   Derived_Ptr = new Derived_Class;

if (...) Base_Ptr = Derived_Ptr;
Derived_Ptr = Base_Ptr;          // What type does Base_Ptr point to ?
```

It is certainly *possible* that Base_Ptr will actually point to an object of the derived type; in this case there is no reason to reject the assignment. On the other hand, if the designated object is actually of the base type, we are attempting a down-conversion and the assignment should be rejected. To take care of this case, C++ defines a *dynamic cast* which is conditional on the type of the designated object:

```
Derived_Ptr = dynamic_cast<Derived_Class*>Base_Ptr;            C++
```

If the designated object is in fact of the derived type, the conversion is successful. Otherwise, the null pointer 0 is assigned and the programmer can test for it.

Already in Ada 83, explicit conversion was allowed between any two types derived from each other. This posed no problem because derived types have exactly the same components. It is possible for them to have different representations (see Section 5.8) but type conversion is perfectly well-defined, because both representations have the same number and type of components.

The extension of derived type conversion to tagged types is immediate in the case of up-conversion from a derived type to a base type. Unneeded fields are truncated:

```
S: SST_Data;                                              Ada
A: Airplane_Data := Airplane_Data(S);
```

In the other direction, *extension aggregates* are used to supply values to fields that were added during the extension:

```
S := (A with Mach => 1.7);                                Ada
```

The fields Speed and so on are taken from the corresponding fields in the value A and the extra field Mach is explicitly given.

When attempting to down-convert a class-wide type to a specific type, a run-time check is made and an exception will be raised if the class-wide object is not of the derived type:

```
procedure P(C: Airplane_Data'Class) is                    Ada
    S: SST_Data;
begin
    S := SST_Data(C);           -- What type is C ??
exception
    when Constraint_Error => ...
end P;
```

15.4 The Eiffel programming language

The central characteristics of the Eiffel programming language are:

- Eiffel was built from the ground up as an object-oriented language, rather than by grafting support for OOP onto an existing language.

- In Eiffel, the only way of constructing a program is as a system of classes that are clients of one another or that inherit from one another.

- Since inheritance is the main structuring construct, a standard library of classes (related by inheritance) is central to the language.

- While not part of the "language", a sophisticated programming environment was developed by the Eiffel team. The environment includes language-sensitive support for displaying and modifying the classes, for incremental compilation, and for testing and debugging.

Eiffel departs from Smalltalk (which has similar characteristics) in its insistence on static type checking to go with dynamic polymorphism as in Ada 95 and C++. Eiffel goes further in its attempts to support reliable programming by integrating assertions into the language as we discussed in Section 11.5.

The only program unit in Eiffel is the class: no files as in C and C++, and no packages as in Ada.[6] The terminology of Eiffel is different from that of other languages: subprograms (procedures and functions) are called *routines*, objects (variables and constants) are called *attributes*, and the routines and attributes that comprise a class are called the *features* of the class. Essentially, no distinction is made between functions and constants: like an Ada enumeration literal, a constant is considered simply as a function with no parameters. Eiffel is statically typed like C++ in the sense that assignment statements and parameter passing must have conforming types that can be checked at compile-time. However, the language does not have Ada's wealth of type checking constructs such as subtypes and numeric types.

When a class is declared, a list of features is given:

```
class Airplanes
feature                           -- "public"
    New_Airplane(Airplane_Data): Integer is
        do
            ...
        end; -- New_Airplane
    Get_Airplane(Integer: Airplane_Data) is
        do
            ...
        end; -- Get_Airplane
feature {}                        -- "private"
    database: ARRAY[Airplane_Data];
    current_airplanes: Integer;
    find_empty_entry: Integer is
        do
            ...
        end; -- find_empty_entry
    end; -- class Airplanes
```

As in C++, a set of features may be grouped and each group can have its accessibility specified differently. A feature-group with a specifier that is the empty set "{}" exports to no other class, like a private-specifier. A feature-group with no specifier exports to every other class in the system; however,

---

[6] A disadvantage of restricting the language to this single construct is that the environment must contain an additional tool to specify how a program is created out of a set of classes.

it is unlike a public-specifier in C++ or the public part of an Ada package specification because only read-access is exported. In addition, you may explicitly write a list of classes in the feature-specifier; these classes will be allowed to access the features within the group, like friends in C++.

There is no real distinction in Eiffel between predefined types and types defined by the programmer. database is an object of class ARRAY which is predefined in the Eiffel library. Of course, "array" is a very general concept; how are we to indicate the component type of the array? The answer is to use the same method that a programmer would use to parameterize any data type: generics. The predefined class ARRAY has one generic parameter which is used to specify the component type:

```
class ARRAY[G]
```

When an object of type ARRAY is declared,[7] an actual generic parameter must be supplied, in this case Airplane_Data. Unlike Ada and C++, which have a special syntax for declaring predefined composite types, everything in Eiffel is constructed of generic classes using a single set of syntactical and semantical rules.

Generics are widely used in Eiffel, because the library contains definitions of many generic classes that you can specialize for your specific requirements. Generics may also be *constrained* to achieve a contract between the generic class and the instantiation similar to Ada (see Section 10.3). Instead of pattern matching, a constraint is expressed by giving the name of a class from which the actual generic parameter must be derived. For example, the following generic class can be instantiated only by types derived from REAL:

```
class Trigonometry[R -> REAL]
```

You may have noticed that the Eiffel class has no separation between the specification of features and their implementation as executable subprograms. Everything must be in the same class declaration, unlike Ada which divides packages into separately compiled specifications and bodies. Thus the Eiffel language pays for its simplicity by requiring more work from the programming environment. In particular, the language defines a *short* form, in effect the interface, and the environment is responsible for displaying the short form upon request.

---

[7]Note that the declaration does not create the array; this must be done in a separate step which will also specify the size of the array.

Inheritance

Every class defines a type and all classes in the system are arranged in a single hierarchy. There is a class called ANY at the top of the hierarchy. Assignment and equality are defined within ANY but may be overridden within a class. The syntax for inheritance is similar to C++: the inherited classes are listed after the class name. Given the class Airplane_Data:

```
class Airplane_Data
feature
    Set_Speed(I: Integer) is ...
    Get_Speed: Integer is ...
feature { }
    ID: STRING;
    Speed: Integer;
    Altitude: Integer;
end; -- class Airplane_Data
```

we can inherit as follows:

```
class SST_Data inherit
    Airplane_Data
        redefine
            Set_Speed, Get_Speed
        end
feature
    Set_Speed(I: Integer) is ...
    Get_Speed: Integer is ...
feature { }
    Mach: Real;
end; -- class SST_Data
```

All the features in the base class are inherited with their export attributes unchanged. However, the programmer of the derived class is free to redefine some or all of the inherited features. The features to be redefined must be explicitly listed in a redefine-clause that follows the inherit-clause. In addition to redefinition, a feature can be simply renamed. Note that an inherited feature can be re-exported from a class even if it was private in the base class (unlike C++ and Ada 95 which do not allow breaking into a previously hidden implementation).

The Eiffel environment can display the *flat* version of a class which shows all the currently valid features even if they were inherited and redeclared somewhere in the hierarchy. This clearly displays the interface of a class and saves the programmer from having to "dig" through the hierarchy to see exactly what was redeclared and what was not.

Eiffel, like C++ but unlike Ada 95, uses the distinguished receiver approach so there is no need for an explicit parameter for the object whose subprogram is being called:

```
A: Airplane_Data;
A.Set_Speed(250);
```

Allocation

Eiffel has no explicit pointers. All objects are implicitly allocated dynamically and accessed by pointers. However, the programmer may choose to declare an object as expanded, in which case it is allocated and accessed without a pointer:

```
database: expanded ARRAY[Airplane_Data];
```

In addition, a class may be declared as expanded and all objects of the class are directly allocated. Needless to say predefined Integer, Character, etc. are expanded types.

Note that given an assignment or equality operator:

```
X := Y;
```

there are four possibilities depending on whether X, Y, neither or both are expanded. In Ada and C++, it is the responsibility of the programmer to distinguish when pointer assignment is intended and when assignment of designated objects is intended. In Eiffel, assignment is transparent to the programmer, and the meaning of each possibility is carefully defined in the language.

The advantage of indirect allocation is that ordinary objects whose type is that of a base class can have values that are of any type whose class is derived from the base type:

```
A: Airplane_Data;
S: SST_Data;

A := S;
```

If the allocation were static, there would be no "room" in the object A to store the extra field Mach of S. Since indirect allocation is used, the assignment is simply a matter of copying the pointer. Compare this with Ada 95 and

C++ which require additional concepts: class-wide types and pointers for assignment that preserves the specific type.

Additionally, Eiffel distinguishes between shallow copy and deep copy in assignment statements. Shallow copy just copies the pointers (or the data in the case of expanded objects) while deep copy copies the entire data structures. By overriding the inherited definition of assignment you can choose either meaning for any class.

Dynamic polymorphism follows immediately; given:

```
A.Set_Speed(250);
```

the compiler has no way of knowing if the specific type of the value currently held in A is of A's base type Airplane_Data, or of some type derived from Airplane_Data. Since the subprogram Set_Speed has been redefined in at least one derived class, run-time dispatching must be done. Note that no special syntax or semantics is required; all calls are potentially dynamic, though the compiler will optimize and use static binding where possible.

Abstract classes

Abstract classes in Eiffel are similar to those in C++ and Ada 95. A class or a feature in a class may be declared as **deferred**. A deferred class must be made concrete by *effecting* all deferred features, that is, by supplying implementations. Note that unlike C++ and Ada 95, you can *declare* an object whose type is deferred; you get a null pointer which cannot be used until a value of an effective derived type is assigned:

```
deferred class Set ...          -- Abstract class

class Bit_Set inherit Set ...   -- Concrete class

S: Set;                         -- Abstract object !
B: Bit_Set;                     -- Concrete object

!!B;                            -- Create an instance of B
S := B;                         -- OK, S gets a concrete object
S.Union(...);                   -- which can now be used
```

Multiple inheritance

Eiffel supports multiple inheritance:

```
class Winged_Vehicle
feature
    Weight: Integer;
    display is ... end;
end;

class Motorized_Vehicle
feature
    Weight: Integer;
    display is ... end;
end;

class Airplane inherit
    Winged_Vehicle, Motorized_Vehicle
        ...
end;
```

Whenever multiple inheritance is allowed, a language must specify how to resolve ambiguities if a name is inherited from more than one ancestor. Eiffel's rule is basically very simple (even though its formal definition is difficult because it must take account of all the possibilities of an inheritance hierarchy):

> If a feature is inherited from an ancestor class by more than one path, it is shared; otherwise features are replicated.

rename- and redefine-clauses can be used to modify names as necessary. In the example, the class Airplane inherits only one Weight field. Obviously, the intention was for the class to have two Weight fields, one for the airframe and one for the motor. This can be achieved by renaming the two inherited objects:

```
class Airplane inherit
    Winged_Vehicle
        rename Weight as Airframe_Weight;
    Motorized_Vehicle
        rename Weight as Engine_Weight;
        ...
end;
```

Suppose now that we wish to override the subprogram display. We cannot use redefine since it would be ambiguous which subprogram we are redefining. The solution is to undefine both inherited subprograms and to write a new one:

```
class Airplane inherit
    Winged_Vehicle
        undefine display end;
    Motorized_Vehicle
        undefine display end;
feature
    display is ... end;
end;
```

The Eiffel reference manual discusses in detail the use of rename, redefine
and undefine to solve ambiguities in multiple inheritance.

15.5 Design considerations

Inheritance and composition

Inheritance is only one method of structuring that can be used in object-
oriented design. A much simpler method is composition which is the inclu-
sion of one abstraction within another. You already know about composition
because you know that one record can be included within another:

```
with Airplane_Package;
package SST_Package is
    type SST_Data is private;
private
    type SST_Data is
        record
            A: Airplane_Data;
            Mach: Float;
        end record;
end SST_Package;
```

and in C++, a class can have an instance of another class as an element:

```
class SST_Data {
private:
    Airplane_Data a;
    float mach;
};
```

Composition is more elementary than inheritance because no new language
constructs are required to support it; any support for module encapsulation
automatically enables you to compose abstractions. Generics, which in any

case are needed in a type-checked language, can also be used to compose abstractions. Inheritance, however, requires sophisticated language support (tagged records in Ada and virtual functions in C++), and run-time overhead for dynamic dispatching.

If you need dynamic dispatching, you must, of course, choose inheritance over composition. However, if dynamic dispatching is not done, the choice between the two is purely a matter of deciding which method produces a "better" design. Recall that C++ requires you to decide when a base class is created if dynamic dispatching is to be done, by declaring one or more subprograms to be virtual; these and only these subprograms will dispatch. In Ada 95, dynamic dispatching will potentially occur on any subprogram declared with a controlling parameter of a tagged type:

```
type T is tagged ... ;
procedure Proc(Parm: T);
```

The actual decision whether binding is static or dynamic is made separately for each call. Do not use inheritance when a simple record would suffice.

The basic difference between the two methods is that composition simply uses an existing closed abstraction, while inheritance has knowledge of the implementation of an abstraction. Users of a closed abstraction are protected against modification of the implementation. When inheritance is used, base classes cannot be modified without considering what the modification will do to the derived classes.

On the other hand, every access to a closed abstraction must go through an interface subprogram, while inheritance allows efficient direct access by derived classes. In addition, you may modify an implementation in a derived class, whereas in composition you are limited to using the existing implementation. To put it concisely: it is easy to "buy" and "sell" modules for composition, while inheritance makes you a "partner" of the supplier of a module.

There is no danger in a well-designed use of either method; problems can occur when inheritance is used indiscriminately as this can create too many dependencies among the components of a software system. We leave a detailed discussion of the relative merits of the two concepts to specialized texts on OOP. For the pro-inheritance viewpoint, see Meyer's book (*Object-oriented Software Construction*, Prentice-Hall International, 1988), especially Chapters 14 and 19. Compare this with the pro-composition viewpoint expressed in: J.P. Rosen, "What orientation should Ada objects take?", *Communications of the ACM*, 35(11), 1992, pp. 71-76.

Uses of inheritance

It is convenient to divide the uses of inheritance into several categories:[8]

Behaves as An SST behaves as an Airplane. This is a simple use of inheritance for code sharing: operations that are appropriate for Airplane are appropriate for SST, subject to overriding as needed.

Polymorphically substitutable for Linked_Set and Bit_Set are polymorphically substitutable for Set. By deriving from a common ancestor, sets that are implemented differently can be processed using the same operations. Furthermore, you can create heterogeneous data structures based on the ancestor type that contain elements of the entire family of types.

Generically substitutable for Common properties are inherited by several classes. This technique is used in large libraries such as those in Smalltalk or Eiffel, where common properties are factored out into ancestor classes, sometimes called *aspect classes*. For example, a class Comparable would be used to declare relational operations such as "<", and any class such as Integer or Float that possesses such operations will inherit from Comparable.

Implemented by A class can be created by inheriting its logical functions from one class and its implementation from another. The classic example is a Bounded_Stack which (multiply) inherits its functionality from Stack and its implementation from Array. More generally, a class constructed by multiple inheritance would inherit its functionality from several aspect classes and its implementation from one additional class.

These categories are neither mutually exclusive nor exhaustive; they are intended as a guide to the use of this powerful construct in your software designs.

Overloading and polymorphism

While overloading is a form of polymorphism ("multi-formed"), the two concepts are used for quite different purposes. Overloading is used as a convenience to give the same name to subprograms that operate on entirely distinct types, whereas dynamic polymorphism is used to implement an operation for a family of related types. For example:

---

[8]This classification is due to Ian Muang and Richard Mitchell.

```
void proc put(int);
void proc put(float);
```
C++

is overloading because the common name is used just as a convenience and there is no relation between int and float. On the other hand:

```
virtual void set_speed(int);
```
C++

is a single subprogram that happens to be implemented differently for different types of airplanes.

There are technical difficulties in mixing overloading and dynamic polymorphism, and it is recommended that you not combine the use of the two concepts. Do not try to overload within a derived class on a subprogram that appears in the base class:

```
class SST_Data : public Airplane_Data {
public:
    void set_speed(float);        // float rather than int
};
```
C++

The rules of C++ specify that this subprogram neither overloads nor overrides the subprogram in the base class; instead it *hides* the definition in the base class just like an inner scope!

Ada 95 allows overloading and overriding to coexist:

```
with Airplane_Package; use Airplane_Package;
package SST_Package is
    type SST_Data is new Airplane_Data with ...
    procedure Set_Speed(A: in out SST_Data; I: in Integer);
            -- Overrides primitive subprogram from Airplane_Package
    procedure Set_Speed(A: in out SST_Data; I: in Float);
            -- Overloads, not a primitive subprogram
end SST_Package;
```
Ada

Since there is no Set_Speed primitive subprogram with a Float parameter for the parent type, the second declaration is simply an unrelated subprogram that overloads on the same name. Even though this is legal it should be avoided, because the user of the type is likely to be confused. Looking just at SST_Package (and without the comments!), you cannot tell which subprogram overrides and which just overloads:

```
procedure Proc(A: Airplane_Data'Class) is          [Ada]
begin
    Set_Speed(A, 500);       -- OK, dispatches
    Set_Speed(A, 500.0);     -- Error, cannot dispatch !
end Proc;
```

15.6 Methods of dynamic polymorphism

We conclude this chapter by summarizing dynamic polymorphism in languages for object-oriented programming.

Smalltalk Every invocation of a subprogram requires dynamic dispatching that involves searching up the inheritance hierarchy until the subprogram is found.

Eiffel Every invocation of a subprogram is dynamically dispatched (unless optimized to static binding). Unlike Smalltalk, the possible overridings are known at compile-time, so the dispatching has a fixed overhead based on a jump table.

C++ Subprograms explicitly declared virtual and called indirectly via a pointer or reference are dynamically dispatched. Run-time dispatching has fixed overhead.

Ada 95 Dynamic dispatching is implicitly used on primitive subprograms of a tagged type when an actual parameter is a class-wide type and the formal parameter is of a specific type. Run-time dispatching has fixed overhead.

The language designs differ in the explicit programming and the overhead required for dynamic polymorphism, and these then influence programming style and program efficiency. A clear understanding of the principles involved will help you compare object-oriented languages and improve your ability to design and create good object-oriented programs in whatever language you choose.

15.7 Exercises

1. Implement the Set packages in Ada 95 and the classes in C++.

2. Can an abstract type in Ada 95 or an abstract class in C++ have data components? If so, what might they be used for?

```
type Item is abstract tagged                                    Ada
   record
      I: Integer;
   end record;
```

3. Write a program for a heterogeneous queue based on an abstract class.

4. Implement the set packages/classes with a generic element type instead of just integer elements.

5. Study in detail multiple inheritance in Eiffel and compare it to multiple inheritance in C++.

6. A standard example of multiple inheritance in Eiffel is that of a fixed-size list implemented by inheriting from both list and array. How would you write such an ADT in Ada 95 which does not have multiple inheritance?

7. What are the dangers of defining protected data in C++? Does this also apply to child packages in Ada 95?

8. Study the structure of the standard library in Ada 95 which makes extensive use of child packages. Compare it with the structure of the standard I/O classes in C++.

9. Study the package Finalization in Ada 95 which can be used to write constructors and destructors. Compare it with the C++ constructs.

10. What is the relationship between assignment statements and constructors/destructors?

11. Give examples of the use of class-wide objects.

PART V

Non-imperative Programming Languages

16 Functional Programming

16.1 Why functional programming?

In Section 1.8 we mentioned that both Church and Turing proposed models of computation long before the first computers were built. Turing machines are very similar to modern computers in that they are based on an *updatable store*, that is, a set of memory cells whose contents are modified when an instruction is executed. This is also known as the *von Neumann* architecture.

Church's formulation of a model of computation (called the *lambda calculus*) is entirely different, being based on the mathematical concept of functions. This formulation is completely equivalent to Turing's in terms of the computations that can be described, but as a practical formalism for computing, the functional approach has been much less popular. The language Lisp, developed in 1956, uses a functional approach to computation similar to the lambda calculus model, though it contains many features that encourage an imperative programming style.

During the 1980's further research into functional programming has resulted in languages that have a very clean theoretical basis and yet can be efficiently implemented. The main difference between modern functional programming languages and Lisp is that types and type checking are basic concepts of these languages, so both the reliability and efficiency of programs are greatly improved.

Many of the problems that we have in writing reliable programs stem directly from the use of an updatable store:

- Memory can be "smeared" because we are directly modifying memory cells (using array indices or pointers), rather than simply computing values.

- It is difficult to construct complex programs from components because subprograms can have side effects. Thus it can be impossible to under-

317

stand the effect of a subprogram in isolation from the entire program.

Strong type checking and the encapsulation techniques of object-oriented programming can alleviate these problems but not entirely eliminate them. By adopting a functional approach, both of these problems disappear.

The discussion will be based on the popular language Standard ML though the concepts hold for other languages.

16.2 Functions

Functions are defined in ML by equating the name of a function with its formal parameter to an expression:

```
fun even n = (n mod 2 = 0)
```

the difference being that there are no global variables, no assignment,[1] no pointers and hence no side effects. Once a function has been defined, it can be *applied* to a value; the *evaluation* of the application will produce a result:

```
even 4 = true
even 5 = false
```

A type is associated with every function just as types are associated with variables in programming languages. The type of even is:

```
even:  int -> bool
```

meaning that it maps a value of integer type into a value of Boolean type.
Expressions used in ML can contain conditions:

```
fun min (x,y) = if x < y then x else y
```

Evaluating an example of an application of the function gives:

```
min (4,5) =
(if x < y then x else y) (4,5) =
if 4 < 5 then 4 else 5 =
if true then 4 else 5 =
4
```

Note that this is not an if-statement but a conditional expression, similar to the C operator:

---

[1]ML actually does have imperative assignment in case you absolutely need it, but we will ignore this aspect of the language.

x < y ? x : y

What is the type of min? In functional programming, a function is considered to have exactly one argument;[2] if you need more than one, you must create a tuple (pair, triple, etc.) using the Cartesian product function. Thus (4,5) is of type int × int and the function min is of type:

min: (int × int) -> int

Instead of using tuples, you can define a function which will be applied one by one to each argument:

fun min_c x y = if x < y then x else y

This is called a *curried function*, named after the mathematician H.B. Curry. When this function is applied to a sequence of arguments, the first application creates another function which is then applied to the second.

The function min_c takes one integer argument and creates a new function, also of one argument:

min_c 4 = if 4 < y then 4 else y

This function can then be applied to another single argument:

```
min_c 4 5 =
(if 4 < y then 4 else y) 5 =
if 4 < 5 then 4 else 5 =
if true then 4 else 5 =
4
```

Curried functions can be used with *partial evaluation* to define new functions:

fun min_4 = min_c 4

```
min_4 5 =
(if 4 < y then 4 else y) 5 =
if 4 < 5 then 4 else 5 =
if true then 4 else 5 =
4
```

---

[2]It is common in functional programming to use the mathematical word argument, rather than the programming word parameter.

16.3 Compound types

Lists

A list can be created from any previously defined type, in particular for predefined types like integer or Boolean. The lists:

> [2, 3, 5, 7, 11]   [true, false, false]

are of types int list and bool list, respectively. Alternatively, a list can be created using *constructors*; the list constructors are [] for the empty list, and element :: list for a non-empty list created by adding an element to an existing list. Constructors can be used when defining functions by *pattern matching*.

```
fun     member [] e = false
|       member [e :: tail] e = true
|       member [e1 :: tail] e = member tail e
```

The type of member is:[3]

> member: int list × int -> boolean

and it can be read as follows:

> When member is applied to a list L and (then) to an element e, the evaluation is based on cases according to the arguments: (1) if L is empty, e is not a member of L; (2) if e is the first element of L, then e is a member of L; (3) otherwise, e1, the first element of L, is not the same as e, so we (recursively) check to see if e is a member of the tail of L.

You do not have to declare the type of a function in ML; the compiler automatically infers the type of the function from the types of the arguments and the type of the result. If the compiler cannot infer the type, you will have to supply enough type declarations to disambiguate the expression. Type checking is static, meaning that when a function is applied to a value, a check is made at compile time that the type of the function matches the type of the argument.

Note that this function is recursive. Recursion is extremely important in functional programming languages; in the absence of "statements" it is the only way of creating loops in expression evaluation.

As a final example, let us show how to write the *insertion sort* algorithm in ML. You use this algorithm to sort your hand when playing cards: take

---

[3]Actually, the type is 't list × 't boolean, but type variables are not introduced until the next section.

each card one by one from the pile in front of you and place it in its correct place:

```
fun     insertion_sort [] = []
|       insertion_sort head :: tail =
            insert_element head insertion_sort tail
and
fun     insert_element x [] = [x]
|       insert_element x head :: tail =
            if x < head then x :: head :: tail
            else head :: (insert_element x tail)
```

These functions are of types:

```
insertion_sort: int list -> int list
insert_element: int -> int list -> int list
```

Once you get used to the notation it is easy to read such programs:

A sorted empty list is the empty list. A non-empty list is sorted by taking the first element x, sorting the remainder of the list tail, and then inserting x in its proper place in the sorted version of the list.

An element x is inserted into an empty list by creating a list of a single element. To insert x into a non-empty list, compare x with the head of the list: (1) if x is less than head, make x the new first element of the list; (2) otherwise create a new list composed of head followed by the list created by inserting x in the remainder of the list.

Note that -> associates to the right:

```
insert_element: int -> (int list -> int list)
```

The function maps an integer into another function that maps integer lists into integer lists. Using partial evaluation, we can create new functions like:

```
fun insert_4 = insert_element 4
```

which is a function that inserts 4 into an integer list.

Compared with an imperative program for the same algorithm, there are no indices and no for-loops. Furthermore, it generalizes immediately to sorting objects of other types just by replacing the operator "<" by an appropriate Boolean function for comparing two values of the type. No explicit pointers are needed to create the list; the pointers are implicit in the data representation. Of course, sorting lists in any language is less efficient than sorting an array in-place but for many applications using lists is practical.

Defining new types

Throughout the book, we have seen that defining new types is essential if a programming language is to model the real world. Modern functional programming languages also have this capability. Let us define a (recursive) type for trees whose nodes are labeled with integers:

```
datatype int tree =
        Empty
|       T of (int tree × int × int tree)
```

This is read:

> int tree is a new data type whose values are: (1) the new constant value Empty, or (2) a value formed by the *constructor* T applied to a triple consisting of a tree, an integer and another tree.

Having defined the new type, we can write functions that process the tree. For example:

```
fun     sumtree Empty = 0
|       sumtree T(left, value, right) =
            (sumtree left) + value + (sumtree right)
```

adds the values labeling the nodes of the tree, and:

```
fun     mintree Empty = maxint
|       mintree T(left, value, right) =
            min left (min value (mintree right))
```

computes the minimum of all the values labeling the nodes, returning the largest integer maxint on an empty tree.

All the standard tree algorithms can be written in the same manner: define a new data type that matches the tree structure, and then write functions on the type. No explicit pointers or loops are required, just recursion and pattern matching.

16.4 Higher-order functions

In functional programming, a function is an ordinary object with a type, so it can be an argument of other functions. For example, we can create a generic form of insert_element by simply adding a function compare as an additional argument:

```
fun      general_insert_element compare x [] = [x]
|        general_insert_element compare x head :: tail =
             if compare x head
             then x :: head :: tail
             else head :: (general_insert_element compare x tail)
```

If string_compare is a function from strings to Boolean:

```
string_compare: (string × string) -> bool
```

applying general_insert_element to this argument:

```
fun string_insert = general_insert_element   string_compare
```

gives a function of type:

```
string -> string list -> string list
```

Note that unlike imperative languages, this generalization is achieved naturally without any additional syntax or semantics like generic or template.

But what is the type of general_insert_element? Well, the first argument must be of type "function from a pair of anything to Boolean", the second argument must be of the same "anything", and the third argument is a list of "anything". *Type variables* are used as a shorthand for "anything" and the type of the function is thus:

```
general_insert_element: (('t × 't) -> bool) -> 't -> 't list
```

where type variables are written in ML as identifiers preceded by an apostrophe.

The use of *higher-order functions*, that is functions that have functions as arguments, is not limited to such static constructs as are generics. An extremely useful function is map:

```
fun      map f [] = []
|        map f head :: tail = (f head) :: (map f tail)
```

This function applies its first argument to a list of values producing a list of the results. For example:

```
map even [1, 3, 5, 2, 4, 6] = [false, false, false, true, true, true]
map min [(1,5), (4,2), (8,1)] = [1, 2, 1]
```

This is practically impossible to achieve in imperative languages; at most we could write a subprogram that receives a pointer to a function as an argument, but we would require different subprograms for each possible argument signature of the function argument.

Note that the construction is safe. The type of map is:

```
map: ('t1 -> 't2) -> 't1 list -> 't2 list
```

meaning that the elements of the argument list 't1 list must all be compatible with the argument of function 't1, and the result list 't2 list will consist only of elements of the function result type 't2.

Higher-order functions abstract away most of the control structures that we find essential in imperative languages. To give another example, the function accumulate compounds the function application instead of creating a list of results like map:

```
fun     accumulate f initial [] = initial
|       accumulate f initial head :: tail = accumulate f (f initial head) tail
```

accumulate can be used to create a variety of useful functions. The functions

```
fun minlist = accumulate min maxint
fun sumlist = accumulate "+" 0
```

compute the minimum of an integer list and the sum of an integer list, respectively. For example:

```
minlist [3, 2, 1] =
accumulate min maxint [3, 1, 2] =
accumulate min (min maxint 3) [1, 2] =
accumulate min 3 [1, 2] =
accumulate min (min 3 1) [2] =
accumulate min 1 [2] =
accumulate min (min 1 2) [] =
accumulate min 1 [] =
1
```

Higher-order functions are not limited to lists; you can write functions that traverse trees and apply a function at each node. Furthermore, functions can be defined on type variables so that they can be used without change when you define new data types.

16.5 Lazy and eager evaluation

In imperative languages, we always assume that the actual parameters will be evaluated before calling the function:

> n = min(j+k, (i+4)/m); `C`

The technical term for this is *eager evaluation.* However, eager evaluation has its own problems which we encountered in if-statements (Section 6.2), and a special construct for short-circuit evaluation had to be defined:

> if (N > 0) and then ((Sum / N) > M) then ... `Ada`

How should a conditional expression:

> if c then e1 else e2

be defined in a functional programming language? Under eager evaluation we would evaluate c, e1 and e2 and only then perform the conditional operation. Of course, this is not acceptable; the following expression fails if eager evaluation is used, since it is an error to take the head of an empty list:

> if list = [] then [] else hd list

To solve this problem, ML has a special rule for evaluation of the if-function: the condition c is evaluated first, and only then is one of the two branches evaluated.

The situation would be much simpler if *lazy evaluation* were used, where an argument is evaluated only if it is needed, and only to the extent needed.[4] For example, we could define if as an ordinary function:

```
fun     if true x y = x
 |      if false x y = y
```

When if is applied, the function is simply applied to its first argument, producing:

```
(if list=[] [] hd list) [] =
if []=[] [] hd [] =
if true [] hd [] =
[]
```

and we don't attempt to evaluate hd [].

Lazy evaluation is similar to the *call-by-name* parameter passing mechanism in imperative languages, where the actual parameter is evaluated anew

---

[4]For this reason lazy evaluation is also known as *call-by-need.*

each time the formal parameter is used. The mechanism is problematic in imperative languages, because the possibility of side-effects makes it impossible to optimize by computing and storing an evaluation for reuse. In side-effect-free functional programming there is no problem, and languages using lazy evaluation (such as Miranda[5]) have been implemented. Lazy evaluation can be less efficient than eager evaluation, but it has significant advantages.

The main attraction of lazy evaluation is that it is possible to do incremental evaluation which can be used to program efficient algorithms. For example, consider a tree of integer values whose type we defined above. You may wish to program an algorithm which compares two trees to see if they have the same set of values under some ordering of the nodes. This can be written as follows:

    fun   equal_nodes t1 t2 = compare_lists (tree_to_list t1) (tree_to_list t2)

The function tree_to_list traverses the tree and creates a list of the values in the nodes; compare_lists checks if two lists are equal. Under eager evaluation, both trees are completely transformed into lists before the comparison is done, even if the first nodes in the traversal are unequal! Under lazy evaluation, it is only necessary to evaluate the functions to the extent necessary to continue the computation.

The functions compare_lists and tree_to_list are defined as follows:[6]

    fun   compare_lists [] [] = true
    | compare_lists head :: tail1 head :: tail2 = compare_lists tail1 tail2
    | compare_lists list1 list2 = false

    fun   tree_to_list Empty = []
    | tree_to_list T(left, value, right) =
               value :: append (tree_to_list left) (tree_to_list right)

An example of lazy evaluation would proceed as follows (where we have abbreviated the functions as cmp and ttl, and the ellipsis indicates a very large subtree):

    cmp   ttl T(T(Empty,4,Empty), 5, ...)
           ttl T(T(Empty,6,Empty), 5, ...) =
    cmp   5 :: append (ttl T(Empty,4,Empty)) (ttl ...)
           5 :: append (ttl T(Empty,6,Empty)) (ttl ...) =

---

[5]Miranda is a trademark of Research Software Ltd.

[6]This traversal is called *preorder* because the root of a subtree is listed before the nodes in the subtree.

```
cmp    append (ttl T(Empty,4,Empty)) (ttl ...)
       append (ttl T(Empty,6,Empty)) (ttl ...) =
       ...
cmp    4 :: append [] (ttl ...)
       6 :: append [] (ttl ...) =
false
```

By evaluating the arguments only as needed, the unnecessary traversal of the right-hand subtree is completely avoided. Programming tricks are needed to achieve the same effect in a language like ML that uses eager evaluation.

An additional advantage of lazy evaluation is that it lends itself to interactive and systems programming. The input, say from a terminal, is simply considered to be a potentially infinite list of values. The lazy evaluator never evaluates the entire list, of course; instead, whenever a value is needed, the head of the list is removed after prompting the user to supply a value.

16.6 Exceptions

An evaluation of an expression in ML can raise an exception. There are predefined exceptions, mainly for exceptions that are raised when computing with predefined types, such as division by zero or taking the head of an empty list. The programmer can also declare exceptions which may optionally have parameters:

```
exception BadParameter of int;
```

The exception can then be raised and handled:

```
fun only_positive n =
    if n <= 0 then raise BadParameter n
    else ...

val i = ...;
val j = only_positive i
    handle
        BadParameter 0 => 1;
        BadParameter n => abs n;
```

The function only_positive raises the exception BadParameter if the parameter is not positive. When the function is called, an exception handler is attached to the calling expression, specifying the value to be returned if the function raises the exception. This value can be used for further computation at the point where the exception was raised; in this case it is only used as the value returned from the function.

16.7 Environments

In addition to defining functions and evaluating expressions, an ML program can contain declarations:

```
val i = 20
val s = "Hello world"
```

Thus ML has a *store*, but unlike imperative languages this store is not updatable; in the example, it is not possible to "assign" a different value to i or s. If we now execute:

```
val i = 35
```

a new named value would be created, hiding the old value but not replacing the contents of i with a new value. ML declarations are similar to const declarations in C in that an object is created but cannot be modified; however, an ML redeclaration hides the previous one while in C it is illegal to redeclare an object in the same scope.

Block structuring is possible by making declarations local to a definition or an expression. The syntax for localization within an expression is shown in the following example which computes the roots of a quadratic equation using a local declaration for the discriminant:

```
val a = 1.0 and b = 2.0 and c = 1.0
let
    D = b*b - 4.0*a*c
in
    ( (-b+D)/2.0*a, (-b-D)/2.0*a )
end
```

Each declaration *binds* a value to a name. The set of all bindings in force at any time is called an *environment*, and we say that an expression is evaluated in the context of an environment. We actually discussed environments at length in the context of scope and visibility in imperative languages; the difference is that bindings cannot be modified in a functional programming environment.

It is an easy extension to include abstract data types within an environment. This is done by attaching a set of functions to a type declaration:

```
abstype int tree =
        Empty
|       T of (int tree × int × int tree)
with
    fun sumtree t = ...
    fun equal_nodes t1 t2 = ...
end
```

The meaning of this declaration is that only the listed functions have access to constructors of the abstract type, similar to a private type in Ada or a C++ class with private components. Furthermore, the abstract type may be parameterized with a type variable:

```
abstype 't tree = ...
```

which is similar to creating generic abstract data types in Ada.

ML includes a very flexible system for defining and manipulating modules. The basic concept is the *structure* which encapsulates an environment consisting of declarations (types and functions), in a way that is similar to a C++ class or an Ada package that defines an abstract data type. However, in ML a structure is itself an object that has a type called a *signature*. Structures can be manipulated using *functors* which are functions that map one structure to another. This is a generalization of the generic concept which maps package or class templates to concrete types. Functors can be used to hide or share information in structures. The details of these concepts are beyond the scope of the book and the interested reader is referred to textbooks on ML.

Functional programming languages can be used to write concise, reliable programs for applications that deal with complex data structures and algorithms. Even if the efficiency of the functional program is not acceptable, it can still be used as a prototype or as a working specification of the final program.

16.8 Exercises

1. What is the type of the curried function min_c?

   ```
   fun min_c x y = if x < y then x else y
   ```

2. Infer the types of sumtree and mintree.

3. Write out the definition of general_insert_element in words.

4. Write a function for appending lists, and then show how the same function can be defined using accumulate.

5. Write a function that takes a list of trees and returns a list of the minimum values in each tree.

6. Infer the types of compare_lists and tree_to_list.

7. What does the following program do? What is the type of the function?

```
fun     filter f [] = []
|       filter f h::t = h::(filter f t),           if f h = true
|       filter f h::t = filter f t,                otherwise
```

8. The standard deviation of a sequence of numbers $(x_1, \ldots, x_n)$ is defined as the square root of the averages of the squares of the numbers minus the square of the average. Write an ML program that computes the standard deviation of a list of numbers. Hint: use map and accumulate.

9. Write an ML program to test for perfect numbers; $n > 2$ is a perfect number if the factors of n (not including n) add up to n. For example, $1 + 2 + 4 + 7 + 14 = 28$. The outline of the program is as follows:

```
fun isperfect n =
      let fun addfactors ...
in addfactors(n div 2) = n end;
```

10. Compare exceptions in ML with exceptions in Ada, C++ and Eiffel.

17

Logic Programming

Logic programming is based on the observation that formulas in mathematical logic can be interpreted as specifications of computations. The style of programming is declarative rather than imperative. We do not issue commands telling the computer what to do; instead, we describe the relationship between the input data and the output data, and let the computer figure out how to obtain the output from the input. To the extent that this is successful, logic programming provides a significantly higher level of abstraction, with the corresponding advantage of extremely concise programs.

There are two major abstractions that characterize logic programming. The first is that control statements such as our familiar for- and if-statements are abstracted away. Instead, the "compiler" supplies an extremely powerful control mechanism that is *uniformly* applied throughout the program. The mechanism is based on the concept of *proof* in mathematical logic: instead of a step-by-step algorithm, a program is considered to be a set of logical formulas which are assumed to be true (axioms), and a computation is an attempt to prove a formula from the axioms of the program.[1]

The second abstraction is that assignment statements and explicit pointers are no longer used; instead, a generalized pattern matching mechanism called *unification* is used to construct and decompose data structures. Implementations of unification create implicit pointers between components of data structures, but all the programmer sees is abstract data structures such as lists, records and trees.

After we discuss "pure" logic programming, we will describe the compromises introduced by Prolog, the first and still very popular, practical logic programming language.

---

[1] More precisely, that the formula is a *logical consequence* of the program. Rather than digress to explain this concept, we will use the more intuitive notion of proof.

17.1 Pure logic programming

Consider the C function that checks if one string is a substring of another, returning a pointer to the first occurrence or zero if there is no such occurrence. This is a non-trivial program with two nested loops and assorted boundary conditions to be checked, just the sort of program that is likely to have an obscure bug. A possible implementation is as follows:

```
/* Is s1 a substring of s2 ? */                                    C
char *substr(char *s1, char *s2)
{
    char *p = s2;           /* Used to index through s2 */
    int len1 = strlen(s1) - 1;   /* Store lengths */
    int len2 = strlen(s2) - 1;
    int i;                  /* Index through strings */

    while (*p != 0) {       /* Check for end of s2 */
        i = len1;
        if (p+i) > (s2+len2)    /* Too few characters */
            return NULL;
        while ( (i >= 0) && (*(p+i) == *(s1+i)) )
            i--;            /* Match from end of s1 */
        if (i == -1) return p;   /* Found - matched all of s1 */
        else p++;           /* Not found - continue loop */
    }
    return NULL;
}
```

Let us try to define exactly what it means for a string s to be a substring of another string t. We denote the substring relation by "$\sqsubseteq$", and the concatenation operator by "$\|$".

$$t \sqsubseteq t$$
$$(t = t1 \| t2) \wedge (s \sqsubseteq t1) \Rightarrow (s \sqsubseteq t)$$
$$(t = t1 \| t2) \wedge (s \sqsubseteq t2) \Rightarrow (s \sqsubseteq t)$$

These are three logical formulas that define substring in terms of the more primitive concept of concatenation. The first formula gives a basic *fact*, namely that every string is a substring of itself. The next two formulas state that if a string t is decomposed into two (smaller) strings $t1$ and $t2$, and ("$\wedge$") s is a substring of one of these components, then ("$\Rightarrow$") s is a substring of t. Of course you know that these are not circular definitions but recursive definitions: reducing the problem to smaller and smaller problems until it can be solved by a base case.

But what does this have to do with computation? Suppose that we reverse the logical formulas:

$$t \sqsubseteq t$$
$$(s \sqsubseteq t) \Leftarrow (t = t1 \parallel t2) \wedge (s \sqsubseteq t1)$$
$$(s \sqsubseteq t) \Leftarrow (t = t1 \parallel t2) \wedge (s \sqsubseteq t2)$$

and suppose that we have two specific strings s and t, and we wish to check if s is a substring of t. The logical formulas tell us exactly how to do this. First check if s is perhaps the same as t; if not, decompose t into two substrings $t1$ and $t2$, and (recursively) check if s is a substring of either one. Perform this check for *every* possible decomposition of t until you find a sequence of decompositions which shows that s is a substring of t. If no such sequence exists, then s is not a substring of t.

The reasoning is done backwards: what would have to be true in order for $s \sqsubseteq t$ to be true? Well, if:

$$(t = t1 \parallel t2) \wedge (s \sqsubseteq t1)$$

were true, that would solve the problem. But in order for $s \sqsubseteq t1$ to be true for some substring $t1$:

$$(t1 = t11 \parallel t12) \wedge (s \sqsubseteq t11)$$

or:

$$(t1 = t11 \parallel t12) \wedge (s \sqsubseteq t12)$$

would have to be true and so on. This recursive reasoning can be continued until a fact such as $s \sqsubseteq s$ is reached which is unconditionally true.

For example, is "wor" $\sqsubseteq$ "Hello world"? "Hello world" can be decomposed in twelve different ways:

""	"Hello world"
"H"	"ello world"
"He"	"llo world"
. . .	. . .
"Hello wor"	"ld"
"Hello worl"	"d"
"Hello world"	""

For every possible decomposition, we must check the two component strings to see if "wor" is a substring of either of them. Of course each such decomposition (except those with the null string as one of the components) results in a further set of decompositions. But eventually, we will decompose a string into "" and "wor" and then successfully conclude that "wor" is a substring of "wor". In fact, there is more than one way of solving the problem, because we could obtain the same components in several different ways, and even obtain the symmetric decomposition "wor" and "".

While the above computation is rather tedious to do by hand, it is just the type of repetitious task at which a computer excels. To execute a logic program, a set of logical formulas (the program) and a goal such as:

$$\text{"wor"} \sqsubseteq \text{"Hello world"} \; ?$$

are submitted to a software system which is called an *inference engine*, because it conducts logical inferences from one formula to another until the problem is solved. The inference engine checks if the goal formula can be proven from the axioms, the formulas of the program which are assumed to be true. The answer could be either yes or no, called *success* or *failure* in logic programming. Failure could be caused because the goal does not follow from the program, for example, "wro" is not a substring of "Hello world", or it could be caused by an incorrect program, for example if we omitted one of the formulas of the program. There is a third possibility, namely that the inference engine searches forever without deciding either way, in the same way that a while-loop in C may never terminate.

The basic concepts of logic programming are:

- The program is declarative and consists solely of formulas in mathematical logic.

- Each set of formulas for the same *predicate* (such as "$\sqsubseteq$") is interpreted as a (possibly recursive) procedure.

- A particular computation is defined by submitting a *goal*, which is a formula that is to be checked to see if it can be proven from the program.

- The compiler is an inference engine that *searches* for a possible proof of the goal from the program.

Thus every logic program has a dual reading: one as a set of formulas and another as a specification of a computation. In a sense, a logic program is a minimal program. In software engineering, you are taught to precisely specify the meaning of a program before attempting to implement it, and a precise specification uses a formal notation, usually some form of mathematical logic. If the specification *is* the program, there is nothing further to do, and thousands of programmers can be replaced by a handful of logicians. The reason that logic programming is not trivial is that pure logic is not efficient enough for practical programming, and thus there is a clear step that must be taken from the scientific theory of logic to its engineering application in programming.

There are no "control statements" in logic programming, because the control structure is uniform over all programs and consists of a search to prove a formula. Searching for solutions to a problem is, of course, not new; what is new is the suggestion that searching for solutions to computational problems be done in the general framework of logical proofs. Logic became logic programming when it was discovered that by limiting the structure of the formulas and the way that the search for proofs is done, it is possible to retain the simplicity of logical declarations and yet search for problem solutions in an efficient manner. Before explaining how this is done, we must discuss how data is handled in logic programming.

17.2 Unification

A *Horn clause* is a formula which is a *conjunction* ("and") of elementary formulas that implies a conclusion which is a single elementary formula:

$$(s \sqsubseteq t) \Leftarrow (t = t1 \parallel t2) \wedge (s \sqsubseteq t1)$$

Logic programming is based on the observation that by restricting formulas to Horn clauses, just the right balance is achieved between expressiveness and efficient inference. Facts, such as $t \sqsubseteq t$, are conclusions which are not implied by anything, that is, they are always true. The conclusion is also called the *head* of the formula because when written in this reversed form, it appears first in the formula.

To initiate a computation of a logic program, a *goal* is given:

$$\text{"wor"} \sqsubseteq \text{"Hello world"} ?$$

The inference engine tries to match the goal and the conclusion of a formula. In this case, there is an immediate match: "wor" matches the variable s and "Hello world" matches the variable t. This defines a *substitution* of terms (in this case constants) for the variables; the substitution is applied to all variables in the formula:

$$\text{"wor"} \sqsubseteq \text{"Hello world"} \Leftarrow (\text{"Hello world"} = t1 \parallel t2) \wedge (\text{"wor"} \sqsubseteq t1)$$

Applying backwards reasoning, we have to show that:

$$(\text{"Hello world"} = t1 \parallel t2) \wedge (\text{"wor"} \sqsubseteq t1)$$

is true, and this leads to another pattern match, namely trying to match "Hello world" to $t1 \parallel t2$. Here, of course, there are many possible matches and this leads to the search. For example, the inference engine can let $t1$ point to "He" and $t2$ point to "llo world"; these substitutions are then carried through the computation.

Did we say "point to"? Using pattern matching, pointers to arbitrary portions of the string can be created without any explicit notation! All the cautions about the dangers of pointers no longer apply, because pointers to components of the data structure are created and maintained automatically (and correctly) by the inference engine. Logic programming abstracts away not only the control structure, but also the necessity for explicit pointers to allocate and manipulate dynamic data.

There is one concept missing in order to make a programming language out of logical formulas, namely, how are answers returned from a computation? In the above example, we just asked if the goal (without variables) is true or not, and the result of the computation is merely success or failure, indicating that the goal is true or false. If the goal contains variables, the computation may succeed provided that certain substitutions are made for the variables. In mathematical logic, this would be expressed using an *existential quantifier*:

$$\exists s(s \sqsubseteq \text{"Hello world"})$$

which is true if *there exists* a value that can be substituted for s such that the formula is true.

Expressed as a goal:

$$s \sqsubseteq \text{"Hello world"}$$

it matches the first formula for substring $t \sqsubseteq t$, *provided* that both s and "Hello world" are substituted for t. This, of course, is possible only if "Hello world" is also substituted for s. The substitution of the string for the variable defines an answer to the goal:

$$[\text{"Hello world"} \rightarrow s]$$

Suppose we ask the inference engine to continue searching. The goal also matches the head of the second formula giving:

$$(\text{"Hello world"} = t1 \parallel t2) \wedge (s \sqsubseteq t1)$$

By choosing one of the possible decompositions of "Hello world", the inference engine will obtain the formula:

$$(\text{"Hello world"} = \text{"Hello w"} \parallel \text{"orld"}) \wedge (s \sqsubseteq \text{"Hello w"})$$

But $s \sqsubseteq$ "Hello w" matches $t \sqsubseteq t$ under the substitution:

$$["Hello w" \rightarrow s]$$

giving another answer to the goal.

Generalized pattern matching, called *unification*, enables links to be maintained between variables and data structures (or components of data structures). Once a variable is *instantiated*, that is once a variable receives a concrete value, that value is instantly propagated to all connected variables. When a computation terminates successfully, the substitutions that have been made to the variables in the goal form the answer.

Note that unification is symmetrical in all arguments of a goal. Suppose the goal is:

$$"Hello world" \sqsubseteq t$$

This means: Is "Hello world" the substring of some string? The answer will be "Hello world", or even "Hello worldxxx". Logic programs are directionless and can be run "forwards" or "backwards", and generate multiple solutions.

Thus logic programming is based on a uniform control structure that searches for logical inferences, and on a uniform data structuring mechanism that composes and decomposes data. It is correct to say that there is only one "statement" in logic programming, namely an inference step that uses unification to match an elementary formula with a formula. It is hard to conceive that a programming language could be much simpler than this, with no bulky manuals containing dozens of rules and regulations to study! Of course, the single "statement" in the language is extremely powerful and it takes a lot of practice until you become adept at writing logic programs.

17.3 Prolog

Computation and search rules

Prolog is a logical programming language that can be used in practice to write concise, efficient programs. Prolog makes two compromises with the ideal logic programming concept that we have discussed. The first is to define *specific* search and order of computation rules on the logical formulas, so that the language can be efficiently implemented. The second is to include *non-logical predicates*, which are elementary formulas that have no logical meaning but instead are used for their side-effects, such as input and output.

Prolog programs consist of sets of Horn clauses (one elementary formula is implied by a conjunction of zero or more other formulas). Each set of Horn clauses with the same head is called a procedure:

```
substring(T, T).
substring(S, T) :- concat(T, T1, T2), substring(S, T1).
substring(S, T) :- concat(T, T1, T2), substring(S, T2).
```

The sign ":-" denotes implication, and variables must begin with upper-case letters. Given a goal:

```
?- substring("wor", "Hello world").
```

computation proceeds by attempting to unify the goal with the head of a formula; if the unification succeeds, the goal is replaced by the sequence of elementary formulas (also called goals):

```
?- concat("Hello world", T1, T2), substring("wor", T1).
```

The goal that results may consist of more than one elementary formula; the inference engine must now choose one of them to continue the attempt to find a solution. The *computation rule* of Prolog specifies that the inference engine always chooses the *leftmost* elementary formula. In the example, the computation rule requires that the concat be chosen before the recursive call to substring.

There may be more than one formula whose head matches the chosen elementary formula, and the inference engine must choose one of them to attempt unification. The Prolog *search rule* specifies that formulas be attempted in the order that they appear in the program text. When attempting to match a goal formula with the formulas of the substring procedure, the search rule requires that the fact substring(T,T) be chosen first, then the second formula with substring(S,T1), and only if these fail, the third formula with substring(S,T2).

The reason for these seemingly arbitrary requirements is that they enable Prolog to be implemented on a stack architecture just like C and Ada, and most computation is Prolog is just as efficient as it would be in imperative languages. The computation is done by *backtracking*. In the above example:

```
?- concat("Hello world", T1, T2), substring("wor", T1).
```

suppose that the computation has proven concat with the substitution:

$$["H" \rightarrow t1, "ello world" \rightarrow t2]$$

Now an attempt is made to prove substring("wor", "H") which obviously fails. The computation backtracks and attempts to find another proof of concat with a different substitution. All the data needed for the computation of substring("wor", "H") can be discarded upon backtracking. Thus the computation rule of Prolog maps naturally into an efficient stack implementation.

To further improve the efficiency of Prolog programs, the language includes a feature called the *cut* (denoted "!"), which tells the inference engine to
refrain from searching part of the potential solution space. It is the programmer's responsibility to ensure that there are no possible solutions that are
"cut away". For example, suppose that we are trying to parse an arithmetic
expression which is defined as two terms separated by an operator:

```
expression(T1, OP, T2) :- term(T1), operator(OP), !, term(T2).

operator('+').
operator('-').
operator('*').
operator('/').
```

and that the goal is expression(n,'+',27). Obviously, both n and 27 are terms,
and '+' is one of the operators, so the goal succeeds. If, however, the goal is
expression(n,'+','>'), the computation will proceed as follows in the absence
of the cut:

```
n is a term
'+' matches operator('+')
'>' is not a term
'+' does not match operator('-')
'+' does not match operator('*')
'+' does not match operator('/')
```

The inference engine backtracks and tries different ways to satisfy opera-
tor(OP), in the hope that a different match will also allow it to satisfy term(T2).
Of course, the programmer knows that that is hopeless; the cut causes the
entire formula for expression to fail if a failure occurs after the cut is passed.
Of course, the cut takes Prolog further away from the ideal of declarative logic
programming, but it is extensively used in practice to improve efficiency.

Non-logical formulas

To be truly practical, Prolog includes features that have nothing to do with
logic programming. By definition, output statements have no logical meaning
on a computation, since their only effect is on some environment outside the
program. Nevertheless, output statements are necessary if we are to write
programs that open files, display characters on the screen and so on.
    Another area in which Prolog departs from pure logic programming is
that of numerical computation. It is certainly possible to define addition in

logic; in fact, that is the only way to rigorously define it:

$$N + 0 = N$$
$$N + s(M) = s(K) \Leftarrow N + M = K$$

0 is the numeral zero and $s(N)$ is the numeral that succeeds N, so for example, $s(s(s(0)))$ is the numeral 3. The formulas define "+" using the two rules: (1) a number plus zero is the number itself, and (2) N plus the successor of M is the successor of $N + M$. Obviously it would be extremely tedious to write, and inefficient to execute, the logical version of $555 + 777$.

Prolog includes the elementary formula:

```
Var is Expression
```

Expression is evaluated and a new variable Var is created with this value. Note that this is *not* true assignment; the value of the variable can never be assigned to again, only used as an argument in some later elementary formula.

Expression evaluation and assignment to a newly created variable can be used to simulate for-loops:

```
loop(0).
loop(N) :-
    proc,
    N1 is N - 1,
    loop(N1).
```

The following goal will execute proc ten times:

```
?- loop(10).
```

The argument is a variable used as an index. The first formula is the base case of the recursion: when the index is zero, there is nothing further to do. Otherwise, the procedure proc is executed, a *new* variable N1 is created, set to N-1, and used as an argument to the recursive call to loop. Unification creates a new variable for each use of the second formula of loop. This is not too inefficient because it can be done on the stack. Also, many Prolog compilers can do tail-recursion optimization which is a method for replacing recursion by ordinary iteration if the recursive call is the last statement executed in a procedure.

The reason that the use of is is non-logical is that it is not symmetric, that is, you cannot write:

```
28 is V1 * V2
```

or even:

    28 is V1 * 7

where V1 and V2 are uninstantiated variables, that is variables which have had values substituted in them. This would require semantic knowledge of arithmetic (how to factor and divide integers), whereas unification performs a purely syntactical matching on terms.

The Prolog database

There is no limit on the number of formulas that a Prolog program can contain, other than any limits imposed by the size of the computer's memory. In particular, there is no limit on the number of facts that can be included, so a set of Prolog facts can fulfil the function of a table in a database:[2]

    customer(1, "Jonathan").   /* customer(Cust_ID, Name) */
    customer(2, "Marilyn").
    customer(3, "Robert").

    salesperson(101, "Sharon").   /* salesperson(Sales_ID, Name) */
    salesperson(102, "Betty").
    salesperson(103, "Martin").

    order(103, 3, "Jaguar").   /* order(Sales_ID, Cust_ID, Article) */
    order(101, 1, "Volvo").
    order(102, 2, "Volvo").
    order(103, 1, "Buick").

Ordinary Prolog goals can be interpreted as database queries. For example:

    ?- salesperson(Sales_ID, "Sharon"),   /* Sharon's ID */
        order(Sales_ID, Cust_ID, "Volvo"),   /* Order for Volvo */
        customer(Cust_ID, Name).   /* Customer of this order */

means: "To whom did Sharon sell a Volvo?". If the query is successful, the variable Name will receive the substitution of the name of one of those customers. Otherwise, we can conclude that Sharon did not sell any Volvos.

Sophisticated database queries become simple Prolog goals. For example: "Is there a customer who was sold a car by both Sharon and Martin?":

---

[2]This type of database is known as a *relational database*.

```
?-  salesperson(ID1, "Sharon"),        /* Sharon's ID */
    salesperson(ID2, "Martin"),        /* Martin's ID */
    order(ID1, Cust_ID, _),            /* Sharon's customer ID */
    order(ID2, Cust_ID, _).            /* Martin's customer ID */
```

Since the variable Cust_ID is common to two elementary formulas, the goal can be true only if the same customer ordered from each of the salespersons.

Is Prolog a practical alternative to specialized database software? The implementation of lists of facts is quite efficient and can easily answer queries on tables of thousands of entries. However, if your tables consist of tens of thousands of entries, more sophisticated search algorithms are needed. Also, if your database is intended for non-programmers, an appropriate user interface is needed, and your Prolog implementation may or may not be an appropriate programming language in this case.

It is important to emphasize that "this was *not* done by professionals." That is, no new language or database concepts were introduced; this is just ordinary Prolog programming. Any programmer can create small databases just by listing the facts and then submit queries at any point during a computation.

Dynamic databases

If all sets of facts exist at the beginning of a Prolog program, the queries are perfectly declarative: they just ask for a conclusion based on a set of assumptions (the facts). However, the Prolog language includes a non-logical facility for modifying the database during the course of an inference. The elementary formula assert(F) is always true as a logical formula, but as a side-effect it adds the fact F to the database; similarly, retract(F) removes the fact F:

```
?-  assert(order(102, 2, "Peugeot")),       /* Betty sells a car */
    assert(order(103, 1, "BMW")),           /* Martin sells a car */
    assert(order(102, 1, "Toyota")),        /* Betty sells a car */
    assert(order(102, 3, "Fiat")),          /* Betty sells a car */
    retract(salesperson(101, "Sharon")).    /* Fire Sharon ! */
```

Database modifications can be used to simulate an assignment statement in Prolog. Assume that a fact count(0) exists in the program, then:

```
increment :-
    retract(count(N)),        /* Erase old value */
    N1 is N + 1,              /* New variable with new value */
    assert(count(N1)).        /* Restore new value */
```

Not one of the three elementary formulas is a logical formula!

Recall that assignment is used to record the state of a computation. Thus the alternative to simulating assignment is to carry every state variable as an additional argument in the formulas, which can become both tedious and confusing. In practice, use of non-logical database operations in Prolog programs is acceptable, either to implement dynamic databases or to improve the readability of the program.

Sorting in Prolog

As an example of the relation between the descriptive and the procedural views of a logic program, we will discuss sort programs in Prolog. We limit ourselves to sorting lists of integers. Notation: [Head|Tail] is a list whose first element is Head and whose remaining elements form a list Tail. [] denotes the empty list.

Sorting is truly trivial in logic programming because all we have to do is to describe what it means for list L2 to be a sorted version of list L1: L2 consists of an arrangement (permutation) of all the elements of L1 with the restriction that the elements are ordered:

```
sort(L1, L2) :- permutation(L1, L2), ordered(L2).
```

where the formulas in the body are defined as:

```
permutation([], []).
permutation(L, [X | Tail]) :-
    append(Left_Part, [X | Right_Part], L),
    append(Left_Part, Right_Part, Short_List),
    permutation(Short_List, Tail).

ordered([]).
ordered([Single]).
ordered([First, Second | Tail]) :-
    First =< Second,
    ordered([Second | Tail]).
```

Just read these descriptively:

- The empty list is a permutation of the empty list. A permutation of a non-empty list is a division of the list into an element X and two parts Left_Part and Right_Part, such that X is appended to the front of a permutation of the concatenation of the two parts. For example:

    permutation([7,2,9,3], [9|Tail])

if Tail is a permutation of [7,2,3].

- A list with zero or one elements is ordered. A list is ordered if the first two elements are ordered, and the list consisting of all but the first element is also ordered.

Procedurally, this is not the most efficient sorting program in the world; in fact, it is usually called *slow sort*! It simply tries (generates) all permutations of the list of numbers until it finds a sorted list. However, it is just as easy to write a descriptive version of more efficient sorting algorithms such as *insertion sort*, which we solved in ML in the previous chapter:

```
insertion_sort([], []).
insertion_sort([Head | Tail], List) :-
    insertion_sort(Tail, Tail_1),
    insert_element(Head, Tail_1, List).

insert_element(X, [], [X]).
insert_element(X, [Head | Tail], [X, Head | Tail]) :-
    X =< Head.
insert_element(X, [Head | Tail], [Head | Tail_1]) :-
    insert_element(X, Tail, Tail_1).
```

Procedurally, the program is quite efficient because it does the sort by directly manipulating sublists without aimless searching. As with functional programming, there are no indices, no for-loops, no explicit pointers and the algorithm generalizes immediately to sorting other objects.

Typing and failure

Prolog is not statically type-checked. Unfortunately, the response of the Prolog inference engine to type errors can cause serious difficulties for the programmer. Suppose that we write a procedure to compute the length of a list:

```
length([], 0).                  /* Length of empty list is 0 */
length([Head | Tail], N) :-     /* Length of list is */
    length(Tail, N1),           /*    length of Tail */
    N is N+1.                    /*    plus 1 */
```

and accidentally call it with an integer value rather than with a list:

```
?- length(5, Len).
```

This is not illegal because it is certainly possible that the definition of length contains an additional matching formula.

The response of the inference engine is simply to *fail* on the call to length, which is not what you were expecting. Now length was called within some other formula p, and the failure of length will cause p to fail (which you were not expecting either), and so on back up the chain of calls. This result is uncontrolled backtracking which eventually causes the original goal to fail for no obvious reason. Finding such bugs is a very difficult matter of tracing calls step by step until the error is diagnosed.

For this reason, some dialects of Prolog are typed, requiring you to declare that an argument is either an integer or a list or some programmer defined type. In a typed Prolog, the above call would be a compilation error. The usual trade-offs apply when assessing such dialects: reduced flexibility as opposed to catching errors at compile time.

17.4 Advanced logic programming concepts

Building on the success of Prolog, other logic programming languages have been proposed. Many languages have attempted to combine the advantages of logic programming with other programming paradigms such as object-oriented programming and functional programming. Perhaps the most intensive effort has been invested in attempts to exploit the concurrency inherent in logic programming. Recall that a logic program consists of a sequence of formulas:

$$t \sqsubseteq t$$
$$(t = t1 \parallel t2) \wedge (s \sqsubseteq t1) \Rightarrow (s \sqsubseteq t)$$
$$(t = t1 \parallel t2) \wedge (s \sqsubseteq t2) \Rightarrow (s \sqsubseteq t)$$

and that at any point during the computation, the inference engine is attempting to reduce a sequence of goals such as:

$$\ldots \wedge (\text{"Hel"} \parallel t1) \wedge \ldots \wedge (t1 \parallel \text{"orld"}) \wedge \ldots$$

The Prolog language computes each goal sequentially from left to right, but it is also possible to evaluate the goals concurrently. This is called *and-parallelism* because of the conjunction that connects formulas of the goal. When matching a goal with the head of a program formula, the Prolog language tries each formula sequentially in textual order, but it is also possible to try the formulas concurrently. This is called *or-parallelism* because each goal must match the first formula *or* the second formula, and so on.

Defining and implementing concurrent logic languages is difficult. The difficulties in *and*-parallelism arise from synchronization: when a single variable appears in two different goals, like $t1$ in the example, only one goal can actually instantiate (write to) the variable, and it must block other goals from reading the variable before the instantiation is done. In *or*-parallelism, several processes perform a concurrent search for a solution, one for each formula of the procedure; when a solution is found, some provision must be made to communicate this fact to other processes so that they can terminate their searches.

There has also been much effort into integrating functional and logic programming. There is a very close relationship between the mathematics of functions and logic, because:

$$y = f(x_1, \ldots, x_n)$$

is equivalent to the truth of the logical formula:

$$\forall x_1 \cdots \forall x_n \exists! y (y = f(x_1, \ldots, x_n))$$

(where $\exists! y$ means "there exists a unique y"). The main differences between the two programming concepts are:

1. Logic programming uses (two-way) unification which is stronger than (one-way) pattern matching used in functional programming.

2. Functional programs are one-directional in that given all the arguments the program returns a value. In logic programs, any of the arguments of the goal can be left unspecified and unification is responsible for instantiating them with answers.

3. Logic programming is based on an inference engine which automatically searches for answers.

4. Functional programming naturally treats higher-level objects, since functions and types are first-class objects that can be used as data, whereas logic programming is more or less limited to formulas on ordinary data types.

5. Similarly, the high-order facilities in functional programming languages generalize naturally to modules whereas logic programming languages tend to be "flat".

A new area of research in logic programming is the extension of matching from purely syntactical unification to include semantic information. For example, if the goal specifies $4 < x < 8$ and the formula head specifies $6 \leq x < 10$, then we can solve for $6 \leq x < 8$, that is $x = 6$ or $x = 7$. Languages that include semantic information in the matching are called *constraint logic programming languages*, because values are constrained by equations. Constraint logic languages must be based on efficient algorithms to solve the underlying equations.

These advances show great promise in improving both the level of abstraction and the efficiency of logic programming languages.

17.5 Exercises

1. Compute $3 + 4$ using the logical definition of addition.

2. What will happen if the loop program is called with the goal loop(-1)? How can the program be fixed?

3. Write a Prolog program that does not terminate because of the specific computation rule of the language. Write a program that does not terminate because of the search rule.

4. The Prolog rules call for a *depth-first search* for solutions, because the leftmost formula is repeatedly selected even after it has been replaced. It is also possible to do a *breadth-first search* by selecting formulas sequentially from left to right, only returning to the leftmost formula when all others have been selected. What is the effect of this rule on the success of a computation?

5. Write a Prolog goal for the following query:

   Is there a type of car that was sold by Sharon but not by Betty?
   If so, what type of car was it?

6. Study the predefined Prolog formula findall and show how it can solve the following queries:

   How many cars did Martin sell?
   Did Martin sell more cars than Sharon?

7. Write a Prolog program for appending lists and compare it with an ML program. Run the Prolog program in different "directions".

8. How can a Prolog procedure be modified so that it will catch type mismatches and write an error message?

9. What types of logic programs would benefit from and-parallelism and what types would benefit from or-parallelism?

A   Where to Get Compilers

For many years it was difficult for students to experiment with programming languages: compilers can be expensive and it can be difficult to persuade a computer center to install and maintain software. Today the situation is changed and it is possible to obtain free compilers for most, if not all, of the languages that we have discussed.[1] These compilers run on workstations and even on personal computers, so you can install them at home or in your lab. Furthermore, the compilers are easily accessible on the Internet.

To obtain information about compilers for a language, look at files called *FAQ*'s (Frequently Asked Questions). These can be downloaded by doing an anonymous ftp to the address rtfm.mit.edu. In the directory /pub/usenet is a (very long) list of subdirectories; you are looking for comp.lang.x where x is one of: ada, apl, c, c++, eiffel, icon, lisp, ml, prolog, smalltalk, etc. Change to one of these subdirectories and download files that have the letters FAQ in them. These files will have lists of available compilers for the language, in particular those that can be downloaded using ftp. While these programs may not be as fancy as commercial packages, they are more than adequate for learning and experimenting with a language.

The FAQ's will also have the names and addresses of professional associations which publish newletters and journals giving up-to-date information on the languages.

C++

A free compiler for C++, call gcc, has been developed by the GNU project of the Free Software Foundation. See the FAQ in the gnu.g++.help subdirectory at rtfm.mit.edu for details. gcc has been ported to most computers, including

---

[1]*Free* means that normal use is permitted without charge. The programs themselves are distributed under different licensing agreements.

personal computers. Since C++ has yet to be standardized, there may be differences between gcc and any other C++ compiler.

Ada 95

New York University has developed a free compiler for Ada 95, called gnat (GNU Ada Translator). gnat uses the back-end of gcc and has been ported to most or all of the computers that gcc supports. See the Ada FAQ for up-to-date information on ftp-sites for gnat; the main site is in directory /pub/gnat at cs.nyu.edu. There you will also find a menu-driven programming environment for gnat that has been developed by the George Washington University.

AdaS

Pascal-S is a compiler for a subset of Pascal that emits *P-Code*, which is machine code for an artificial stack machine. An interpreter for P-Code is also included. This author has developed a version of Pascal-S, called AdaS, which compiles a small subset of Ada. The source code of AdaS can be found in the file adasnn.zip (where nn is a version number) in the directory /languages/ada/crsware/pcdp in the Public Ada Library (PAL) on host wuarchive.wustl.edu.[2]

AdaS is not suitable for serious programming, but it is an excellent tool for studying implementation techniques for programming language constructs, in particular the stack manipulations during subprogram call and return.

---

[2]The PAL, a collection of documents, software and training materials on Ada, is also available at ftp.cdrom.com and at ftp.cnam.fr in Europe.

B Selected Bibliography

General

Surveys of programming languages can be found in:

> Ellis Horowitz (ed.). *Programming Languages: A Grand Tour.* Springer Verlag, 1983.

> Jean E. Sammet. *Programming Languages: History and Fundamentals.* Prentice Hall, 1969.

> Richard L. Wexelblat. *History of Programming Languages.* Academic Press, 1981.

Wexelblat's book is particularly interesting; it is the record of a conference where the inventors of the first programming languages describe the origin and purpose of their work.

An excellent introduction to the theory of computation (logic, Turing Machines, formal languages and programming verification) is:

> Zohar Manna. *Mathematical Theory of Computation.* McGraw-Hill, 1974.

Advanced textbooks that discuss formal semantics of programming languages are:

> Michael Marcotty and Henry Legrand. *Programming Language Landscape: Syntax, Semantics and Implementation.* SRA, Chicago, 1986.

> Bertrand Meyer. *Introduction to the Theory of Programming Languages.* Prentice Hall International, 1991.

For compilation see:

Alfred Aho, Ravi Sethi and Jeffrey D. Ullman. *Compilers: Principles, Techniques and Tools.* Addison-Wesley, 1986.

Charles N. Fisher and Richard J. LeBlanc. *Crafting a Compiler.* Benjamin Cummings, 1988.

A good introduction to object-oriented design and programming is:

Bertrand Meyer. *Object-oriented Software Construction.* Prentice Hall International, 1988.

Note that the version of Eiffel described there is obsolete; if you wish to study the language, the up-to-date specification is:

Bertrand Meyer. *Eiffel: the Language.* Prentice Hall, 1992.

Specific languages

We will not even attempt to list the dozens of textbooks on C, Ada and C++!

The formal definition of Ada can be found in:

Ada 95 Reference Manual. ANSI/ISO/IEC-8652:1995.

The reference manual is very formal and requires careful study. There is a companion document called the Rationale that describes the motivation of the language constructs and gives extensive examples. Files containing the text of these documents can be downloaded free as described in the Ada FAQ.

The C standard is ANS X3.159-1989; the international standard is ISO/IEC 9899:1990. Currently (late 1995), C++ is not yet standardized; for information on obtaining the latest proposed draft of the C++ standard see the FAQ. More accessible is the annotated reference manual:

Margaret A. Ellis and Bjarne Stroustrup. *The Annotated C++ Reference Manual.* Addison-Wesley, 1990 (reprinted 1994).

The following book is a "rationale" for C++ and should be read by all serious students of the language:

Bjarne Stroustrup. *The Design and Evolution of C++.* Addison-Wesley, 1994.

Other widely used object-oriented languages that are worth studying are Smalltalk and CLOS:

Adele Goldberg and David Robson. *Smalltalk-80, the Language and its Implementation.* Addison-Wesley, 1983.

Sonya E. Keene. *Object-Oriented Programming in Common Lisp: a Programmer's Guide.* Addison-Wesley, 1989.

In Section 1.3, we recommended that you study one or more languages based on a specific data structure. The following list of texts will get you started:

Leonard Gilman and Allen J. Rose. *APL: An Interactive Approach.* John Wiley, 1984.

Ralph E. Griswold and Madge T. Griswold. *The Icon Programming Language (2nd Ed.).* Prentice Hall, 1990.

J.T. Schwartz, R.B.K. Dewar, E. Dubinsky, and E. Schonberg. *Programming with Sets: An Introduction to SETL.* Springer Verlag, 1986.

Patrick H. Winston and Berthold K.P. Horn. *LISP (3rd Ed.).* Addison-Wesley, 1989.

Finally, introductions to languages and language concepts that were just surveyed in this book can be found in:

M. Ben-Ari. *Principles of Concurrent and Distributed Programming.* Prentice Hall International, 1990.

Ivan Bratko. *Prolog Programming for Artificial Intelligence (2nd Ed.).* Addison-Wesley, 1990.

Chris Reade. *Elements of Functional Programming.* Addison-Wesley, 1989.

Leon Sterling and Ehud Shapiro. *The Art of Prolog.* MIT Press, 1986.

Jeffrey D. Ullman. *Elements of ML Programming.* Prentice Hall, 1994.

Index